THE CRUSADES

THE CRUSADES

by

Robert Silverberg

Writing as Franklin Hamilton

THE BORGO PRESS

MMX

INTRODUCTION TO THE BORGO EDITION

From Franklin Hamilton to Robert Silverberg

Since 1955 I have primarily been a writer of science fiction, but in the early 1960s, when I was about six years along in what had been a very successful career, science fiction fell into hard times, with diminishing sales of books and magazines and a corresponding aversion to artistic risk by most of the editors who remained at work in the greatly shrunken field. (Things were so bad that many leading writers, editors, and readers took part in a famous symposium, *Who Killed Science Fiction*, that won an award at the next World Science Fiction Convention.)

Since it now had become impossible for me to continue earning a living as a full-time freelancing specialist in science fiction, I turned my writing activities elsewhere, and soon, drawing on my own interests in history and science, had established myself as a writer of non-fiction books for high school and college readers. The major publishers of such books—Holt, Putnam, Doubleday, Macmillan, and several more—welcomed them, and quickly I began winning awards for them and the attention of librarians, who readily bought each new one as it appeared. The first of the books was *Lost Cities and Vanished Civilizations* (1962), swiftly followed by several others on archaeological subjects—*Empires in the Dust, Man Before Adam, Sunken History, To the Rock of Darius,* etc. I wrote a book about Socrates. I wrote one about great medical men. I wrote one on Copernicus and Galileo. I wrote one about nuclear physics. I wrote one on the Indians of the Pueblos. It was a busy decade.

I wrote so many books on so many themes between 1961 and 1970, in fact, that it started to seem implausible that one writer could master such a wide range of subjects, although I have always been a good researcher and a very prolific writer. My publishers and I feared that book buyers would begin to question the quality of the work. So it became commercially desirable to conceal my prolificacy behind pseudonyms. When I did a couple of books about famous explorers, I used the byline "Walker Chapman." A biography of Winston Churchill was credited to "Edgar Black." And when, in 1964, I wrote a book about the Norman conquest of England, it was published (by the Dial Press, an important publisher of the day) under the name of "Franklin Hamilton."

There were three Franklin Hamilton books in all: *1066*, the Norman Conquest book, followed in 1965 by *The Crusades*, and in 1967 by *Challenge for a Throne*, which dealt with the Wars of the Roses. (A projected fourth book about the Byzantine Empire got caught in a publishing change and was abandoned.) They were good, solid books, beautifully illustrated by my friend Judith Ann Lawrence (the wife of science-fiction writer James

Blish), they were well received by reviewers, and they sold very well for many years.

Now, after several decades in publishing limbo, here they are back in print again—and, since I am no longer so prolific that my books jostle against each other for the attention of readers, I see no reason to continue to hide them behind a pseudonym, so I have placed my own name on them at last.

—Robert Silverberg
Oakland, California
August, 2010

chapters

i promise you in the name of the Father, and of the Son, and of the Holy Ghost, that all those who take part in this war and die while bearing arms, if their hearts are contrite and if they have been confessed, shall enter into possession of that Kingdom which the Lord has conquered for us by the Cross, and here and now I invest you with that Kingdom by that same cross, by the cross which I offer you. Come therefore, and may no one of you refuse to accept so glorious an investiture, so formal a warranty of the throne which is waiting for you above. . . .

HUMBERT OF ROMANS,
about 1256 A.D.

GOD WILLS IT

ON an August day in 1095, workmen appeared at the cathedral of the French town of Le Puy. Wielding picks, they began to smash a hole in the wall of the building. No sacrilege was involved; Bishop Adhemar himself had given the orders. A new entrance was to be cut into the cathedral—an entrance to be used only once, on a high ceremonial occasion, and then to be sealed forever.

The occasion was the arrival of Pope Urban II in Le Puy. The Pope, head of Western Christendom, had been journeying westward all summer. When he entered the cathedral, Bishop Adhemar felt, it would be a moment of such historic importance for Le Puy that nothing less than a new entrance was necessary.

On the fifteenth of August, Pope Urban celebrated a solemn mass in the cathedral of Le Puy. From miles around crowds flocked to see him, for it was not every day that a Pope visited Le Puy. And this was an unusual Pope, a Frenchman himself, vigorous and wise, tall and handsome, with a grave, courteous manner. Great things were expected of him. He had come to the Throne of St. Peter in difficult times; Christianity was divided and the Holy Land, Christ's birthplace, was under the rule of Turks and Arabs who followed the teachings of Mohammed.

After the ceremonies, the people scattered again, telling each other they had witnessed a great occasion. But greater events were afoot. That day, in private, Pope Urban conferred with Adhemar, the Bishop of Le Puy. Adhemar had been a knight, a warrior, before entering the Church. Noble in bearing, a true prince of God, Adhemar was respected by all. The two men met and spoke, and the Pope told the Bishop of his grand dream: to free the Holy Land from the grip of the Mohammedans, and make it once again a place where Christian pilgrims could go in safety. A crusade! A holy war! Would Bishop Adhemar support such a scheme, the Pope asked? Adhemar took Urban's hand in his and pledged his backing.

It was important for the Pope to secure the support of such men as Adhemar before he made his plans public. In those days, the Pope was by no means absolute master of Christianity. Urban had had to struggle to claim his title. The Cardinals of the Church had elected him Pope in 1088, but, for political reasons, a rival had been put forth by Henry IV, the Holy Roman Emperor, who ruled Germany and much of Italy. Henry's candidate, Guibert, had taken control of Rome itself. Not until May of 1095 was the true Pope able to oust the Antipope. Now, only a few months later, Urban was making his triumphant journey through Europe in the full flush of his victory.

After his conference with Adhemar, Urban sent out messengers to all the abbots and bishops loyal to him. There would be a general council of the Church in the town of Clermont in November. The Pope did not reveal the purpose of the council. That announcement would come in due time.

As November's chill winds swept across France, the notables of the Church gathered in Clermont. More than

God Wills It

250 bishops and abbots arrived. There were clerical princes from many parts of France, from Spain, from the Duchy of Normandy, even from the Holy Roman Empire. Some were aged men, close to death, who made the journey to show their support of Pope Urban. Some, like Adhemar of Le Puy, were younger and stronger, in the prime of life. The townspeople of Clermont looked on in awe as the glittering prelates swarmed into their town accompanied by retinues of priests, clerks, and servants. Clermont overflowed; tents had to be pitched in the open fields.

From November 18 to November 26, the council transacted the business of the Church in closed session. Certain decrees were passed: one forbade monks to frequent taverns, another granted the right of sanctuary to any criminal who fled from pursuers into a church or other holy place. The Pope spoke harshly of Philip I, King of France, who had put aside his lawful wife to take another. Quarrels between high churchmen were settled.

Then, when the matters before the council had been dealt with, Pope Urban let it be known that he planned to speak in public on Tuesday, November 27. A platform was built outdoors in the marketplace of Clermont. Bishops and monks, barons and knights, peasants and merchants gathered by the thousands to hear the Pope's words. Few had any idea in advance of what he was going to say. An excited hush fell as Urban rose to speak.

Four chroniclers have left us their accounts of the Pope's words. At least one seems to have been an eyewitness: Fulcher of Chartres, a monk in the service of a nobleman named Stephen of Blois. According to Fulcher, the Pope began by speaking of the sad plight of the Christians who lived in the East, in that far-off center of civilization, the Byzantine Empire:

11

"It is necessary that you bring to your brothers in the East the help so often promised and so urgently needed. They have been attacked, as many of you know, by Turks and Arabs. . . . Churches have been destroyed and the countryside laid waste. If you do not make a stand against the enemy now, the tide of their advance will overwhelm many more faithful servants of God."

The Pope spoke of the holiness of Jerusalem, the city where Christ had spent his last days on earth, where the crucifixion had taken place—a city that Christians had regarded as the holiest of shrines for a thousand years. He told of the pilgrims who had ventured there, and of their sufferings at the hands of the unbelievers. Then he delivered this ringing appeal:

"I beg and beseech you—and not I alone but Our Lord begs and beseeches you as heralds of Christ—rich and poor alike make haste to drive this evil race from the places where our brothers live and bring a very present help to the worshipers of Christ. I will send the news to those who are far off; but it is the voice of Christ which commands your obedience!"

In the past, the Church had always spoken out bitterly against war. How could the followers of Jesus, that man of peace, be encouraged to take up arms? Urban was careful to draw the distinction between a holy war and the evil strife of the past:

"Before this, you have waged unjust warfare, slaying each other and sometimes wielding mad weapons for the sake merely of greed and pride. For this you have earned everlasting death and the ruin of certain damnation. Now we set before you wars which have in themselves the glorious reward of martyrdom and the halo of present and everlasting fame.

Bishop Adhemar takes the Cross

"If anyone who sets out should lose his life either on the way, by land or by sea, or in battle against the infidels, his sins shall be pardoned from that moment. This I grant by right of God's power to me," Urban promised.

He cried out to the warlike barons, to all men of blood, to brigands and hired killers, to put aside their grim sports and join the holy army. "Join us without delay!" he implored. "Let those who are going settle up their affairs and collect what they will need to pay their expenses, so that when the winter is over and the spring comes they may set off joyfully under the guidance of Our Lord."

There was silence as the Pope finished. His listeners were stunned. So great a dream! So glorious a goal! To liberate the Holy Land, to smite the infidel and drive him out. It was a prospect to set the blood pounding and the head spinning. A deafening shout rang out across the market square of Clermont. *"Deus lo volt!"* God wills it! God wills it!

Who would come forth, the Pope asked, to join the crusading army? Who would vow to go to Jerusalem, for the sake of true religion, not for honor or riches but in order to free the Church of God? He held forth his hands, and Bishop Adhemar of Le Puy came forward and begged to be the first to join.

Red cloth was brought, and eager hands cut from it a little cross that was sewn to the shoulder of Adhemar's robe. The Cross, the red insignia of Christianity, became the symbol of the Crusades. After Adhemar came others, hundreds of them, demanding to take the Cross too.

Pope Urban had kindled a fire that day, a blaze of religious zeal that was destined to burn for centuries, now flickering fitfully, now leaping furiously to the heavens. Under the hot Asiatic sun lay the Holy Land, in unbelievers' hands, and freeing it became the goal of every Christian. Wars would follow, thousands would perish, and European knights would become kings in Jerusalem. A procession of noble heroes and black villains was about to form; the Crusades were beginning, the central and guiding enterprise of the early Middle Ages, and by the time they had run their course the path of world events would have been greatly changed.

Men would soon be going east—some out of religious zeal, others in search of gold and glory, a few simply from the desire to kill or be killed. An epic was beginning, a romantic tale of chivalry and of greed, of bravery and of treachery, of virtue and of wickedness. Pope Urban had spoken better than he knew that November day in Clermont. The answering shout, "God wills it," was heard in many lands. All Europe heard it and responded. It echoed in gleaming Constantinople, the capital of Eastern Christianity. Its roar reverberated as far as the Holy Land itself, to the ears of the sultans and caliphs of the Moslem world. They frowned, and then smiled, and wondered if anything would ever come to pass from all this fervor.

The holy Land

JERUSALEM, the heart of the Holy Land, was sacred to men of many creeds. Jews venerated it because it had been the capital of the ancient Kingdom of Israel in the time of David and Solomon. To Christians the city was sacred because of its many associations with Jesus. And Mohammedans came to revere it because Allas—God—had brought the Prophet Mohammed there one night before revealing heaven itself to him.

At the time that Christ lived and died in Jerusalem, the entire area that would later be called the Holy Land was under Roman rule. Rome had built a vast empire that stretched from the boundaries of Persia in the east to England in the west, from the Danube River in the north to the sandy wastes of the Sahara in the south. Rome was pagan, then; but the religion of Christ, at first an underground movement, took root and flourished, and by the early fourth century the Emperor Constantine had made it the official religion of the empire. It was Constantine, too, who built an eastern capital for the empire. In No-

16

vember, 324, he journeyed to the place where Europe and Asia meet, where the strait called the Bosporus links the Black Sea and the Mediterranean. An ancient town called Byzantium stood at that point, and near it Constantine established the magnificent city of Constantinople, or New Rome.

By 364, the Roman Empire was divided, with one Emperor ruling at Rome and another at Constantinople. While hordes of barbarians were descending from the north to crush Rome, the eastern empire was thriving and growing ever more powerful. Within a century, the Rome of the Caesars was only a memory, but the eastern empire, now called the Byzantine Empire, reigned in splendor over much of eastern Europe and also over such former Roman territories as Egypt, Asia Minor, Syria, Lebanon, and Palestine.

So Jerusalem came under the control of the Byzantines as the heirs of Rome. That fact alone made Constantinople the real center of the Christian world. There was a Pope in Rome, but Rome was under the thumb of rough barbarian chieftains. By a decree of the year 451, the Pope was the head of the Church in name, but his eastern rival, the Patriarch of Constantinople, was actually his equal in power. And it was through the fabulous city of Constantinople that all pilgrims had to pass on their way to Jerusalem.

Jerusalem was a magnet for Christians. A pilgrimage to the Holy Land was the goal of every worshiper: to see the places where the story of Jesus had been acted out, to kneel where the Savior had knelt, to pray where Christ had prayed. Folk who knew the Bible as they knew no other book were steeped in tales of Palestine. They knew its geography and envisioned its landmarks; they yearned to see it all with their own eyes. There are many accounts of early pilgrimages, such as that of the Abbess Etheria of Gaul, who journeyed to the Holy Land in 386, and that of an unknown man of Bordeaux who made the trip fifty years before her. By 500 A.D., with the Byzantines firmly in control of the eastern world, a steady flow of pilgrims traveled to Jerusalem.

The travel was a good business for Byzantium. The pilgrims had to pay heavy tolls as they passed through Constantinople, and more cash had to be handed to the Byzantine guardians of the holy places of Palestine. Despite the high costs and the severe hardships, the pilgrims came gladly. And, obligingly enough, the Byzantines took them on tours, showed them the sacred relics. Where the relics no longer existed, or had never existed at all, it was always possible to manufacture them. In a pilgrim's account written about 525 the traveler says he was able to see in Jerusalem "the horn with which David and Solomon were anointed . . . . the Holy Lance, made of the wood of the Cross, which shines at night like the sun in the glory of the day . . . . the earth of which Adam was formed . . . . the cup of the Last Supper . . . . the crown of thorns . . . . the rod with which Jesus was whipped." It was possible to follow the footsteps of Christ as he walked through the city toward the place of his crucifixion. At nearby Nazareth could be seen "the book from which our Lord learned his A B C." Bones of the saints, dishes from which the apostles had eaten, and other relics just as unlikely, all made the pilgrims glow with joy. It was thought that seeing and handling such things brought the sinner into contact with God and helped him to obtain pardon for sin.

All this was changed by the coming of Mohammed.

The Holy Land

He was a man of Arabia, born about 570 A.D. in the city of Mecca. His family was poor, and he entered the service of Khadijah, the widow of a rich merchant. Though she was about fifteen years older than he was, she became fond of him and took him as her husband. The marriage, when Mohammed was about twenty-five, freed him from the need to earn a living and gave him time to ponder questions of religion.

Arabia then was a land of idol worshipers. Jews and Christians dwelled in Mecca, and no doubt Mohammed had occasion to discuss their religion with them. Meditating as he rode from city to city on merchant's business, jogging on camelback through the baking desert heat, Mohammed turned away from the multitude of gods that Arabia followed and embraced the Judaeo-Christian idea of One True God.

"There is no God but God, and Mohammed is his Prophet," his followers declare to this day. Mohammed had the gift of leadership, granted to him as it has been to few others. This not very dynamic businessman of Mecca was transformed into the voice of Allah, and men listened to him. The religion that he preached owed much to Judaism and Christianity, which Mohammed did not deny; he recognized Moses and Jesus as great prophets also. But his creed, simple and direct, went to the hearts of the Arabians. It had no rituals, no elaborate doctrines, no priesthood. Mohammed called on all men to bow to God, to accept Allah's will, and to recognize all other men as brothers. The name of the religion, *Islam*, meant "surrender," and Mohammed's followers were called *Moslems*, "those who surrender themselves."

Not all Arabs accepted Islam's severe, pious teachings. In 622, Mohammed was attacked by assassins. He narrowly escaped and was forced to flee from Mecca. He made his way to the city of Medina. This journey, called the *hegira* or Flight of the Prophet, is so important in Moslem history that the year 622 A.D. has become Year One of the Mohammedan calendar.

In Medina, supporters flocked to Mohammed's cause. He formed an army of men willing to shed blood in Allah's name, and the Moslem conquests began. Islam was a strange combination of the austerely religious and the bloodthirsty; the wars of the Moslems were wars of piety which used the sword to bring the message of Allah's justice to unbelievers.

Mohammed sent a message to Heraclius, the Byzantine Emperor, asking him to embrace Islam. Heraclius paid no attention to the desert prophet; he had bigger enemies to cope with. Between 613 and 620, Persian armies had conquered Syria, Egypt, and Asia Minor, murdering thousands of Christians and carrying off the True Cross on which Christ was said to have been crucified. From 622 to 628, Heraclius led what could be called the first of all the Crusades. He drove the Persians from the Holy Land and recaptured the True Cross.

The glorious victory brought him letters of congratulations from as far away as France and India. Heraclius had emerged as the hero of Christendom. Giddy with his triumph, he could not be disturbed by the ravings of an Arabian prophet. Safe in mighty Constantinople, with its shrines blazing with bright mosaics, the Byzantine Emperor, conqueror of the Persians, had little to fear from Mohammed.

But Islam spread. When the Prophet died in 632, his friend Abu Bakr succeeded him, taking the title of Caliph, or Commander of the Faithful. Arab armies marched against the already battered Persians and destroyed them. Steadily the Moslems advanced out of Arabia, under Abu Bakr and then under his successor, the Caliph Omar. The trumpet rang; the curved swords gleamed in the sunlight; Moslems surged onward through Palestine, Syria, Egypt, North Africa.

A clash with Byzantium was inevitable. In 636, Moslem met Christian in Palestine, and a fierce battle took place on the banks of the Yarmuk, near the Sea of Galilee. In a blinding sandstorm, the Arabs slew thousands of Byzantine troops. Twelve thousand Christian Arabs deserted Heraclius and converted to Islam *en masse*. Byzantium, wearied by its bitter war with Persia, could not withstand the Moslem onslaught.

So Jerusalem passed into Moslem rule. The Church of the Holy Sepulchre built by the Emperor Constantine was demolished, but otherwise the Arabs did not harm the shrines of Christendom. Even in these harsh times, a few Christian pilgrims continued to make their way east.

The Arab advance continued. They crossed the Mediterranean and conquered Spain; they crushed Persia completely; they attacked Constantinople itself in 718, but were thrown back. Fourteen years later, at the battle of Tours, they met another defeat when Charles Martel halted their invasion of France. After that, the tide of Moslem expansion slowed, and Christianity began to come to terms with the powerful new religion.

With their early lust for battle wearing off, the Arabs grew more peaceful. Except in occasional moments of fanaticism, they tolerated Christians and Jews in the lands they had conquered. The Christians of the Holy Land found them easy masters. Taxes were lower than they had been under the rule of Byzantium, and the Moslem sense of justice created an atmosphere of tranquility. There had long been sharp quarrels between different sects of Christianity, and the Byzantine Christians had sometimes been savage in their persecution of those who did not worship Christ in the same way they did. Now, under the Arabs, all the squabbling divisions of Christianity had equal protection before the law, and the persecutions ended.

Meanwhile, in Western Europe, great changes were occurring. The barbarians who had swamped Rome had had time to grow civilized and Christianized, and out of the Dark Ages of the fifth through eighth centuries had come new order. The Franks, a Germanic people, had beaten the Arabs in the days of Charles Martel; now that leader's grandson forged an empire that claimed to succeed that of ancient Rome. He was Charlemagne, the first Emperor of the West, who regarded himself as the rival of the Byzantine Emperor.

Charlemagne communicated with Haroun al-Rashid, the Caliph of that day, who ruled from the new Arab capital of Baghdad. Haroun, a wise and tolerant man, acknowledged that Christians had the right to visit Jerusalem. By the year 800, monasteries and churches again were being built by Christians in the Holy Land, and the stream of pilgrims grew. So long as they paid their tolls, visiting Christians were as welcome as they had been when the Byzantines governed the Holy Land.

The Arab civilization grew rich and complex. Poets, physicians, scholars clustered at Baghdad, and also in Spain, at the western end of the Moslem domain. The Arabs translated into their own language the great philosophical and literary manuscripts of the Greeks and Romans. Universities came into being. Baghdad was the center of an astonishing cultural upsurge that made the Arabs the intellectual leaders of the world.

The Holy Land

Constantinople, too, was still a great city, the most opulent in the Christian world. Western Europe remained backward and barbaric by comparison. The pilgrims who journeyed to Constantinople and then into the Arab lands were awed by the sights they saw.

The Byzantines never forgot that they once had been masters of the Near East. Now their empire no longer reached beyond Asia Minor; Syria, Palestine, and Egypt were regarded as lost provinces that might someday be reconquered. Several times, they unsuccessfully invaded the Arab-held lands. They were in difficulty at the other end of their territory, too. In the west ambitious princes of reviving Western Europe were nibbling away at the Byzantine lands. The most fearsome were Normans, descendants of Viking rovers who had settled in northern France. Looking for new lands to conquer, the Normans invaded Byzantine-held Sicily and took possession of it.

Hemmed in by Christian enemies to the west and Arab enemies to the east, the Byzantines felt increasingly isolated. They were resentful of the unruly men of Western Europe, whom they called Latins because their religious services were held in that language. (The Byzantines, though they traced their power back to the Roman Empire, spoke Greek now.) And they eyed the Arab overlords of the Near East jealously.

The situation remained fluid for centuries. The Byzantines schemed to recapture all the territory that had been theirs in the time of Emperor Heraclius. Finally, dissension in the Moslem world gave them their chance.

The Arabs had been masters of Islam for four hundred years. But out of the wastelands of Central Asia came nomad tribes, the Turks, who swept into the Arab dominion as furiously as the Arabs themselves had invaded the Persians and the Byzantines. The Turks were Moslems too, but that did not prevent them from attacking and conquering their fellow-worshipers, the Arabs.

Of all the Turkish tribes, the most powerful were the Seljuks, ruled by a single family of warriors. It was the Seljuks who now seized the Holy Land. Their rise to power began about 1040, when they defeated several rival tribes of Turks. Within ten years, the Seljuks were strong enough to become rulers of Persia. Next they moved westward into Iraq. The Caliph of Baghdad, frightened by these warlike Turks, accepted their "protection" in 1055 and became a Turkish puppet. Asia Minor, which was held by the Byzantines, was the next target. The Seljuks marched into Armenia and Georgia, pulling down crosses and destroying cathedrals. By 1070, they had advanced deep into Byzantine territory.

Byzantium had been torn by civil wars during the years the Seljuks were growing strong. Now, with danger threatening even Constantinople, a strong new emperor, Romanus IV Diogenes, came to the throne. At a time when the Seljuks were busy on two fronts, trying to conquer Egypt as well as Asia Minor, Romanus Diogenes assembled an army of about 200,000 men and led it eastward.

Hurriedly the Seljuk Sultan, Alp Arslan, returned from Egypt and met the attack. In a valley near Manzikert in Asia Minor Alp Arslan outmaneuvered the Byzantines, led them into a trap, and slew them in multitudes. Emperor Romanus himself was captured and forced to submit to Seljuk wishes. The Turks took a firm grasp on Asia Minor.

To the south, in Egypt, the Seljuks had powerful enemies. An Egyptian dynasty called the Fatimids opposed them and held out against them. The Seljuks seized Jerusalem in 1076, but they were unable to continue southward into Egypt. Back and forth across Syria and Palestine the

The Holy Land

Turks and Arabs contended. Some cities fell to the Turks, others continued to be held by the Fatimid Arabs.

From the point of view of the Christian pilgrims, the rise of the Seljuks was a disaster. They held most of Asia Minor, blocking the only land road to the Holy Land. Unlike the tolerant Arabs, the Seljuk Turks were hostile to Christianity. It was increasingly difficult to make the dangerous journey to Jerusalem.

The Byzantines bemoaned the Seljuks' rise, too, for a much more practical reason. They had lost nearly all of Asia Minor to them, and how long would it be before the Turks were hammering at the walls of Constantinople? Byzantium was not strong enough to hold them off; the catastrophe at Manzikert in 1071 had broken the strength of the Byzantine army. In 1073, the new Byzantine Emperor, Michael VII, began to hint that he would not mind some aid from the Christians of Western Europe. Pope Gregory VII, an ambitious, energetic man, was thinking along the same lines. He conceived the idea of sending Christian knights to help Byzantium drive the Turks out of Asia Minor. But nothing came of the project.

Eight years later, Alexius Comnenus came to the Byzantine throne. He invaded Asia Minor without western help and forced the Seljuks back a fair distance. Then a truce was agreed upon, dividing Asia Minor between the Byzantines and the Seljuks. Alexius, a highly capable ruler, was willing to settle for this victory for the time being.

The situation continued to change rapidly. The Seljuks quarrelled among themselves as rival princes of the same family struggled for power. The Fatimids of Egypt continued to harass the Turks. After a high point about 1080, the Seljuks found themselves divided and in difficulties. By 1095 it looked as if the Seljuk empire would split apart as rapidly as it had been formed.

Every city seemed to have a different master. In Asia Minor the Seljuk Sultan Kilij Arslan ruled; in Syria, his cousins, Ridwan of Aleppo and Duqaq of Damascus, quarrelled with each other and with a third Turk, Kerbogha. The coastal city of Tripoli was governed by a clan of independent Arabs. The Fatimids of Egypt were recapturing southern Palestine. In Jerusalem, the sons of a Turkish soldier named Ortoq were in control. All was in confusion in the Moslem world.

The Byzantine Emperor Alexius had been watching with glee as the Turks fell out with one another. He had ruled for fourteen years, rebuilding Byzantium's strength, biding his time. It seemed to him the right moment to return to the attack and sweep all the Turks aside, joining Asia Minor, Syria, Lebanon, and Palestine once more to the Byzantine Empire.

He sent envoys to Pope Urban II. Alexius wanted the Pope to send him some knights, a few hundred experienced soldiers who could serve in the campaign against the Seljuks. In return, Alexius got a great deal more than he asked for and much more than he wanted. The Pope spoke at Clermont; and soon, to his horror, Alexius found that nearly every warrior of Europe was marching toward Constantinople.

The Armies
Gather

THE call went out from Clermont, and the knights of Europe began to take the Cross. Pope Urban's instructions were quite clear. No one should join the Crusade without first consulting his priest; no one should go who was elderly or ill; no one should take the Cross who did not intend to go all the way to Jerusalem. No monk or priest was to take the Cross without the permission of his superior. The expedition would depart on August 15, 1096.

Adhemar of Le Puy, the first man to volunteer, was placed in charge of the Crusade. He was a bishop, but he had had military experience, and in that time it was not unusual for prelates to be warriors as well. Adhemar was wise, clearheaded, a good diplomat, a skilled negotiator. The Pope had chosen him as leader because he knew that the army would be made up of proud and unruly noblemen who might, without the calm Adhemar to control them, fight against each other as much as they did against the Moslems.

Not every knight in Europe was equally enthusiastic about going Crusading. The richest and most powerful had little interest in leaving their lands to fight in Asia. They had too much to lose and nothing to gain except spiritual glory. So most of the kings and counts stayed home.

The Crusaders were likely to be restless knights of high family who, because they were younger sons, could not expect to inherit land, power, or titles in Europe. Such men hoped to found new domains for themselves in the East. For them, the Crusade was a chance to grow rich and mighty. It also happened to be a blessed enterprise, but that was incidental. Typical of this group was Bohemond of Taranto, a Norman adventurer who had little hope of inheriting his family's territories in Sicily. Another was Godfrey of Bouillon, whose older brother, Eustace of Boulogne, was the heir to the family lands. Godfrey's younger brother, Baldwin of Lorraine, had even less chance of gaining power in his homeland and also joined the Crusade.

But some of the Crusaders were men of rank and substance. Count Raymond of Toulouse was the first baron to answer Pope Urban's call, sending his messenger to Clermont on November 28, 1095. At fifty-five, Raymond was older than most of the Crusading knights, a wealthy man who ruled over wide dominions. For him, the Crusade was a chance to add to his fame; he saw himself as the leader of all the warrior princes who were destined to recapture Jerusalem.

All during the winter of 1095–96, such men as Raymond of Toulouse, Godfrey of Bouillon, Baldwin of Lorraine, and Bohemond of Taranto made their plans and gathered their followers. They would march across Europe, each force taking a separate route, and would meet at Constantinople. There, joining together, they would cross over into Asia Minor and surge first eastward and then southward into the Holy Land. There was no question of going by sea; it would be fearfully expensive to transport armies the whole length of the Mediterranean, and it would be dangerous, besides. The ports of Syria all were held by Moslems. The land route was the only route.

These were the great men of the First Crusade, the leaders, the noblemen. Valiant deeds lay ahead for them; all would win new titles, and Baldwin would become a king. But while the barons hatched their plans, other Crusaders were already on the move. A strange and motley band of peasants and paupers, inflamed by a bizarre little preacher, marched toward the Holy Land long before the knights were ready to go. And so the grand drama of the Crusades opened with a touch of farce.

Peter the Hermit was the man who launched this first thrust against the infidels. "He was a little man, and looked a poor, stunted creature," wrote the chronicler William of Tyre a hundred years later, "but he was wondrously endowed with a great heart and a shining spirit, with wisdom and straightforward speech."

Peter went barefoot and clad himself in filthy rags. He touched neither meat nor bread, living on fish and wine. Swarthy of skin, long and lean of face, he cut a comic figure indeed. Yet he had the power to command men. Guibert of Nogent, a historian who saw Peter the Hermit at first hand, wrote, "In all that he did or said it seemed that there was something divine in him, so that people even went so far as to pull out hairs from his mule to keep them as relics."

Within weeks after the Council of Clermont had

Peter the Hermit preaches the Crusade

proclaimed the Crusade, this shaggy, foul-smelling hermit
was moving through France and into Germany, preaching
a holy war against the Moslems. Wherever he spoke, men
came to listen, and when he moved on they went with
him. They were not knights. They were peasants, men of
the soil, whose life was one of constant labor and little
comfort. They had no love for their noble masters nor for
their endless toil. Now Peter stood before them, telling
them that they had the Pope's blessing to quit their farms
and seek adventure in the Holy Land.

It was an alluring idea. Better to die a warrior in Jerusalem than to live a serf in France. If they perished in the Holy Land, they went to heaven, cleansed of all their sins—the Pope had said so. If they lived and conquered who knew what glory might be theirs?

By the time Peter the Hermit reached Cologne, as many as 15,000 had joined this People's Crusade, and thousands more flocked to his side in Germany. Around him were brigands and idlers, peasants, disinherited knights, women and children, old men, the lame, the halt, the blind, all swept up in the fervor of Peter's preaching. It was not really an army; it was a mass migration. There was no control, no discipline. Guibert of Nogent shows us these Crusaders at Cologne in April, 1096: "You might see a marvelous and most laughable sight, a troop of poor folk with two-wheeled carts drawn by oxen whom they had shod after the fashion of horses, bearing their few possessions in these little carts, while their very children, as soon as they came to some walled town, would ask again and again if this were Jerusalem."

The People's Crusade seemed funny to Guibert, but those whose lands lay in its path did not find it at all amusing. Peter's hordes had to eat; since they had little or no money, they looted and pillaged when hunger overcame them. He attempted to maintain order, but the marchers left havoc in their path.

Peter realized that he could not fight the Turks without true warriors to lead his ragtag band. So he stopped in Cologne to preach the Crusade to local knights. Several minor noblemen, including Count Hugh of Tübingen and Walter of Teck, joined him. One band of Crusaders could not wait for Peter to recruit men. Led by a certain Walter the Penniless, they broke away from Peter and set out on their own early in April.

Walter the Penniless and his troop followed the Danube River to the Hungarian border, got permission to cross Hungary, and by the end of May reached Belgrade, a western outpost of the Byzantine Empire. The military commander at Belgrade was aghast when the horde of rabble appeared and announced its intention to go on to Constantinople. He held Walter in check for a while, hurriedly sending a messenger to the capital for instructions.

The Armies Gather

Walter and his men grew restless while waiting for word from Constantinople. They grew hungry, too, and began to rob local farmers of their grain. The Byzantines, with growing uneasiness, finally let the Crusaders continue eastward—accompanied by an armed escort to keep them from getting out of hand. By the middle of July, they were in Constantinople.

Peter the Hermit, his knights finally recruited, left Cologne on April 20. Following Walter's route, the immense, ill-disciplined army marched into Hungary, traveling on foot at a rate of about twenty-five miles a day. Through May and early June, all went well, but trouble broke out at the Hungarian frontier town of Semlin. Guibert of Nogent writes that Peter's "unruly followers, finding all the necessities of life in great abundance in Hungary, soon began to commit outrageous excesses against the very gentle inhabitants of it."

It was harvest time, and the Crusaders made free with the grain of the Hungarians. At Semlin, authorities tried to control the invaders, and the result was a pitched battle in which four thousand Hungarians were killed. Peter, who had been completely unable to control his men, feared now that the vengeance of the Hungarian king would be swift. Hastily, the Crusaders built rafts and made their way across the river into Byzantine territory.

The Byzantine commander at Belgrade, who had had his difficulties with the band of Walter the Penniless, was even more appalled when the new torrent of Crusaders descended upon him. He quickly withdrew from Belgrade, leaving the city to the mercy of Peter's horde. The Crusaders looted Belgrade and managed to set fire to it. Then they continued on to the town of Nish, in what is now Bulgaria.

Here the Byzantines were waiting with a large force of soldiers under an officer named Nicetas. He met Peter and explained that he would provide an escort from Nish to Constantinople. Peter agreed to the arrangement, and shortly the Crusaders were on the road once more. In a day's time, some German Crusaders had quarreled with the Byzantine escort. Peter could not calm the Germans, and the infuriated Byzantines attacked without mercy. Guibert of Nogent declares, "Some [of the Crusaders] perished by the sword, others were drowned in the waters of a river, others returned to France worn out with fatigue, penniless, in the most terrible state of want, and, worse still, overcome with shame."

Peter reassembled the survivors, discovering that he had lost 10,000 of his 40,000 men. In a more subdued mood, the Crusaders proceeded on through the Byzantine lands, and on August 1, 1096, Peter's band arrived at Constantinople. The journey had been disastrous, but it was at its end.

Emperor Alexius was hardly delighted to see the newcomers. He had asked for warriors; instead he had received an army of hungry peasants, so many locusts to lay waste the countryside. The Emperor's daughter, Anna Comnena, who wrote a history of these events, commented, "They made up a throng of men and women such as had never before been seen in the memory of man. . . . They outnumbered the grains of sand on the seashore and the stars in the sky."

Alexius was civil enough. He invited Peter the Hermit to come to court. The ragged hermit came before the magnificent Emperor and was treated with courtesy. Alexius, seeing that Peter's Crusaders were no warriors, advised him to remain in Constantinople until the knights and barons arrived later in the year. Within a few days, though, he had changed his mind. As Guibert of Nogent tells us, "The pilgrims behaved with the utmost insolence, pulling down the palaces in the town, setting fire to public buildings, removing the lead from the roofs of churches and selling it afterwards to the Greeks." Alarmed by their behavior, Alexius decided to get them out of town as fast as possible and offered free transportation for the Crusaders across the Bosporus into Asia Minor.

On August 6, the People's Crusade invaded Asia Minor. Peter the Hermit made his headquarters at a Byzantine fortress called Civetot, on the Asian shore. Almost at once, a faction of Germans and Italians broke away from Peter and elected an Italian lord named Rainald as their leader. Only the Frenchmen remained loyal to Peter, but even they paid little heed to his words now that they were beyond Constantinople.

Cautiously, the Crusaders crept forward, pillaging as they went. Though the region around Civetot was Byzantine property and inhabited by Christian Greeks, the Crusaders attacked them as fiercely as though they were Turks. Then, in mid-September, a few thousand Frenchmen raided the suburbs of Nicaea, the capital of the Seljuk Sultan Kilij Arslan. They massacred the villagers, who were mostly Christian, and gathered up their herds of sheep. Returning to Civetot, they sold their booty at a good price.

The Germans and Italians under Rainald were jealous of the adventure. They also set out into Turkish-held territory, avoiding the walled city of Nicaea but going some miles past it. Coming to a castle called Xerigordon, they slew its Turkish garrison and occupied it.

Kilij Arslan had merely been amused by the first

35

raids of the Crusaders. Now he thought they had gone too far. He sent a detachment of crack troops to besiege Xerigordon. The Turks cut off the castle's water supply, and for eight days the Crusaders suffered the agonies of thirst. An anonymous chronicler writes, "Our men suffered so much from thirst that they opened the veins of their horses and donkeys to drink their blood . . . . others dug up the damp earth and spread it over their chests." At last Rainald agreed to surrender. The Turks promised to spare the life of any man who would become a Moslem. Rainald and many of his men renounced Christianity on the spot and were sent into slavery in Syria; the rest were slaughtered.

Peter the Hermit was in Constantinople during the Xerigordon massacre. He had gone back to confer with Alexius and to arrange for supplies and other assistance. While he was away, a soldier named Geoffrey of Burel persuaded the other leaders that the army should march out to avenge the disaster at Xerigordon. All the remaining soldiers took to the road, leaving only women and children in camp at Civetot. The noisy army of Crusaders swaggered straight into a Turkish ambush. Many were slain; the rest fled back to Civetot followed by the Turks. Only a handful escaped, among them Geoffrey of Burel. Walter the Penniless, Hugh of Tübingen, Walter of Teck, and nearly all the rest, perished.

So ended the People's Crusade—in total defeat. A year later, when the regular army of Crusaders passed through this part of Asia Minor, the chronicler Fulcher of Chartres saw "a mass of severed heads and bones of slaughtered men," the remains of Peter's Crusaders. And Anna Comnena wrote, "These bones made up a huge pile, or rather mound, or, better still, a hill or a high mountain of considerable size. Some time later men of the same race as these murdered barbarians, while building walls like those of a city, used their bones instead of mortar to fill the gaps and thus, in a sense, made a tomb for them as they built the town."

Nothing else endured of the People's Crusade.

While this comic adventure was drawing to its tragic close, the true Crusaders, the professional soldiers of Europe, were on their way toward Constantinople.

They were traveling in four groups, each an army with its own generals. One army consisted of men of southern France and Italy, led by Count Raymond of Toulouse. His wife, Princess Elvira of Aragon, was related to the royal house of Spain. He was a veteran warrior who had fought against the Spanish Moslems. Proud and pious, stubborn, envious by nature, Raymond was in his own eyes the chief of all the princes who went Crusading. He was the oldest, the wealthiest, the most experienced in battle, and therefore he felt that the other leaders of the Crusade should defer to him. He was a confidant of Pope Urban II; the Pope's own representative in the Crusade, Bishop Adhemar of Le Puy, traveled with Raymond's army.

A second Crusading army was led by three brothers: Eustace of Boulogne, Godfrey of Bouillon, and Baldwin of Lorraine. It consisted of northern Frenchmen and Germans. Eustace, the eldest brother, had only a lukewarm interest in the Crusade and spent little time in the Holy Land. His territories in Europe had more attraction for him. But his two brothers were destined to win fame there.

Godfrey of Bouillon, who was about thirty-five years old, was a tall, sturdy man with yellow hair and beard. Robert the Monk, one of the contemporary chroniclers of the First Crusade, wrote that Godfrey "was a man of goodly countenance, tall stature, pleasant speech, worthy behavior, and so mild of disposition that he seemed more like a monk than a soldier; but when the enemy was at hand he was a dreadless lion." As a younger son, he had not inherited any land, but the Holy Roman Emperor, Henry IV, had given him the Duchy of Lower Lorraine to rule. Godfrey had proved a poor ruler, unable to cope with the details of administration, and it was quite likely that Emperor Henry would soon discharge him from his duties. Partly because his future in Lorraine looked bleak and partly out of religious enthusiasm, Godfrey took the Cross. He was an amiable, popular man, heroic-looking rather than truly heroic, and much of his later fame seems undeserved.

His younger brother Baldwin of Lorraine was also a landless man; like many youngest sons, he had been marked by his family for a career in the Church, but he found holy orders not much to his taste, and became a warrior instead. Baldwin was even taller than his towering brother Godfrey; his hair was dark and his skin was strangely white. The gigantic Baldwin was a cool-mannered, haughty man with a taste for pomp and luxury. When he took the Cross, he was saying goodbye to Europe forever, for, as Raymond of Toulouse had also done, Baldwin took a vow to spend the rest of his days in the Holy Land. Both men brought their wives with them on the Crusade.

The third army of Crusaders was considered the main one. It was composed of men from the north and center of France and was under the joint leadership of three men: Robert, Duke of Normandy, his brother-in-law Count Stephen of Blois, and his cousin Count Robert II of

The Armies Gather

Flanders. Robert of Normandy was the eldest son of William the Conqueror, the Norman duke who had taken possession of England in 1066. Robert had received Normandy upon William the Conqueror's death, while another son, William Rufus, had become King of England. Robert of Normandy, forty years old, was a mild-mannered, easygoing man, bold in battle but not a very dynamic figure; he was usually in debt and had to borrow heavily from his brother King William Rufus in order to outfit his army for the Crusade.

Stephen of Blois was another half-hearted Crusader. He had not wanted to go at all, but he was ordered to do so by his wife, the fierce Adela. She was the daughter of William the Conqueror, and she was quite capable of ruling Stephen's lands while he went off to win glory in the name of God in the Holy Land. Stephen took with him, fortunately, the monk Fulcher of Chartres, who kept a careful chronicle of the war.

Robert of Flanders was more forceful than his two fellow generals. He had family reasons for taking the Cross; his father, Count Robert I of Flanders, had made a pilgrimage to Jerusalem in 1086, and on his way back had served for a while in the army of Emperor Alexius. There had been a bond of friendship between the elder Robert and the Emperor until the Count's death in 1093, which led his son now to go to Alexius's aid.

The fourth of the armies of the First Crusade joined the others as an afterthought. It was made up of the most fearsome breed of warriors in Europe at that time: the Normans of southern Italy. These stormy men, descendants of the Vikings, had left their homes in Normandy to carve new dominions for themselves in Byzantine-held Sicily. It had been easy enough to drive the Emperor's men out, but then, for more than a generation, the Sicilian Normans busied themselves in a bloody civil war, brother against brother and cousin against cousin. When Pope Urban proclaimed the Crusade, they paid little heed.

But in the fall of 1096, knights began to arrive in Sicily on their way toward Constantinople, and one of the Normans of Sicily was inspired to join them. He was Bohemond of Taranto, son of the great Norman leader Robert Guiscard, who had conquered Sicily practically single-handed. Bohemond had been on the losing end of the civil wars in Sicily and saw little future for himself there. It was much more probable, he thought, that he could win a kingdom for himself in the Holy Land. So, on the spur of the moment, he rounded up some followers and took the Cross, not out of religious zeal but from the hunger to rule.

Bohemond was totally unscrupulous though he could act the part of an honorable man when he felt it was to his advantage. Those who knew him feared him. He was a masterly leader, whose personal bravery insured the complete loyalty of his men. A clever politician, a subtle planner, a bold strategist, Bohemond was too complex to be dismissed as a barbarian. Anna Comnena, Emperor Alexius's historian-daughter, wrote that Bohemond "had a certain charm, somewhat spoiled, however, by the feeling of terror that he inspired. The man's tough and savage personality was revealed in his whole person, in the way he stood and in the way he glanced about him. Even his laugh could make his followers shiver. Courage and passion raged in his body and in his soul, and both these qualities were directed towards war. His mind was flexible and cunning, always devious."

The Byzantines had good reason to fear Bohemond.

He and his ferocious father had fought against them in Sicily and had inflicted terrible defeats upon them. The news that Bohemond was coming to Constantinople, supposedly to help them, did not please the Byzantines. "Everyone admired his appearance and shivered at his reputation," wrote Anna Comnena. "Nobody in the Byzantine Empire had met a man like this before, whether barbarian or Greek. He was more than a foot taller than anyone else, slender, with broad shoulders and chest, and strong arms. . . . He had powerful hands, an erect carriage, burly shoulders. . . . Remarkably white skin was tinged with red on his cheeks. His hair was fair and was not allowed to hang to his shoulders in the barbarian fashion. He did not like long hair, but had it cut short to his ears."

With Bohemond came his nephew Tancred, hotheaded and crafty, a young man who thirsted for glory. Like Bohemond, Tancred had no scruples; but he was more blatant in his ambitions, altogether a less attractive personality. There was a certain savage nobility about Bohemond that was missing from Tancred.

Just how many soldiers were included in the four armies of the First Crusade has long been a matter for debate. The chroniclers are of little help: Fulcher of Chartres tells us that there were 600,000 soldiers in all, which is much too high to be probable, while another chronicle speaks of 300,000, and a third gives the figure as 100,000. The real size of the fighting forces must have been much smaller, though the expeditions were swelled by the presence of women, children, servants, and clergy. A reliable contemporary source says that Bohemond went to Constantinople with 500 knights. Sir Steven Runciman, the foremost modern historian of the Crusades, has calculated from this and other plausible figures that the army of Crusaders consisted of, at best, about 4,500 cavalrymen and 30,000 infantry. It was a small force compared with the size of the Moslem hordes that awaited it, but it was made up of the finest soldiers of Christendom.

ON TO
CONSTANTINOPLE!

THE first of the Crusading knights to leave his home was Hugh, Count of Vermandois, the brother of King Philip I of France. Hugh set out late in August, 1096, riding at the head of a small army. By October, he had reached Italy, where he found Bohemond and Tancred beginning to organize their forces. At the Italian town of Bari on the Adriatic Sea, Hugh decided to journey by sea to the shores of Greece on the opposite side of the Adriatic. There he could enter the Byzantine Empire.

Hugh sent a messenger ahead to Constantinople, requesting the Emperor to greet him with a reception party worthy of a prince of royal blood. Alexius agreed and ordered a local governor to welcome Hugh. But the Crusader was shipwrecked and came ashore in Greece wet and bedraggled, all his belongings lost. He was taken into Byzantine hands and treated with great respect, given new clothing and housed at Byzantine expense. When he finally was taken to Constantinople, escorted by the Byzantine admiral Manuel Butumites, however, it was virtually as a prisoner. Alexius was taking no chances with these Crusading princes. Though he greeted Hugh warmly and loaded him with gifts, he kept close watch over him.

Emperor Alexius was troubled by the prospect of having the Crusaders descend upon his land. He had already watched with displeasure as the rabble of the People's Crusade arrived and departed in the summer of 1096. Now it was fall and a much more dangerous host was coming. Hugh of Vermandois was only the first of many. All Byzantium buzzed with worried talk about the Franks, the name by which the Western Europeans were known when they were not simply called Latins. The rumor was, as Anna Comnena wrote, that "all the West and all the barbarian tribes from beyond the Adriatic . . . were moving in a body through Europe towards Asia, bringing whole families with them."

According to Anna, Alexius "dreaded the arrival of the Franks, for he knew their impetuosity, their unstable and fickle character. . . . He knew how grasping the sight of riches made them and that at the first opportunity they would violate their treaties without scruple. Yet far from being discouraged he made all arrangements to be ready to fight if the need arose."

Alexius was not a man given to panic. He had been on the Byzantine throne for fifteen years, since 1081, and that in itself was a mark of his strength: there had been six Emperors in twenty-five years before Alexius emerged. Though not tall, he was a sturdy man of true imperial bearing. Gracious, sophisticated, relaxed in manner, he saw himself as the heir to fifteen centuries of Greek and Roman civilization, and he felt quite competent to deal successfully with the Turkish barbarians who threatened him on the one side and the Frankish barbarians who menaced him on the other.

On to Constantinople

What worried him most about the Crusaders was the thought that they had come to the East not to restore the lost Byzantine possessions, but to win kingdoms for themselves. In this he was quite correct, of course. It did not take much subtlety to realize that men like Bohemond would not fight to capture cities from the Turks and then meekly surrender them to Alexius. The Emperor's strategy, then, was to get each Crusader to swear an oath of allegiance to him, recognizing Alexius as his overlord and granting him control over the lands he might conquer.

Hugh of Vermandois, dazzled by the splendor of Constantinople and the generosity of Alexius, swore the oath without a second thought. But the next Crusaders to arrive were more cautious.

The army of Godfrey and Baldwin followed the route of the People's Crusade, down the Danube and through Hungary. King Coloman of Hungary had already had two groups of Crusaders led by Walter the Penniless and Peter the Hermit pass through his country. There had been looting both times, particularly by Peter's men, and Coloman was scarcely eager to have more Crusaders within his boundaries. But Godfrey offered his brother Baldwin as a good-conduct hostage, a gesture that did not altogether delight Baldwin. By telling his soldiers that any act of violence would be punished by death, Godfrey got his army safely through Hungary into the Byzantine Empire, and Baldwin was released.

Everything remained orderly as the Crusaders passed across Bulgaria, but there was a brief outbreak of rioting as they neared Constantinople. The news failed to cheer Emperor Alexius. On December 23, 1096, Godfrey's army arrived at Constantinople, and, at Alexius' suggestion, pitched camp just outside the city. Alexius sent for Godfrey, but Godfrey did not come. He had learned of the disaster that had overtaken Peter the Hermit's Crusaders two months earlier, and he suspected some sort of treachery on Alexius's part. Unlike the gullible Hugh of Vermandois, Godfrey did not want to expose himself to the sly Byzantine Emperor until the other leading Crusaders were present. The atmosphere of distrust between Emperor and Crusaders thus was marked at the very outset of the great enterprise.

During January and February, Alexius tried in vain to get Godfrey to appear and swear allegiance to him. Godfrey refused. Alexius struck back by blockading the camp of the Crusaders and shutting off its food supply. At once, Baldwin began to raid the suburbs. Matters grew more tense until, by early April, there was virtual war between the Crusaders and the Byzantines. Godfrey and Baldwin captured a platoon of Byzantine soldiers and put them to death; then, on April 2, the Crusaders drew up outside the walls of Constantinople and began to lay siege to the city.

Alexius was horrified. It was Holy Week, the day before Good Friday, and it seemed the highest sacrilege that Godfrey should attack on such a day. But the Emperor sent archers to the walls, ordering them to shoot over the heads of the Crusaders. Godfrey retreated. The next day, Hugh of Vermandois came out of the city to speak to Godfrey. Hugh asked him to end the foolhardy little war and submit to Alexius's wishes. Godfrey mocked him as a puppet of the Emperor and attacked Constantinople once more.

Losing his patience, Alexius sent his best troops into action. The Crusaders, not yet accustomed to fighting together, were no match for the well-disciplined Byzantines. They fled. On Easter Sunday, Godfrey and Baldwin swal-

lowed their pride and consented to take the oath of allegiance. It had not been a very auspicious start for their
Crusade; their first battle had been against fellow Christians, and it had ended in defeat.

The brothers swore to recognize Alexius as overlord
of any conquests they might make and to restore to the
Byzantines any land they seized that had once been part
of the Empire. Alexius gave a lavish banquet for the Crusaders, heaped them with gifts of gold, and then hustled
them across the Bosporus into Asia Minor where they
would be out of his way. For more Crusaders were about
to reach Constantinople, and Alexius did not want them
to join forces with Godfrey's army in his city.

The next to arrive were minor vassals of Godfrey—
bold, half-wild men who also balked at the oath of allegiance. Alexius brought them under control, and they
swore as he wished. During the ceremony, one of the
knights casually sat himself on Alexius's throne. Baldwin,
who was present, snapped at the man to get up, but the
knight replied angrily, like a naughty child. Alexius, that
polished and civilized man, was relieved to get these rude
warriors across the Bosporus too.

On April 9, Bohemond and his Normans appeared.
They had crossed the Adriatic safely, continuing by land
through Greece and Bulgaria. Bohemond had reminded
his men that they were traveling across a Christian country and through iron discipline had kept them from running wild in the usual Crusader manner. But in Byzantine
Bulgaria the discipline was relaxed, and Bohemond allowed his men to provision themselves at the expense of
the natives. They fought back, but, a chronicler of the
expedition declares, "We assailed them on all sides and
soon had the upper hand. Wherefore, we set fire to it

47

and burned the town with all that dwelt therein." Bohemond excused this act of aggression with the excuse that the town was inhabited by a sect of heretic Christians, not "true" Christians.

The Emperor sent an escort of troops to keep watch on Bohemond after that, making sure that the Normans did no plundering and never remained more than three days in the same place. There was only one battle, arising out of confusion, when Tancred became embroiled with the Byzantines and slew several. Bohemond, shrewdly trying to avoid offending Alexius, calmed his hotheaded nephew, and the rest of the journey to Constantinople was uneventful.

Bohemond did not make the mistake of Godfrey and Baldwin, who had stiffly refused to yield to Alexius. He took the oath of allegiance immediately—for, to Bohemond, oaths were only words and it was foolish to waste time quarreling with the Byzantines when there was land to be won in Asia. Bohemond had another motive for cooperating with Alexius. He asked that the Emperor name him as commander-in-chief of all the Byzantine forces in Asia.

Alexius hesitated. He privately feared Bohemond's ambitions and hardly wished to fan their flame with so lordly a title. He told Bohemond that it was too soon to make such an appointment, but hinted in vague terms that Bohemond might earn it in due time. Alexius also promised in a cloudy way that Bohemond might have "a little land" in the vicinity of the Syrian city of Antioch—a promise the Norman did not forget.

On April 26, Bohemond's army was ferried across the Bosporus to join the forces of Godfrey on the Asian shore. Tancred, who did not understand why his uncle was playing Alexius's game, refused to take any oaths. He passed through the city at night to avoid having to face the Emperor, but Alexius, with Bohemond sworn to support him, was not concerned about the unruly nephew.

On the next day, the army of Raymond of Toulouse made its appearance at Constantinople. Raymond had crossed northern Italy, following the coast into what is now Albania, then had marched across Byzantine territory with the customary disturbances and minor battles against the Emperor's troops. Raymond's men were boisterous and hard to restrain, and they resented the presence of Byzantine police. In one skirmish, Raymond himself was attacked by the Byzantines. Another time, Bishop Adhemar strayed from the road and was wounded by the police before they realized who he was. He was forced to drop out of the march to recuperate, and without his influence as a peacemaker the progress of Raymond's forces became ever more uproarious. Raymond left his army and went ahead to Constantinople, arriving on April 21, six days before the others. While he was gone the soldiers raided the countryside. In one furious battle the Byzantines soundly drubbed the Crusaders.

Raymond would swear no oaths of allegiance to Alexius. He regarded himself as bound only to the Pope, and to the Pope's representative, Adhemar of Le Puy. Since in his own view he was the military leader of the Crusaders, he could not bring himself to bow to Alexius. Bohemond and even Godfrey urged Raymond to submit. But Raymond was in no mood to take advice from his rivals in the Crusade, either.

At last, Alexius produced a compromise. On April 26, Raymond swore a lesser oath, promising to respect the life and honor of the Emperor and to see that nothing would be done to injure Byzantine interests. With this, Alexius was content, and Raymond did not see it as contrary to his own position. Two days later, Raymond took his army across the Bosporus.

The fourth of the Crusading armies, that of Robert of Normandy, Robert of Flanders, and Stephen of Blois, showed up at Constantinople in the middle of May. They had lingered through the winter in the warmth of southern Italy, after visiting Pope Urban near Rome. (Rome itself was once more in the hands of the supporters of the Antipope Guibert.) The leaders of this army were clearly not eager to go Crusading, and the fact was reflected in their late arrival. They made no objections to taking the oath. Stephen of Blois in particular was awed by Alexius, who treated him with royal generosity. Writing home to his wife, William the Conqueror's daughter Adela, Stephen said, "Your father, my love, made many great gifts, but he was almost nothing compared to this man."

To his great relief, Alexius now had all the troublesome Crusaders on the far side of the Bosporus. About a hundred thousand Franks had come eastward between the summer of 1096 and the spring of 1097, in what had amounted to a vast invasion of Byzantium. Anna Comnena, writing with obvious distaste for the Franks, tells us that "they arrived on each other's heels with arms, horses, and full military equipment. These men were so full of ardor and impetuosity that they swarmed all over the roads. They were accompanied by a multitude of unarmed people carrying palms and with crosses on their shoulders. . . . They were as numerous as leaves and flowers in spring." She could not bring herself to list the names of the leaders, because there were so many of them, and because the "barbarous sounds" were so hard to pronounce.

On to Constantinople

Alexius had fed all these Crusaders, had given them shelter, had in one way or another persuaded them to take oaths to him, and had eased them into Asia Minor. He did not trust the Crusaders, and they certainly did not trust him. To Alexius, the Franks were brutal brigands; to the Crusaders, Alexius was a tricky schemer. But each side needed the other: Alexius depended on the Crusaders to destroy the Turks, and the Crusaders needed Byzantium as its source of provisions and equipment.

And now began the holy war.

The first task was to drive the Seljuk Turks out of Asia Minor. That would clear an overland route from Constantinople to Syria, and Syria was the gateway to Palestine. With naval transportation such an uncertain thing, the Crusaders did not attempt to seize such coastal ports as Beirut, Tyre, and Acre and fight their way inland toward Jerusalem. Instead they planned to make their way through the deserts and mountains of Asia Minor into Syria, then downward by land until they were in a position to capture the Holy City.

They called their enemies the Saracens, by which they meant any sort of eastern Moslem, whether Turk or Arab. It was a word derived from the Byzantine Greek *sarakenos* and the Arabic *sharkeyn,* both meaning "eastern people." The Arabs themselves drew the distinction between the *sharkeyn* and the *maghribe,* or "western people," referring to the Moslems of North Africa and Spain. But to the Crusaders, all Moslems were Saracens.

The Seljuks were the first Saracens to be encountered. The Crusaders marched toward the city of Nicaea, the Seljuk capital, sixty-five miles from Constantinople. The Turks had captured it in 1081, and since then it had been a constant threat to Byzantium. Like most important cities of its time, Nicaea was surrounded by sturdy walls, and was fortified by 240 watchtowers. The only way to take such a city was to besiege it, pen its defenders inside, and attempt to smash through the walls.

The Crusaders arrived at Nicaea early in May, 1097, after passing the grisly site where the bones of the People's Crusade lay bleaching in the sun. Sultan Kilij Arslan was not in his capital; he had gone eastward himself to do battle against a rival Turkish clan, the Danishmends, in Armenia. He did not regard the Crusaders as a serious threat, remembering how easily his troops had slaughtered the peasant soldiers of Peter the Hermit the previous October.

The Crusaders laid siege to Nicaea. The city stood on the shore of a lake, so it was impossible to blockade it completely. The Turks were able to bring in supplies by water. Unless the lake could be taken, the siege might last forever.

While the Crusaders pondered this problem, Sultan Kilij Arslan arrived with his army to relieve Nicaea. For the first time the Christian armies clashed with those of the Saracens. The Sultan's men attempted to cut their way through the ranks of Crusaders and enter the walled city. They were met by the troops of Raymond of Toulouse and Robert of Flanders in a battle that raged all day.

The fighting methods of the two forces were quite different. Man for man, the Crusaders were bigger and stronger, and they used swords and lances while the Saracens depended on bows and arrows. The Crusaders were armored when they fought, but not in the shining metal suits that we usually think of as armor. Heavy steel plates were used for armor only from the fifteenth century onward, after the invention of firearms. In the closing decade

The Battle of Nicaea

of the eleventh century, men wore light, flexible coats of chain mail and helmets that left the face exposed except for a narrow vertical bar that protected the nose. A light cloth garment called a surcoat was worn over the chain mail so that the knights would not be blinded by the reflection of sunlight from one another's armor.

Their swords were heavy—no lightweight fencing foils
—and their shields were long and bulky. The knights, who
fought from horseback, wielded lengthy lances to great
effect. The foot soldiers, protected only by helmets and
leather armor, carried bows as well as swords. Some of
them swung the deadly spike-studded hammers known as
maces. Another weapon of the Crusaders was the crossbow, which Anna Comnena called "a truly diabolical
weapon." Its cord was pulled back by a windlass or lever,
instead of by a man's arm, and it released its short thick
bolt with such force that it could penetrate all but the
finest armor. The crossbow was devastating and murderous,
so much so that the Crusaders did not think it was quite
sporting to use it. Its biggest drawback was the time it
took to load; while a crossbowman struggled to wind up
his weapon, he could be shot half a dozen times by men
armed with ordinary bows.

The Saracens had swords, long and curving weapons
of superb Damascus steel. They used them with skill, making up in agility what they lacked in brute strength. They
relied greatly on their archers, sending squadrons of bow-
men into battle to make a quick attack, retreat, and attack
again somewhere else like troublesome mosquitoes. The
chronicler William of Tyre, who wrote in the twelfth
century, describes their tactics:

"When our forces met, the Turks shot so many arrows
at us that the sky could hardly have been darker in rain
or hail, and many of our people had great cause for grief
from them. When the first group had emptied their
quivers and shot off all their arrows, the second followed
them, and, going to a place where there still were many
knights, they began to shoot arrows more thickly than we
could believe possible."

On to Constantinople

In this first battle, before the walls of Nicaea, the Crusaders had the upper hand. Feeling the strength of the brawny Franks, the Sultan withdrew at the end of the day, heading for the mountains and abandoning Nicaea to its fate.

The siege continued. Raymond and Adhemar attempted to mine the walls, that is, to tunnel into them and cause their collapse. The unknown author of a chronicle called *The Deeds of the Franks* describes how the Count and the Bishop selected a watchtower along the wall and "chose some men to mine it, with crossbowmen and archers to protect them. They dug down to the very foundations of the wall, and then piled up the beams and the wood and set fire to them. That evening the tower collapsed, when night had already come; and because of the darkness there could be no fighting. During the course of the night the Turks rose hastily and repaired the wall so solidly that, when day came, it was impossible to do them any damage on that side."

So long as the lake remained open and the Turks could get fresh provisions, there was no hope of taking the town. The Crusaders asked Emperor Alexius to lend them ships. Alexius agreed, and a Byzantine fleet sailed to the port of Civetot. It was seven miles overland from Civetot to the landlocked Lake of Nicaea, but the Crusaders ingeniously rigged wagons to carry the ships and dragged them to the lake. During the night, the Byzantine ships took up positions in the water off Nicaea, and in the morning the Turks were horrified to find themselves blockaded on all sides.

On June 19, the Crusaders planned to launch a general attack that would make them the masters of the besieged city. They marshalled their forces under cover of darkness and drew near. But when dawn broke, a stunning surprise awaited them. The Byzantine flag fluttered over Nicaea's walls!

The city had surrendered in the night—not to the Crusaders but to Alexius. The Emperor had moved swiftly and cleverly. He knew that if the Crusaders broke into Nicaea after having besieged it for seven weeks, they would lay waste to the city, plundering it and slaughtering its people. But the Nicaeans were Christians, and until fifteen years before the city had belonged to Byzantium. Alexius had no desire to see the riches of Nicaea fall into the hands of the Franks. He wanted the city restored to the Empire, intact and unharmed.

With the legendary Byzantine skill at intrigue, Alexius had persuaded the Turkish garrison in Nicaea to yield without further battle. He promised them safe conduct to Constantinople, whereas the Crusaders would certainly have massacred them.

The maneuver was infuriating to the Crusaders. They had toiled for nearly two months to take Nicaea only to be cheated of the pleasure of plundering the city. Perhaps some of the commanding officers had entertained thoughts of claiming Nicaea for their own, but now that was impossible also. Alexius had outsmarted them. What little trust there had been between the Franks and the Byzantine Emperor evaporated entirely.

Alexius soothed their disappointment by presenting every Crusader with splendid gifts, allowing the leaders to dip freely into the gold and jewelry of the Seljuk Sultan's treasury. In return, though, he asked that those who had not earlier sworn allegiance to him do so now. The lesser lords took the oath, reluctantly. Only Tancred held out, demanding a mountain of gold before he swore. Bohemond finally talked him into submitting.

On to Constantinople

The Crusaders were disappointed by Alexius's cleverness, but the fact still remained that the capital of the Seljuks had fallen. The taste of victory was sweet. "In five weeks' time we shall be at Jerusalem," Stephen of Blois wrote to his wife. "Unless," he added in a prophetic moment, "we are held up at Antioch."

iv

CRUSADER
AGAINST SARACEN

THE Turks began to show alarm. Before Nicaea had fallen, they had been confident. During the siege of Nicaea, the Sultan had written to its citizens, speaking derisively of the Franks:

"There is no need to be afraid of these people in spite of their vast numbers. They have come from that far country where the sun sets, and they are worn out with the exertions and the labors of the way. . . . Remember that we have already wiped out a swarm of them without trouble, killing more than fifty thousand in one day. Take heart, then, and have no fear."

Now the Seljuk Sultan hastened to patch up his quarrel with the Danishmend Turks and regroup his forces to meet the invaders as they proceeded eastward. The Franks came over the mountains into the plain of Dorylaeum. To make the gathering of supplies easier, they had divided into two sections marching a day apart. Bohemond led the first group, Raymond of Toulouse the second.

On the evening of June 30, five days after leaving

vanquished Nicaea, Bohemond made camp near Dorylaeum, half suspecting that the Turks might be lurking
nearby. At dawn came the attack. A huge army of Saracens
led by Sultan Kilij Arslan swarmed down upon the Franks.
The chronicler Raymond of Aguilers says there were
150,000 Turks; Fulcher of Chartres claims that "they
numbered 360,000 fighters, all on horses and armed with
bows."

Bohemond drew his forces together and ordered them
to remain strictly on the defensive, for he saw they would
be cut to pieces if they broke ranks to attack. The camp
was surrounded by Turks. "We were all huddled together,"
declares Fulcher of Chartres, "indeed, like sheep shut in
a pen, trembling and frightened, surrounded on all sides
by enemies, so that we were unable to advance in any
direction. It was clear to us that this befell us as a punishment for our sins."

Saracen arrows showered down out of the blazing
summer sky. Nearly every Crusader in the front line suffered at least one wound. For six hours Bohemond held
out, but he saw defeat as inevitable. The proud Norman
had not expected to win holy martyrdom so early in the
Crusade.

Then, about midday, the second section of the Frankish army began to arrive, first the troops of Godfrey of
Bouillon and Hugh of Vermandois and then those of Raymond of Toulouse. The Turks had thought they had
trapped the entire Crusading force. Suddenly they were
themselves trapped between two armies of Franks. They
hesitated, and the Crusaders took the offensive. Abruptly,
Bishop Adhemar of Le Puy came down a mountain pass
leading yet another contingent of troops, and at the sight
of the new army the Turks panicked and fled.

"We pursued and slew them the whole day long,"

it is recorded in *The Deeds of the Franks*. "And we got much spoil; gold and silver, horses and asses, camels and sheep and oxen, and many other things." The glorious triumph that had been denied the Crusaders at Nicaea was theirs at Dorylaeum. The Franks were generous in their appreciation of the valor of their defeated foes. As one chronicler wrote, the Turks might have been unconquerable if they had only been Christians. "No man could have found stronger or braver men, or more skilled in warfare; yet, by God's grace, our men had the upper hand."

By God's grace, the Crusaders had no more battles to fight as they crossed Asia Minor except the battle against the elements of nature. Kilij Arslan, having lost thousands of men and an untold quantity of treasure to the Franks, had decided to risk no more contests with them. He kept out of their way from then on, ravaging the countryside instead so that they would be hard put to find provisions. In the July heat, the Crusaders forced themselves onward through the inhospitable desert that occupies the heart of Asia Minor: "an uninhabitable land without water," says the unknown author of *The Deeds of the Franks*, "which we had difficulty in coming through alive. Hunger and thirst beset us everywhere and we had hardly anything left to eat except thorns, which we pulled up and rubbed in our hands; such was the food on which we wretchedly lived."

Most of the horses perished on the fearful desert passage, so even the haughty knights journeyed on foot, sweltering in their armor. After the heat and thirst came cold drenching rain which fell four and five days at a time. By mid-August, when they reached the city of Iconium (the modern Konya), the Crusaders were in desperate need of rest.

They rested and moved on, harassed by Turks who destroyed all food supplies that lay in their way. Now the Crusaders ascended the mountain ranges of the Taurus and the Anti-Taurus, and we read in their accounts how they "penetrated into a diabolical mountain pass that was so lofty and narrow that none dared go before the others on the path. The horses fell headlong into the ravines and each pack animal dragged another down. On every side the knights gave way to despair and beat their breasts for sorrow and sadness."

But in time they left the "accursed mountains" behind and came to a town called Marash, inhabited by Christians who welcomed them joyfully and gave them provisions. "At last," the chronicle declares in relief, "our knights reached the valley where lies the royal city of Antioch, capital of all Syria."

A thousand years before, Antioch had been the most magnificent city in Asia. It lay twelve miles from the shores of the Mediterranean, on the banks of the River Orontes, which gave it an outlet to the sea. It was holy to Christians, for Saint Peter had preached there, and one of the earliest Christian churches had been established in Antioch. Earthquakes and Persian attacks had humbled the city in the sixth century, and afterward, under the Arabs, it had prospered not nearly as well as its nearby inland rival, Aleppo. But the Byzantines had reconquered Antioch in the tenth century and had made it great once more, the mightiest fortress of the Syrian frontier. For all its greatness, Antioch had fallen to the Seljuks in 1085, and was ruled by Yaghi-Siyan, a Turk of independent ways who in theory was a vassal of Ridwan, the Turkish Emir of Aleppo, but in practice did as he pleased.

The Franks were awed by the fabled city. Camped beneath it, they looked up at its enclosing wall, eight miles long, topped with 360 watchtowers. Stephen of Blois, writing to his wife from Nicaea, had told her it would be only a matter of days to take Antioch; but now, actually before the city, it did not seem that simple.

Most of the inhabitants of Antioch were Christians. Yaghi-Siyan, fearing that they might act as a fifth column to aid the besiegers, drove many of them from the city and threw others into prison. Only through treachery had the Turks been able to take the impregnable city in 1085, and Yaghi-Siyan was determined not to be a victim of treachery.

From late October on, the Crusaders encircled Antioch. A chronicler named Albert of Aix describes them, "in all the splendor of their shields of gold, green, red and other colors, unfurling banners of gold and purple. They were mounted on war horses and wore glittering helmets and shields." But they could not entirely surround the city, for on the south there were steep mountains where no troops could be stationed.

Only Raymond of Toulouse argued for an immediate attempt to storm the walls. The other leaders advised waiting and resting until the troops were fresh. The army was not at full strength, for two of its most important leaders had gone off on private adventures. In September, Tancred and a few hundred soldiers had invaded the Syrian city of Tarsus. Tancred had claimed it for his own. But Baldwin of Lorraine had followed him, accompanied by his cousin, Baldwin of Le Bourg, and several thousand men. Baldwin of Lorraine compelled Tancred to surrender Tarsus to him. He had no more right to the city than Tancred did, for by oath the Crusaders were supposed to hand over such conquests to Emperor Alexius. But Tancred, outnumbered, was forced to yield.

Furious with Baldwin, Tancred rampaged onward into Syria. Baldwin rejoined the main army at Marash, but did not continue with it on its southward march to Antioch. Instead, mindful of his own interests, he turned sharply to the east and entered Armenia, where he hoped to found a principality for himself. Already some of the Crusaders were beginning to lose sight of Jerusalem. Early in the winter of 1097, Baldwin of Lorraine captured the fortresses of Ravendel and Turbessel, and in February, 1098, moved on to the Armenian city of Edessa, which had maintained an uneasy independence despite the presence of Turks around it. Edessa welcomed Baldwin as its savior. He wiped out the Turks in the vicinity. In March, after conspirators had slain the Christian ruler of Edessa, the citizens of the city offered the post to Baldwin.

Thus Baldwin of Lorraine became the first Crusader to win a dominion for himself in Asia, not in the Holy Land itself, but far to the northeast. He had broken his oath to Alexius, and had possibly dishonored himself by conniving at the murder of his predecessor. But now this landless youngest brother who had left Europe without rank or fortune was Count of Edessa. He withstood all attempts by the Saracens to displace him, and in a way he helped the Crusaders at Antioch. A great army of Turks heading for Antioch to attack the Franks paused to lay siege to Edessa and was defeated by Baldwin.

With Baldwin ruling Edessa and Tancred plundering the minor cities of Syria, the rest of the Crusaders before the walls of Antioch decided to wait. Perhaps Tancred would arrive, or perhaps Alexius would send reinforcements; in any event, they would have a chance to rest.

They rested. They ravaged the plain of Antioch and built fortified towers to cut off Turkish raiding parties that came down from the mountains. Winter came, and the Crusaders shivered in the rain. Their food supplies were running low. The fact that there could be cold winters in the East had never occurred to the Crusaders; Stephen of Blois told his wife, "We have suffered for the sake of Christ bitter cold and torrential rain. It is not true to say that the heat of the Syrian sun is unbearable, for winter here is very like winter in the West."

In December, Bohemond and Robert of Flanders departed with twenty thousand men to raid the Syrian villages of the countryside, in order to collect food. Godfrey of Bouillon was a sick man at that time, so Raymond of Toulouse was the only leader of the Crusade in command at Antioch. One night the impatient Raymond nearly captured the city while his rival Bohemond was away. A party of Turks emerged from a gate in the wall and attacked Raymond's troops. Though caught by surprise, Raymond led a countercharge and almost reached the open gate. In the darkness, there was a moment of confusion, and the Franks were thrust aside before they could enter Antioch.

Bohemond and Robert of Flanders had little luck collecting food and came back empty-handed to Antioch. Men began to desert, hoping to make the impossible journey back to Constantinople. Surprisingly, one of the deserters was Peter the Hermit, who had joined the Crusaders at Constantinople late in 1096 after the failure of his own Crusade. The man whose fervor had led so many foolhardy peasants to take the Cross now lost his own faith and ran away. Tancred, who had rejoined the Crusaders by now, followed him and brought him back.

Yaghi-Siyan had appealed to his fellow Turkish potentates for help. Duqaq of Damascus provided nothing but promises; Kerbogha of Mosul sent an army, but it became sidetracked besieging Baldwin in Edessa; only Ridwan of Aleppo managed to get aid to Antioch. No sooner did his troops arrive than Bohemond charged them in a surprise attack. Ridwan's men broke ranks and fled back to Aleppo.

Food was running lower all the time, and the grim winter had left many of the Crusaders unable to fight. It seemed as though the siege might have to be lifted. Retreat would mean the failure of the Crusade. Antioch had to be taken or there would not be a safe land route to Jerusalem.

The problems of the Crusaders were multiplied by the presence of spies among them. William of Tyre tells us how these men slipped out of Antioch and into the Crusader camp, posing as Christians: "Some said they were Greeks, others Syrians, others Armenians, and each was careful to assume exactly the language, manners, and customs of the part he was playing. . . . It was no easy task to expel from our camp men whom no difference of customs or language distinguished from the rest of the people."

Bohemond dealt with the spy problem his own way. He ordered that some Turkish prisoners be brought forth and executed. Then, lighting a great fire in the camp, he told his men to prepare the bodies of the dead prisoners as though they were going to be roasted and eaten. Bohemond made certain that the Turks of Antioch were told that the Crusaders "had decided in council that in future all enemies or spies who were taken prisoner should be treated in this way and used for the nourishment of the princes and the people." After that, few spies penetrated the Crusader camp.

It was Bohemond, too, who brought the siege to its

end after it had lasted from October to May. The Norman knight made contact with a certain Firouz, an Armenian Christian who had converted to Islam and taken service with Yaghi-Siyan. Firouz was secretly disloyal to his Turkish master and agreed to let the Crusaders into Antioch— for a price.

Bohemond said nothing to his comrades about his negotiations with Firouz. He had been planning for some time to make himself the lord of Antioch after its capture, in direct violation of his oath to Alexius. Armed with the knowledge that Firouz would betray the city to him, Bohemond called the Crusaders together and said, "We are in a wretched state. It is time for action. Let one among us attempt to seize the city, and if he manages to accomplish it, let us grant him with one voice the possession of it."

The others refused. "None shall receive the possession of this city, but we will all share it equally among us," they replied. "We have borne the same labors; we will all receive the same honor."

Soon the Crusading knights changed their mind. News came that Kerbogha, the terrifying Emir of Mosul, had given up the siege of Edessa and was at last on his way to Antioch with 200,000 men. Some of the Crusaders deserted outright at this report. Among those who hastily set out for home was Stephen of Blois, one of the high leaders. The others were eager to capture Antioch before Kerbogha's army arrived. Again Bohemond spoke to them, telling them that he knew a way to take the city, but that he would put his plan into effect only if they agreed to hand the town over to him. Such men as Raymond of Toulouse and Godfrey of Bouillon, who were jealous of Bohemond's ambitions, grumbled, but finally agreed. They made one condition: "That if Emperor Alexius comes to our help, we will hand over the town to him according to our oaths, even if Bohemond has it in his possession."

Bohemond made contact with his friend Firouz again and arranged the details of Antioch's betrayal. Firouz advised him to assemble the Crusaders and lead them away from the city, toward the east, as though marching out to attack Kerbogha. Then, when darkness fell, they were to creep quietly back to the western wall of Antioch, bringing ladders to scale the tower. Firouz would do the rest.

On the morning of June 2, 1098, Bohemond explained the scheme to Raymond, Godfrey, Robert of Flanders, and Bishop Adhemar. Raymond in particular was distressed to see that Bohemond appeared to have Antioch in his grasp. But taking the city was more important than the personal rivalries of the Crusaders, and they all agreed to follow Bohemond's plan.

Late in the day, the Franks set out toward the east. "If God's grace favors us," Bohemond declared, "this night Antioch will be surrendered to us." The Turks, seeing them go, relaxed. By midnight, the Crusaders had begun to turn back and shortly before dawn Bohemond's troops reached the walls of Antioch. A rope ladder was thrown to the top of the tower, where Firouz was waiting to fasten it in place.

Bohemond himself was the first to mount the ladder. He arrived at the top. As his hand appeared on the rim of the wall, Firouz grasped it, crying, "Long live this hand!" Moments later, sixty Frankish knights followed Bohemond into the tower. They slew the dozing Turks and took possession of the towers nearby. The rope ladder broke; but the Franks climbed down into the city and, with the help of the Christian inhabitants that remained, flung open the great gates.

The Crusaders thundered into Antioch. They slaughtered every Turk they found, and the first bright rays of morning revealed Bohemond's purple banner floating triumphantly from the highest point in the city. The Christians of Antioch, long oppressed by the Turks, joined in the massacre; Yaghi-Siyan himself was caught and beheaded by a group of Armenian peasants, who were handsomely rewarded by Bohemond.

Some of the Saracens were able to flee to a citadel on the hills above the town. The rest perished. By nightfall on June 3, there was not a Turk left alive in Antioch. The Crusaders allowed themselves a joyous sack of the town, pillaging the houses and seizing any treasures they found. "Every open space in the town was littered with corpses, so that none could stay there because of the stench," declares the author of *The Deeds of the Franks*. "It was not possible to walk in the roads without walking on the corpses of the dead." Antioch had been taken, and Bohemond was its master.

The victory celebration was shortlived. By June 7, Kerbogha and his vast horde of warriors were camped outside the walls of Antioch. The Crusaders, so recently the besiegers, were now the besieged.

Bohemond's sense of strategy had failed him, and it appeared that he had carried the whole Crusade to its doom. In his haste to become overlord of Antioch, he had led the entire army into a trap. Now, hemmed up in Antioch, a city whose food supplies were depleted by many months of siege, the Crusaders would have to withstand the same treatment they had dealt out.

Panic threatened the Franks. Hundreds of them climbed over the walls at night, only to be cut down by Kerbogha's men. Within the city the dead were buried quickly, for fear of an epidemic, and the defenses were strengthened. Kerbogha did not try to attack, though. He was content to starve the Crusaders into submission.

Food was in short supply. A loaf of bread cost a gold piece, an egg two gold pieces, a chicken fifteen. Men ate the flesh of horses and donkeys, or tried to live on the leaves of trees. The siege stretched into a second week and a third, and hunger gnawed at the trapped Franks.

The only hope for them was the arrival of Alexius and the Byzantine army. The Crusaders knew that the Emperor had been campaigning in western Asia Minor that spring, and that he was planning to join the Crusaders at Antioch some time in the summer. But Alexius did not arrive. The reason was an ironic one. Early in June, as he marched through Asia Minor with the intention of going to Antioch, Alexius was visited in his camp by Stephen of Blois. Stephen had abandoned the Crusade at Antioch only a few hours before Bohemond had announced his plan for invading the city. Stephen had no knowledge of Bohemond's deal with Firouz, and, naturally, no inkling that by this time Bohemond had already captured Antioch.

Well aware that Kerbogha was descending on Antioch, Stephen jumped to the obvious conclusion: that by now the Crusaders had probably been annihilated by the Turks outside Antioch. He told this to Alexius. The Emperor, who trusted Stephen's judgment, realized that such a defeat was the most likely fate for the Frankish army. Under the circumstances, he did not care to take the risk of going on to Antioch himself. The cause of the Crusade seemed lost. Alexius turned back toward Constantinople.

In a short while, the tale had reached Antioch. Bohemond and his companions were furious with Alexius for what they considered more Byzantine treachery. They could not see his point of view, for, no matter how hopeless their position appeared, they thought it was Alexius's obligation to come to their defense. Stephen of Blois came in for his share of abuse too; he was openly denounced as a coward by his former friends. More trouble was in store for him when he reached France many months later. His wife Adela gave him a fierce tonguelashing for having abandoned the Crusade, and ordered poor Stephen to return to the Holy Land at once to redeem his honor.

All looked grim within Antioch. The leaders of the Crusade bickered; the soldiers were weak with hunger; the summer heat was fearful. Only a miracle could save the Crusade. But the eleventh century was a fertile time for miracles. Men had strong faith in the mystic and the supernatural, particularly these men of the Crusade who believed they were fighting for God. It did not seem at all unusual to them that God should send dreams and visions to them, or that He should work a miracle to save them. And a miracle came to pass.

A disreputable French civilian named Peter Bartholomew, who was the servant of a pilgrim called William-Peter, came to see Bishop Adhemar and Raymond of Toulouse. He told them that in the past six months he had been visited many times by visions of an old man with silver beard and a youth of great beauty. "Arise, and do not be afraid," the old man told Peter Bartholomew. "I am the apostle Andrew."

Saint Andrew and the young man, whom Peter Bartholomew knew to be Jesus, conducted him to the Cathedral of Saint Peter, which the Turks had used as a mosque, while they held Antioch. Saint Andrew disappeared into the ground and returned carrying the Holy Lance, the

The vision of Peter Bartholomew

lance with which Christ's side was pierced by a Roman
soldier as he hung upon the Cross. Peter Bartholomew
wished to take the sacred relic, but the saint told him to
wait until the proper time.

All these months, Peter Bartholomew had ignored the
visions, though Saint Andrew and Jesus repeatedly came
to him and ordered him to reveal the existence of the

Holy Lance to Bishop Adhemar and Count Raymond. In June, just after the capture of Antioch, Peter narrowly escaped death in a battle with the Turks, and Saint Andrew came to him once again, sternly commanding him to reveal his visions. And this time he went to the Bishop and the Count.

Adhemar was skeptical. He regarded Peter Bartholomew as a fool at best, a liar at worst. But Raymond of Toulouse, a simpler man than Adhemar, insisted on searching for the Holy Lance. Had not Saint Andrew told Peter Bartholomew that the Lance would bring victory to the side that carried it into battle?

The story spread through the besieged city. The demoralized Crusaders took heart; if saints and even the Savior were visiting them, their cause could not be lost. Soon other visions were reported: Saint Peter was seen by one man, and the Virgin Mary, and Jesus once more. A meteor flashed above the Turkish camp one night, another sign from heaven, perhaps.

In the middle of June, a dozen Crusaders including Count Raymond accompanied Peter Bartholomew to the Cathedral and began to dig for the Holy Lance. From morning to night they dug, opening a deep trench, but finding no sacred relic. They grew discouraged and weary. But, according to Raymond of Aguilers, who was present at the scene, Peter Bartholomew "took off his belt and shoes and, barefoot and in his shirt, descended into the ditch we had dug." Praying loudly, he groped in the earth and, with a cry of joy, discovered the iron point of a lance embedded at his feet!

The weapon looked suspiciously like an eleventh-century Norman lance, and not like a relic of the time of Jesus, but those who had doubts wisely kept them to themselves. To the common soldiers, it was the Holy Lance, miraculously provided by heaven as the symbol of victory. New courage inspired them. They did not pause to suspect that someone, perhaps Peter Bartholomew, perhaps Raymond of Toulouse, had taken the trouble to plant the Lance where it could later by found.

While the Crusaders were buoyed by the discovery, the besieging Turks were beginning to lose interest in surrounding Antioch. They were men of far-off Mosul, and they wanted to get back to their homes and families. Kerbogha was clearly having difficulties keeping his army loyal, and the Franks could see that there were wholesale desertions. So on June 27, in the third week of the siege and the famine, they sent an ambassador to Kerbogha to persuade him to agree to a truce.

The ambassador was Peter the Hermit, he who once had preached the Crusade with such prophetic zeal. Shivering in his sandals, he went to Kerbogha to negotiate. The Turk would not listen. Despite the desertions in his own forces, he still felt confident that he could taken Antioch and shatter the Crusade.

Bohemond took command now. He argued for an immediate attack on the Turks. This was the ideal moment; the Crusaders were inflamed by the discovery of the Holy Lance, and Bohemond knew that if they delayed much longer, hunger would rob them of their remaining strength.

The gates of Antioch were thrown open, and the Crusaders rode forth. Their eyes were glazed from fasting, and for the last three days they had prayed almost continuously, until they were in what was almost a hypnotic trance of religious fervor. The historian Raymond of Aguilers was given the honor of carrying the Holy Lance.

They were a bedraggled, tattered lot. The Turks could scarcely believe their eyes as they saw the Frankish host advance. Kerbogha, frightened now by the strange intensity of the Christian foe, suddenly offered to parley for a truce, but it was too late. The Crusaders charged, riding into a barrage of arrows with no sign of fear.

Priests stood on the walls of the city, calling for God's help. The soldiers themselves imagined that they saw Saint George leading the heavenly hosts to their aid on white horses. "It seemed to us that there were among us five extra ranks of soldiers," wrote Raymond of Aguilers. The Saracens began to flee. One division of Turks had been sent by Duqaq of Damascus, Kerbogha's chief rival, and Duqaq was eager to see Kerbogha defeated. At a critical moment, Duqaq withdrew his men from the field, and the rest of the Turks, seeing them leave, broke into wild disarray. The Crusaders followed them, inflicting tremendous slaughter. Kerbogha himself slipped away in the confusion, but the field ran red with Saracen blood. The defeat was crushing to the Turks. Kerbogha's treasury fell into the hands of the Crusaders. One of the prizes, William of Tyre declares, was the Emir's tent. "It was constructed like a town, adorned with towers, walls, and ramparts, and covered with sumptuous hangings of silks of many colors. From the center of the tent, one could see many compartments opening out on all sides and forming as it were roads, in which again were many other dwellings, like inns. It was said that two thousand men could easily be housed in this vast edifice."

The double siege of Antioch had left the city in the control of the Franks. In the aftermath of victory came angry disputes. Bohemond again stated his claim to the city. Alexius had not come to the aid of the Crusaders, and

Bohemond no longer considered his oath to the Emperor binding. Godfrey of Lorraine backed Bohemond, seeing it was unwise to thwart him.

But Raymond of Toulouse, always envious of Bohemond's increasing glory, objected. Though he had no love for Alexius himself and had, in fact, refused to swear the full oath of allegiance to him, Raymond preferred to see Byzantium get Antioch rather than let Bohemond have the city. He argued that Antioch had always been part of the Empire before the Turkish conquest, and that by rights it should be returned to Alexius now. Bishop Adhemar took the same stand, pointing out that if Bohemond kept Antioch, it would offend Alexius and drive the wedge of discord even deeper between the Crusaders and the Byzantines.

For five months, the Crusaders remained at Antioch while Raymond and Bohemond jockeyed for power. It was too hot to continue into the Holy Land anyway, and the Crusaders were fatigued by the year-long campaign. In July, a plague of typhoid struck the city, and among its victims was Bishop Adhemar of Le Puy. His death was a severe blow to the Crusade, for he was the chief voice of harmony, and now he no longer would be on hand to restrain the boiling ambitions of the barons.

The summer passed. November came, and men began to talk of setting out for Jerusalem. But the question of Antioch remained unsettled. Bohemond would not leave the city, and Raymond refused to depart so long as Bohemond stayed on. It began to seem as though the Crusade would bog down permanently in Antioch.

JERUSALEM
REGAINED

THE stalemate among the Crusaders dragged on toward the end of 1098. Late in November, galled by inaction, Raymond of Toulouse and Robert of Flanders decided to leave Antioch in order to capture Marra, the next town on the road to Jerusalem. They did not plan to go past Marra until the Antioch question was settled, but at least the town would be in Frankish hands when the time came to head south.

But Marra proved a tougher nut to crack than they expected. For two weeks the Crusaders surrounded the town and tried in vain to scale its walls. Peter Bartholomew, who was still having holy visions, announced that victory soon would come. On December 11, Raymond's carpenters finished building a huge siege machine, the chief offensive weapon in any attack on a walled city. The description in *The Deeds of the Franks* gives a good idea of how such an attack was made:

"Raymond had a tall, strong wooden castle built. It stood on four wheels which were part of the structure.

Several knights were stationed in the upper storey, including Everard the Huntsman, who sounded the trumpet very loudly. Below on the ground were armor-clad knights who pushed the castle near the walls, against a tower. When they saw this, the pagans at once constructed an engine which hurled great stones at the castle, so that nearly all our knights were killed." The Saracens also hurled Greek fire on the attackers—oil of naptha, sealed in clay pots. When the pots were flung, they broke open, scattering the inflammable oil over the enemy, and it then was set afire by white-hot splinters of stone hurled by slings or catapults. The flaming substance could burn even on water, to the great terror of its victims. "But," the chronicler tells us, "almighty God willed it that the castle should not burn this time."

While Crusaders atop the siege castle flung great boulders onto the defenders within the city, other men were at work mining the walls. An attempt to scale the tower failed, but in the evening the mined wall collapsed and the Crusaders were able to enter the town.

During the two-week siege of Marra, Bohemond had joined the forces of Raymond. As the city fell, the clever Norman engineered a maneuver that put control of it in his hands, and Bohemond's men carried off the greater part of the loot. Raymond was furious at having been tricked by Bohemond once again. He tried to force a showdown on the matter of Antioch, with the hope of upsetting Bohemond's grasp on the great city.

Raymond's own soldiers objected. Let Bohemond have Antioch, they said. They were eager to march on to Jerusalem, the real goal of the Crusade. By Christmas, Raymond reluctantly began to give in. He made one last attempt to foil Bohemond: he offered cash payments,

77

virtual bribes, to Godfrey, Tancred, Robert of Flanders, and Robert of Normandy, if they would recognize him as the grand commander of the Crusade. But they refused. Raymond had no choice but to let Bohemond have Antioch and to go on to Jerusalem.

On January 13, 1099, Raymond led his men southward from Marra. He went barefoot, as a sign of penitence, for this was a pilgrimage to Christ's city as well as a campaign of war. The other leaders of the Crusade were unwilling to let Raymond have the glory of capturing Jerusalem alone, and so, shortly, Tancred and Robert of Normandy set out to join him. A few weeks later, Godfrey of Bouillon and Robert of Flanders did the same.

But three of the original princes of the Crusade were missing as the holy war approached its climax. Stephen of Blois was at home in his castle, being harangued by his wife. Baldwin of Lorraine, now Count Baldwin of Edessa, was ruling the lands he had captured in Armenia. And Bohemond of Taranto, content with possessing Antioch, did not join the march to Jerusalem.

While the Crusaders prepared for their attack on Jerusalem, other warriors were looking toward the Holy City as well. The Arab dynasty of the Fatimids decided to take advantage of the weakness of the Turks to seize Palestine.

The Fatimids were stubborn foes of the Turks. Although Moslems, they were quite willing to ally themselves with the Christian Crusaders against their Seljuk enemies. As early as the spring of 1098, while the Crusaders still were laying siege to Antioch, a Fatimid ambassador had come to their camp with a proposal to divide the Seljuk empire: the Franks could have Syria, and Egypt would take Palestine.

Jerusalem Regained

The Crusaders had no objections to doing business with Moslems when they thought it would help their cause, but they could hardly agree to a treaty that would leave the Holy Land controlled by Islam. Politely, they declined the Fatimid offer.

A year later, the Fatimids moved into Palestine anyway, without an agreement with the Crusaders. The Turks were in a state of disarray after their defeats at Dorylaeum, Antioch, and Edessa, and they were in no position to withstand an Egyptian offensive. The Fatimid Grand Vizier, al-Afdal, laid siege to Jerusalem for forty days, battering its walls and compelling the Turks to surrender. So while the Crusaders marched southward the Holy City was passing from Turk to Arab power.

There were other Arab dynasties, independent of the Fatimids, controlling such coastal cities as Shaizar and Tripoli, which lay on the Crusaders' route. The rulers of these cities saw that it was hopeless to oppose the Franks and made treaties of peace with them instead. Town after town sent gifts to the Crusaders and promised them safe conduct through their lands. Where a city failed to yield, the Crusaders besieged and took it without great difficulty.

By April of 1099, they had reached Arqa, on the Mediterranean coast. There they encountered tougher resistance. The siege of Arqa went on and on. Once more, the chief Crusaders began to bicker. With Bohemond elsewhere, the main opponents were Raymond and Godfrey, whose ambitions collided constantly now. Tancred, Robert of Flanders, and Robert of Normandy tended to side with Godfrey.

In the course of the quarrel, Peter Bartholomew spoke up with a new revelation. He announced that on April 5 he had been visited by Christ, Saint Peter, and Saint Andrew, who had instructed him to tell the Crusaders to get on with the conquest of Arqa. This time Peter Bartholomew had had one vision too many. Some of Robert of Normandy's men began to mutter that Peter was in the pay of Raymond of Toulouse, and that his visions were being conveniently arranged to further Raymond's wishes. Soon Raymond's enemies were openly expressing their belief that Peter Bartholomew was a fraud, visions, saints, Holy Lance and all.

But Peter by now believed in his own divine support. Angrily he demanded to be subjected to the ordeal by fire, a common medieval form of judgment. He would run between two huge bonfires built close together. If he emerged unharmed from the flames, the truth of his visions would be proved. If he perished in the blaze, it would show that he had been deceitful or that his visions had been sent by the Devil.

The bonfires were built on Good Friday, April 8. Before a huge audience, Peter Bartholomew ran through the flames. Exactly what happened is a matter for doubt. Raymond of Aguilers, who believed in the truth of Peter's visions, wrote that he came unscathed through the ordeal. Reaching the end of the flaming path, he emerged safely, only to be forced by the Normans to run back the other way. Once more he was untouched by the flames. Then, says Raymond, the crowd became convinced that Peter was a holy man, and rushed forward to seize relics as good-luck charms: a shred of his shirt, a lock of hair, anything they could grab. Peter Bartholomew was pulled from side to side by the screaming, clutching mob, and was trampled so severely that he died a few days later.

More skeptical chroniclers tell a different version more acceptable to modern thinking: that Peter was terribly burned as he passed through the flames, and died of his burns twelve days after the ordeal. But the followers of Raymond of Toulouse insisted that the flames had not harmed him, and continued to regard the Holy Lance as sacred.

A month later, Raymond was persuaded to leave Arqa untaken and move along down the coast. And so the Crusaders went, from Arqa to Tripoli, from Tripoli to Jebail, from Jebail to Beirut, from Beirut to Tyre. They met with little or no opposition as they proceeded through the ancient land, rich with history, where so much of the Bible's story had taken place. From the old Phoenician city of Tyre they went to Sidon, then to Acre and Haifa. Early in June the Crusaders came to Bethlehem, the birthplace of Christ. The citizens, who were Christians, mistook them in the distance for an Egyptian army. But when they realized the truth, the whole populace came out in a joyful procession, carrying crosses and holy relics from the Church of the Nativity. That night there was an eclipse of the moon, which the Crusaders took as an omen of victory.

On Tuesday, June 7, 1099, more than three years after they had first arrived in Constantinople, the army of the Cross ascended a hilltop called Montjoie, and looked upon a magnificent city whose towers and walls were unmistakably those of Jerusalem.

"They all wept for joy," a chronicle declares, "when they heard the cry 'Jerusalem,' moved by the knowledge that after striving for so long in suffering and danger they had at last come near the Holy City. . . . They pushed on hurriedly, sorrow and weariness forgotten, until they reached the walls of Jerusalem, and they sang and shouted and wept for gladness as they went."

81

Jerusalem was a mighty fortress. Its towering walls were the work of the Roman Emperor Hadrian, who had rebuilt the city after its destruction by Roman soldiers in the time of Emperor Titus. The Byzantines had strengthened those walls, and after them the Arabs and Turks had continued to restore and add to them. When the Fatimids had besieged Jerusalem in 1098, they had done some damage to the walls, but it had since been repaired. The Holy City had superb natural defenses, too: on the east, southeast, and west it was protected by deep ravines. Only on the north and the southwest could the city be easily attacked.

The army that hoped to seize this fortress-city faced stern odds. Raymond of Aguilers claimed that Iftikhar, the Fatimid governor of the city, had 60,000 fighting men at his service. As for the Crusaders, said Raymond, "at the most we did not have more than twelve thousand able to bear arms, for there were many poor people and many sick. There were twelve or thirteen hundred knights in our army, as I reckon it, not more."

But these were remarkable men. Bronzed by three Asian summers, toughened by cruel winters, veterans of countless battles, survivors of thirst and famine and siege, they were capable of withstanding any new hardship with ease. "Rejoicing and exulting," according to *The Deeds of the Franks*, "we reached the city of Jerusalem . . . and began to besiege it in a marvelous manner."

The siege began at once. Robert of Normandy took his position on the north with Robert of Flanders. Godfrey and Tancred attacked from the west. Raymond's forces were stationed to the south. But it soon became clear that it was going to be a terrible struggle. Iftikhar had blocked or poisoned all the wells outside the city as the Crusaders neared it and had rounded up the flocks of sheep and taken them within the walls. The only source of pure water for the besieging Crusaders was the pool of Siloam, just below the south walls, where water gatherers would be slain by arrows from above. It was necessary to carry water to the camp in leather bags from a muddy brook six miles away. Nor was there any food supply available to the attackers.

By contrast, the defenders were in a good position. Jerusalem had ample supplies of food and water and could hold out a long time. By way of making the provisions last longer—and to insure against treason within the city—Iftikhar drove all Jerusalem's Christian inhabitants outside the walls. He planned to sit tight and let thirst and famine conquer the Crusaders, but he also sent a messenger to Egypt with an urgent plea for reinforcements.

The Crusaders, William of Tyre wrote, "began to suffer horribly from thirst," made worse by "the burning heat of the month of June." Clouds of dust blew over them, choking their already parched throats. There was no shade in the treeless plain. The warriors fried in their armor and helmets. "What with the foul drink and the barley bread," declared *The Deeds of the Franks*, "we were daily in utter need and affliction. The Saracens lay in wait for us at every fountain and pool."

It was plain that a prolonged siege was impossible. Jerusalem had to be taken by storm and quickly, but the Crusaders were poorly equipped. They lacked the wood to build siege towers, and they had only a few ladders for scaling the walls. On June 13, they attacked anyway, but were repulsed.

Then came good luck. Six Christian vessels arrived at the harbor town of Jaffa: two galleys from Genoa and four from England. They brought food supplies and weapons for the Crusaders, and, most important, ropes, nails, and bolts to be used in building siege machines. With great difficulty, the Crusaders met the ships and conveyed the supplies overland to Jerusalem. Tancred and Robert of Flanders now went foraging for wood in forests many miles away and came back with logs and planks loaded on the backs of camels and of Moslem prisoners. Hurriedly, Raymond and Godfrey each began to construct a siege machine.

At the beginning of July, word came that an army had set out from Egypt to relieve Jerusalem. The Crusaders, wearied by the heat and hardship, realized that they would be destroyed unless they could capture the Holy City and take refuge behind its walls. But their morale was low; there had been more bickering among the leaders, this time between Raymond and Tancred, over such questions as who would take possession of Bethlehem —Tancred claimed it for himself—and who would rule Jerusalem when and if it fell.

The third prophetic Peter of the First Crusade provided the necessary spark of enthusiasm. He was Peter Desiderius, a priest, who claimed that Bishop Adhemar had come to him in a dream with instructions for the Crusaders. "You who have come from distant lands to worship God and the Lord of Hosts," Adhemar was supposed to have said, "purge yourselves of your uncleanliness, and let each one turn from his evil ways. Then with bare feet march around Jerusalem invoking God, and you must also fast. If you do this, and then make a great attack on the city on the ninth day, it will be captured. If you do not, all the evils that you have suffered will be multiplied by the Lord."

Jerusalem Regained

Even those who had lately sneered at Peter Bartholomew's visions accepted the vision of Peter Desiderius. A fast was proclaimed, and on July 8 a solemn procession filed around Jerusalem: first the bishops and the priests, then the princes and the knights, lastly the infantrymen and the civilian pilgrims, all of them barefoot. Amused Saracens jeered at them from the walls. The Crusaders gathered on the Mount of Olives, where Christ had risen to heaven, and heard sermons by Raymond of Aguilers, Peter the Hermit, and another priest, Arnulf of Rohes. In a rare moment of unity, all the feuding princes vowed to fight together to capture Jerusalem.

In the days that followed, the siege towers were completed and wheeled into position against the walls. While the Arab defenders cast stones and Greek fire on the

The Crusaders march around Jerusalem

Crusaders, they labored to wheel the towers over ditches that blocked the path to the walls. By the evening of July 14, Raymond had his tower against the south wall, but Iftikhar himself commanded the defenders, and the Franks could not scale the ramparts. The next morning, Godfrey brought his tower into place on the north wall. By midday, Godfrey's men were on the wall and driving the Arabs back.

Scaling ladders were put into position. The Crusaders swarmed over the wall and into the city, throwing wide the gates. While Godfrey remained atop the wall encouraging his forces, Tancred led the troops deep into Jerusalem.

The Saracens fled, withdrawing to the Mosque of Omar, which stood on the site of the ancient Temple of Solomon. They hoped to seal themselves up in the mosque and use it as a fortress, but Tancred was upon them before they could protect themselves. They gathered in fright on the roof of the building and offered to surrender. Tancred accepted, making them promise to pay a large ransom, and his banner was raised above the mosque.

On the southern side of the city, Iftikhar was still holding Raymond's forces at bay, showering them with Greek fire and stones. While embroiled in this deadlocked conflict, news came to Raymond that the troops of Godfrey and Tancred were already within the city. It was the final humiliating blow for the proud Count, whose ambitions had been frustrated at every step of the way. "What are you waiting for?" he roared to his men. "All the Franks are already within the town!" In the frenzied assault that followed, Iftikhar was driven back and Raymond's men streamed over the wall.

Iftikhar and his surviving officers took refuge in a citadel called the Tower of David. Surrounded by Raymond's army, the Fatimid governor sent word that he wished to surrender. He offered a monumental ransom of gold and precious gems if Raymond would spare his life and the lives of his men and allow them to leave the city. Raymond accepted, and on the evening of Friday, July 15, Iftikhar and his men were escorted to the gates and permitted to make their way to the Moslem-held city of Ascalon.

The rest of the Saracens were less fortunate. The Crusaders, maddened by victory, went on a brutal rampage through the Holy City. *The Deeds of the Franks* describes how "our men followed the Saracens and harried them, killing and felling them right up to the Temple of Solomon, where there was such a carnage that our men were wading in their blood up to their ankles. . . . Soon the Crusaders were running all over the town, carrying off gold, silver, horses, and mules, and plundering the houses, which were crammed with riches."

The Saracens who had surrendered to Tancred were deceived in their hope of safety. Despite Tancred's promise and apparently against his wishes, they were slaughtered too. They were still atop the Mosque of Omar, which the Crusaders called the Temple of Solomon, when death came. The passage in *The Deeds of the Franks* that tells of the massacre seems to sum up the whole contradictory nature of the Crusade, shifting as it does from an expression of religious piety to one of ferocious savagery:

"Then, full of happiness and weeping for joy, our people went to worship at the Sepulchre of Our Lord Jesus and discharged their debt to Him. The next morning they climbed up to the roof of the Temple, attacked the Saracens, both men and women, and drawing their swords, cut off their heads."

With this butchery of helpless prisoners, the conquest

87

of Jerusalem was complete. Friday, July 15, 1099, saw the Crusaders in command of the Holy City. The corpses of Saracens were everywhere. "It was impossible to see without horror that mass of dead," wrote William of Tyre, "and even the sight of the victors covered with blood from head to foot was also a ghastly thing to behold."

The Crusaders had achieved their goal, but their work was far from ended. Now that Jerusalem was in the hands of Christians again, the Holy Land had to be made secure against reconquest by the infidels. The heroism of the past three years would be meaningless unless a permanent Christian state could be founded in the Holy Land. Many cities bordering Palestine still remained under Moslem rule. The coastal towns except for Jaffa were Saracen-held, as were such important inland cities as Damascus and Aleppo. It was a time for consolidating the gains that had been made and for planning the next steps.

Above all else, the conquered lands had to be parcelled out among the victors. When the Crusaders met in solemn conclave two days after their triumph, they knew that matters of great concern would have to be settled, and that the settling might not be easy.

VI

THE KINGDOM
OF JERUSALEM

WHO was to govern the Holy City?

In theory, the Crusaders were bound by oath to name Emperor Alexius as their overlord. But since his failure to come to their aid at Antioch, Alexius had been regarded as a traitor, not as an ally. He was out of the reckoning.

The clergymen argued that Jerusalem should become the property of the Pope, the leader of the Christian world. There was some logic to the argument, and had Adhemar of Le Puy been alive, he might have been placed in command of the city as Pope Urban's representative. But Adhemar had died in the plague a year earlier, and none of the other priests or bishops present at Jerusalem had his universal popularity or his ability to govern wisely.

Nor did Pope Urban have an opportunity to offer his advice. On July 29, 1099, two weeks after the taking of Jerusalem but before the news had reached Europe, Pope Urban died at Rome, never to know that the movement he had launched had been a success. It might be months before a new Pope could be elected, and Jerusalem needed a government at once.

One of the princes of the Crusade would have to rule Jerusalem. But which one? Baldwin still lorded it in Edessa, and Bohemond at Antioch. Stephen of Blois had gone home. Robert of Normandy was planning to return to his native land now that Jerusalem was taken. Robert of Flanders also intended to leave the Holy Land soon.

That left Raymond of Toulouse, Godfrey of Bouillon, and Tancred. No one trusted Tancred, and he had few followers. Raymond, as the senior prince of the Crusade, a man of rank and authority, could appear as a reasonable choice, but Raymond's envious spirit had earned him too many enemies among his fellow princes. Only Godfrey remained, a weak leader and not a particularly intelligent man. He had no outstanding qualifications for the position, but he was known to be godly and honorable, a man much given to prayer and lacking in serious faults of character. Most important, he had few enemies.

As a matter of form, the leaders of the Crusade approached Raymond first and asked him to become King of Jerusalem. Everyone knew that Raymond had no real political support and would be forced to refuse the honor. He did. He went so far as to say that he did not think Jerusalem should have a king at all—hoping to keep Godfrey from gaining the crown that he himself was unable to possess.

The electors turned next to Godfrey. He pretended to be unwilling to accept, but allowed himself to be coaxed. Taking a leaf from Raymond, though, Godfrey put forth one condition. "I do not wish to wear a crown of gold in the city where our Savior wore a crown of thorns," Godfrey declared. He would rule, but not as a king. He asked for the title of *Advocatus Sancti Sepulchri,* "Defender of the Holy Sepulchre."

Thus the Kingdom of Jerusalem was born without a king. Godfrey, as its ruler, would be an uncrowned monarch, but not an absolute monarch. He would be recognized as overlord of the Frankish possessions in the Near East; in practice, though, he and his successors had only as much power over the other barons as they were strong enough to demand. The King of Jerusalem—for Godfrey's successors took the title—was merely first among equals and could not act without the consent of the other knights. Before he made war, levied taxes, or negotiated treaties, he would have to consult with the barons. He needed the backing of his council in making law; once, in the thirteenth century, a regulation governing the sweeping of streets would be declared void because the King had proclaimed it without support of the barons and townsmen.

Though his powers were limited, the King of Jerusalem would still be the central leader of the Franks in the Holy Land. There would be strong kings and helpless ones in the years to come, and the strife between the Crusading princes would never cease.

Raymond sulked when Godfrey began to rule. Gloomily, he left Jerusalem and went on a pilgrimage to the River Jordan, bathing in it near Jericho. He talked of returning to France, despite his vow to remain in the Holy Land till his death. The rest of the Crusaders began to scatter, leaving only a handful of men at Godfrey's court. Robert of Flanders and Robert of Normandy prepared to go home; Tancred set off in search of cities to conquer; some of the minor knights made ready to leave for Europe. But an army was on its way from Egypt.

In his first act as ruler, Godfrey set out from Jerusalem

to meet the Egyptians early in August. He recalled the Crusaders who were about to leave and some that had left already, and came upon the Arab army near Ascalon. The Arabs were taken by surprise. One large group took refuge in a grove of trees and were burned to death. Raymond of Toulouse, who had stopped sulking long enough to join the Crusaders, pursued a host of Arabs and drove them into the sea. In a few hours, the Fatimid threat to Jerusalem was removed and enormous booty fell into the Crusaders' hands.

With the victory achieved, the breakup of the Crusade began in earnest. The two Roberts finally left at the beginning of September. Raymond accompanied them up the coast; he was not going home, but simply looking for likely territory to conquer. Cheated of his crown in Jerusalem, Raymond hoped to imitate Baldwin and Bohemond and found a principality elsewhere. He looked toward central Syria, which was held by Arabs who were not noted as valiant warriors.

About three hundred knights remained with Godfrey in Jerusalem. By Christmas of 1099, though, he had two noble visitors. His brother Baldwin of Edessa, who had been sitting out the Crusade since the fall of 1097, decided it was time to make the pilgrimage to Jerusalem. Bohemond, who had dropped out of the Crusade after the capture of Antioch in 1098, did the same. They paid their respects to Godfrey, and no doubt the thought was in their minds that Godfrey could not live forever. He had no children, and a successor would be needed.

After a brief visit, they returned to their capitals. Godfrey spent the first months of 1100 extending his control over Palestine, helped by the arrival of reinforcements from Europe. Such towns as Ascalon and Acre avoided devastation by submitting peacefully to Godfrey. He allowed the Moslem princes of these cities to retain their positions so long as they paid tribute to him and agreed to maintain the peace. It was the beginning of mutual understanding between the local emirs and the ruler of the new Christian state that had thrust itself into their midst.

Godfrey's successes in diplomacy were interrupted in June. The Defender of the Holy Sepulchre fell ill. He seemed to be dying, but then he rallied, and at the start of July it appeared as if he would recover. Then, on July 18, Godfrey sank into his final coma and died.

There was no understanding concerning the succession to Godfrey's powers. Nor was there any important knight in Jerusalem when he died. Baldwin and Bohemond were far away; Raymond and Tancred were out campaigning in Syria. The members of Godfrey's household kept his death a secret for a few days while conferring on how to deal with the situation.

They feared that power might be seized by Daimbert, an unscrupulous prelate who had been sent from Europe to replace Adhemar of Le Puy as the Pope's representative in the Holy Land. There even was a chance that fierce Bohemond or shifty Tancred might claim the throne. To forestall such an event, Godfrey's followers decided to offer the crown to Baldwin of Edessa. As Godfrey's brother, he was the most logical heir.

While Godfrey's household pondered the situation, Daimbert and Tancred were conspiring to give control of Palestine to Bohemond, reserving great powers for themselves. But Daimbert's letter to Bohemond never reached him; it was intercepted on its way to Antioch by agents of Raymond of Toulouse, who destroyed it. All ignorant of the situation in Jerusalem, Bohemond set out in the opposite direction on an expedition of conquest in Armenia. Leading only three hundred knights and a contingent of infantry, Bohemond overconfidently marched into a narrow valley where Danishmend Turks were waiting in ambush. The Frankish troops were wiped out, and Bohemond, the boldest warrior of the Crusade, was laden with chains and carried off into captivity deep in the mountain country of Armenia.

Baldwin of Edessa prepared to take the throne. In September, 1100, he turned Edessa over to his cousin, Baldwin of Le Bourg, who became the second Count Baldwin of Edessa. The first Baldwin set out for Jerusalem in October and arrived a month later. He was hailed enthusiastically by the people as their King.

Tancred and Daimbert left the city in disgust. On November 11, 1100, Baldwin was crowned as King Baldwin I of Jerusalem. He did not hesitate to accept the royal title that Godfrey had refused.

It was an impressive climax to Baldwin's career. To leave home a penniless younger brother, and to become a king in the Holy Land—it was glorious! And the new monarch showed his strength at once. He ordered Daimbert to return to Jerusalem and compelled him to submit to his authority. Making peace with Tancred was a little more difficult, but by March of 1101 Baldwin I had the belligerent Norman off his hands: he sent Tancred to Antioch to govern it as regent during Bohemond's captivity. That left King Baldwin without a serious rival to his power. Bohemond was in Turkish chains, and Raymond of Toulouse, old and bitter and still without territory of his own in the East, had temporarily gone back to Constantinople.

No one, probably not even Baldwin, had imagined in 1096 that within four years the supreme power of the Holy

The Kingdom of Jerusalem

Land would be in his grasp. But he had maneuvered cleverly, taking no undue risks, outlasting the other princes, and now the kingdom was his.

The position of the Franks was far from secure, though. As of 1100, they held three small principalities, widely separated by great stretches of Saracen territory. The Kingdom of Jerusalem covered the mountainous inland country of Palestine, but the coastal cities except for a few ports like Haifa were held by Moslems. It was a poor country, lacking in wood and water, and badly injured by years of warfare.

In the North were the two other states, the Principality of Antioch in Syria, and the County of Edessa to the northeast in Armenia. Antioch was a wealthy city, well situated to defend itself against Moslem attack, but the Franks did not have a clear title to it since by rights it belonged to the Byzantine Empire. There was constant danger that Alexius might send his powerful navy to take the city, especially now that Bohemond was a prisoner. Edessa was much more secure; it was well defended by fortresses, and its land was fertile and productive.

The rest of the region was held by the Saracens, but they were far from unified. The Fatimid Arabs of Egypt loathed the Turks every bit as strongly as they did the Christians, perhaps more so. The Turks were divided among themselves, the Seljuks contesting with the Danishmends. Even the Seljuks were split, with men like Duqaq of Damascus, Ridwan of Aleppo, and Kerbogha of Mosul scheming to limit one another's power. Minor semi-independent Arab dynasties held such cities as Shaizar and Tripoli. The rich seaports of Beirut, Sidon, Tyre, and Acre were ruled by Arabs who had a purely theoretical allegiance to the Egyptian Fatimids.

All these Moslem rulers controlled cities that were

populated chiefly by Christians, but the native Christians of the Holy Land were as divided as their Saracen masters. There were many different sects—Nestorians, Maronites, Greek Orthodox, Armenians, Jacobites, and more—separated by broad disagreements over matters of ritual and doctrine. The devotees of these creeds preferred to be ruled by Moslems rather than to allow another Christian sect to get the upper hand, an inclination which explained why a relative handful of Saracen warriors could subdue and administer territories populated by thousands of Christians. Nor were the native Christians particularly eager to cooperate with the Frankish Crusaders, who, as Latins, were regarded as heretics.

The situation was complex and confused. The Turks and Arabs were at odds, as were the native Christians, while the Crusaders themselves were chiefly concerned with their personal fortunes. At no time were the Crusades a clear-cut war of Christians against Moslems. The battle lines were always blurred by disunion on both sides.

Baldwin I hoped to unite the Crusaders and make their grip on the Holy Land permanent. He began by touring his kingdom, which was unfamiliar territory to him, since he had not taken part in the conquest of Jerusalem. Early in 1101 Baldwin marched through the outlying wilderness east of Jerusalem to demonstrate his strength to the wild Arab tribes of the Jordanian desert. Fulcher of Chartres, who traveled with the King, tells of visiting "the place, some forty miles from Jerusalem, where, in the tombs of the patriarchs, lie buried in glory the bodies of Abraham, Isaac, Jacob, and of their righteous son Joseph." Five hundred years before, superstitious pilgrims had also been shown the tomb of Adam there, but Fulcher makes no mention of it.

The Kingdom of Jerusalem

He did view the spring that appeared when "Moses, instructed by God, struck a rock twice with his rod," and noted, "This spring still flows today no less abundantly than then. . . . I myself, Fulcher of Chartres, made my horses drink from it." And when the good historian came to the Dead Sea, he tasted its water, found it bitter, and offered some intelligent theories on why the Dead Sea was so salty.

When Baldwin I and his entourage returned to Jerusalem, they were heartened to learn that new Crusaders were on their way from Europe. Baldwin was badly in need of reinforcements, since many of the original Crusaders had gone home. Now, fresh forces were arriving. Some were knights who hoped to follow the glorious path of Bohemond, Godfrey, and Baldwin, but there were also Crusaders of a new kind: seamen from the merchant towns of Pisa, Genoa, and Venice, Italian cities that were then independent and powerful rivals for Mediterranean commerce. As businessmen, the men of these towns were concerned with profit and loss, not with the spiritual benefits to be had from possessing the Holy Land. They saw a good chance for a profitable trade between the new Frankish states and Europe, so they sent naval forces to help the Crusaders conquer the Mediterranean seaports of Lebanon. In return, the merchant towns expected to be granted trading privileges in the ports.

The new Crusaders who came by land followed the same route as the earlier ones, crossing Hungary and the Byzantine Empire. They behaved the same way too, brawling and looting as they traveled. Most of the men of the First Crusade had come from France and the western provinces of Germany; the newcomers were chiefly Italian. German and French Crusaders also set out in the spring of

1101, and among them was the unhappy Stephen of Blois, who had been sent back to the Holy Land by his nagging wife under orders to cleanse his tarnished reputation.

The new men met at Constantinople and were joined by Raymond of Toulouse. There they debated their next step. Raymond and the Emperor Alexius wanted them to invade Asia Minor, which, despite the Crusaders' victories of 1096 and 1097, was still harassed by Turks and unsafe for pilgrims. But the Italian Crusaders wanted to go off into the far northeast to rescue the imprisoned Bohemond before they did anything else.

The Italians had their way. Marching into mountainous Armenia, they met the same fate as the army of Bohemond: the Turks ambushed them and cut them to pieces before they could begin to fight. Four-fifths of the new army was butchered; the survivors straggled back in humiliation to Constantinople. Bohemond remained a prisoner. Turkish morale, damaged by past defeats, began to rise once more.

There were further setbacks for the would-be Crusaders as they attempted to reach Jerusalem. Hugh of Vermandois, the first knight to reach Constantinople in 1096, was slain late in 1101 in another Turkish ambush. Only a few Crusaders reached Antioch alive. The road across Asia Minor remained unsafe, and the three Crusader states in the South were isolated by land. It became more important than ever to capture the coastal ports and open a sea route to the Holy Land.

The three chief rulers, Baldwin I at Jerusalem, Baldwin of Edessa, and Tancred at Antioch, were busily strengthening their defenses and extending their territories. Tancred in particular was active in this respect, now that he had land to govern at last. King Baldwin, who had never trusted Tancred, began to wish that Bohemond would return from captivity and take control of Antioch once more. Baldwin I had been cool to earlier Turkish suggestions that he pay a ransom for Bohemond, but now he opened negotiations.

In the spring of 1103, after almost three years in prison, Bohemond was ransomed. Contributions toward the huge price came from all the Crusaders except Tancred, who probably was interested in having his uncle languish in chains a while longer. Bohemond immediately went to Antioch. Tancred unwillingly handed the city back strengthening their defenses and extending their territories. he had conquered during Bohemond's absence. Finally he was forced to yield.

Before long, Tancred was a ruler again. Moslems attacked Edessa, and the Frankish army under Count Baldwin left the city and charged the enemy violently. The Saracens immediately fled, and the Franks gave chase. But it was a feigned retreat. At a signal, a hidden Moslem army fell upon the pursuers. Count Baldwin was taken prisoner. Edessa needed a ruler until Baldwin could be freed. Bohemond, uneasy about his nephew's presence in Antioch, arranged for Tancred to become regent in Edessa.

Tancred took command of the remnants of Edessa's army and restored the city's defenses. Before long, the Turks attacked again. Edessa withstood the onslaught, and under cover of darkness Tancred led his men into the camp of the sleeping Turks and put them to rout. He took many prisoners, among them a Seljuk princess.

Jekermish, the local Turkish leader, immediately offered to return Count Baldwin in exchange for the princess. King Baldwin of Jerusalem urged Tancred to accept the proposal, but Tancred did not mean to let the rightful

Count return so soon. Backed by Bohemond, Tancred accepted a cash ransom for the princess and left Count Baldwin a prisoner. Such casual backstabbing was a far cry from the lofty ideal of Christian unity that Pope Urban had envisioned when he first called for a holy war against the Saracens.

The shifting patterns of Frankish rule took another turn in late 1104. Bohemond felt himself threatened by Byzantium. The fleet of Emperor Alexius had captured certain Syrian cities and seemed to be closing in on Antioch. Lacking a navy himself, Bohemond could not intercept the Byzantine ships, and his army had been thinned by many battles. Bohemond resolved to go back to Europe and recruit new troops for the defense of Antioch. The wheels turned; Tancred returned to Antioch again as regent and appointed his cousin, Richard of Salerno, to look after Edessa, since Count Baldwin was still a captive.

Bohemond reached his Italian home early in 1105, after an absence of nine years. He spent some months getting his personal affairs in order. Visiting Rome, Bohemond had an interview with the new Pope, Paschal, and persuaded him that another Crusading army had to be assembled—with the enemy not the Saracens but the Byzantines. Pope Paschal agreed. He regarded the Byzantines as dangerous Greek heretics whose Christian allegiance to the Pope was highly doubtful. Bohemond painted Alexius in the most villainous light. According to Bohemond, Alexius had remained in the background, doing nothing and risking nothing while the Franks defeated the Saracens for him. Now that the victory was won, said Bohemond, Alexius planned to move in and thrust the Franks aside.

When Bohemond went from Italy to France, he was

accompanied by a representative of the Pope who was authorized to preach a Crusade against Byzantium. Men began to join Bohemond's new army. It was a significant moment in the story of the Crusades: the first time that fellow Christians had been branded openly as enemies.

Bohemond was a busy man in France. He visited Adela of Blois, the wife of the unwarlike Stephen. She introduced him to her brother, King Henry I of England, and got his support for Bohemond's Crusade against Byzantium. She also helped him arrange two royal marriages, one for himself and one for his nephew Tancred. Bohemond's bride was Constance, the daughter of King Philip of France. For Tancred, Bohemond and Adela provided Constance's younger sister, Cecilia.

By October, 1107, Bohemond was invading the Byzantine Empire. He landed on the Greek coast at the head of a large army and marched inland to besiege the fortress of Dyrrhachium. Alexius was engaged in war with the Seljuks; but he quickly made peace with Sultan Kilij Arslan and, with typical Byzantine flexibility, arranged to hire Seljuk troops to fight against Bohemond. The joint Byzantine and Seljuk army closed in around Bohemond and held him in an unbreakable grip all through the spring and summer of 1108. By September, he knew he was beaten. He had overreached himself by challenging Byzantium.

Bohemond surrendered and was taken before Alexius. Possibly it was their first meeting since 1096 at Constantinople when Bohemond had pretended to be the Emperor's loyal vassal. It was a chilly interview. The gigantic Bohemond loomed over the short, soft-spoken Alexius, but Emperor Alexius held all the high cards this time. He presented Bohemond with a peace treaty to sign. The terms were bitter. Bohemond had to apologize formally for

101

Bohemond before Emperor Alexius

breaking his earlier oath to the Emperor. He would be allowed to remain as Prince of Antioch, but only if he acknowledged the Byzantine Emperor as his overlord. Certain towns conquered by Bohemond and Tancred were to be restored to Byzantium. There were other provisions equally humbling to Bohemond.

Bohemond signed the treaty. Alexius had vanquished the proudest of all the Crusaders. Unwilling to show his face in the East after such a defeat, Bohemond returned to Italy a broken man. The glory he had won at Antioch was only a faded memory now. He died within five years, leaving two small sons as heirs to Antioch.

But Antioch was under Tancred's rule, and Tancred did not grieve to see his uncle crushed by Alexius. Nor had Tancred signed any treaties with the Emperor. He did not regard himself as bound to Byzantium by Bohemond's oath. Bolder than ever, Tancred led new expeditions against the Arabs and Turks and extended Antioch's holdings far to the south and east. He seized the Syrian cities that the Byzantines had captured a few years earlier; he routed the Saracens; he kept control over Edessa through his cousin Richard of Salerno. By the end of 1108, Tancred was the most powerful Frank in the East, though he did not even have a formal title. The coins that he struck for his territories called him simply "The Servant of God." He was in a far stronger position than King Baldwin of Jerusalem.

But there were other ambitious men in the East, and Tancred would not be supreme for long.

THE TRIUMPH
OF KING BALDWIN

BALDWIN I, King of Jerusalem, had not been idle during the machinations of Bohemond and Tancred against Byzantium. He had been powerless to prevent Tancred's rise, and he was far from pleased by it. But during those years the King had been strengthening his own position in Palestine.

The Saracens feared him, remembering his skill in battle from the days when he had been carving out his domain in Edessa. Within a few months after he took the throne, Baldwin received embassies from the Moslem rulers of the coastal cities of Tyre, Acre, Arsuf, and Caesarea, offering tribute in return for peace. King Baldwin gladly accepted their gold, for Jerusalem's treasury was low. Then, allying himself with naval men from Genoa, he attacked the ports anyway. Arsuf fell, and then Caesarea, where the Franks perpetrated a terrible massacre. Baldwin committed the treachery deliberately to inspire terror in the remaining Moslem-held cities.

The Fatimids of Egypt, meanwhile, were determined

The escape of King Baldwin

to avenge their earlier defeats in Palestine. They sent an army of great size—11,000 cavalrymen, 21,000 infantrymen —toward Jerusalem. King Baldwin met them with about 1,200 soldiers. But the Franks were picked men, battle-hardened and capable, and the Arabs were inexperienced. At a battle near Ramleh in 1101, the Arabs were scattered in panic and fled with heavy losses.

A year later a tougher Egyptian army appeared at Ramleh. King Baldwin, remembering his easy victory of 1101, miscalculated and rode against the Fatimids with no more than 500 knights. When he reached the plain of

Ramleh and saw thousands of Saracens stretching almost to the horizon, he realized the extent of his error. The Egyptian cavalry cut off the Franks' line of retreat. King Baldwin ordered his men to charge headlong in the hope of stampeding the Arabs into flight.

In the first moment of surprise, the Egyptians broke ranks and allowed the Crusaders to get through. A few managed to escape altogether; the rest fought their way into the small fortress at Ramleh, which was immediately surrounded by Saracen troops. King Baldwin was among those who entered the fortress. That night, riding his swift steed, Gazelle, the King slipped from the fortress with three companions. Somehow they managed to thread their way through the Egyptian lines to safety. In the morning the Egyptians attacked and stormed the fortress. They set fire to the tower in which the knights had taken refuge. The Franks made a last valiant charge and were cut down to the last man. Among the victims was Stephen of Blois, who was granted a hero's death at last.

King Baldwin made for the port of Jaffa, through countryside roamed by Egyptian troops. He arrived safely and was greeted with surprise by his men there, who had heard that he had perished at Ramleh. Gathering reinforcements, the King returned to battle. He led heavy cavalry against the Egyptians, and this time sent them in pell-mell flight to the Saracen-held city of Ascalon.

With the Egyptians temporarily out of the picture, Baldwin I continued to tighten his grip on the coast of Lebanon. In May of 1104 he took the vital port of Acre, the best harbor along the coast. Now he was in a truly commanding position both inland and at the sea.

In the summer of 1105, the Fatimids made one more attempt to drive the Franks out of Palestine. Once again an Egyptian army marched north to Ramleh. For the first time, the Fatimids joined forces with their old enemies, the Turks. The Seljuks of Damascus sent 1,300 mounted archers to aid the Egyptian army, which numbered 5,000 horsemen and infantrymen. King Baldwin met them with some 2,500 men on Sunday, August 27. The Franks attacked first, but were met by an unexpectedly fierce counterattack by the Turks of Damascus. Waving his banner high, King Baldwin rallied his men and drew victory from defeat. By nightfall the Moslems were in retreat. It was the last large-scale effort by the Fatimids to recapture Palestine, although they continued to send small raiding forces northward and in 1110 were able to reach Jerusalem itself before being driven off.

While King Baldwin I was capturing coastal cities and resisting the Egyptians, another of the Crusading princes was continuing his pathetic quest for power. He was Raymond of Toulouse, the aging, wealthy Count who had joined the Crusade with such proud hopes, only to meet constant reverses. Raymond had become the forgotten man of the Crusade. Godfrey and now Baldwin of Lorraine were rulers in Jerusalem; Bohemond was the Prince of Antioch; even Baldwin of Le Bourg, a minor knight, had come to wear the title of Count of Edessa. Raymond had nothing. Even his hope of winning land in central Syria had vanished when he came into direct conflict with Tancred in 1101. Tancred, less than half as old as Raymond, had taken him prisoner and forced him to sign away any claims he might have to Syrian territory, which Tancred coveted for himself.

Late in 1101, the dejected Raymond began to look toward the only remaining possibility for his domain: the cities of the Lebanese coast. King Baldwin had already begun to seize them to add to the lands of Jerusalem, but the city of Tripoli remained in Arab hands. If he could take it, Raymond could use it as the core of a dominion extending inland across the main land route from Antioch to Jerusalem.

He began his campaign by capturing the port of Tortosa without difficulty. Then, with only 300 men, he laid siege to Tripoli. The Arab army gathered, and the Turkish Emir of Damascus, Duqaq, obligingly contributed 2,000 soldiers of his own to it in the hope of eliminating Raymond permanently. Outnumbered by twenty to one, Raymond's army stood firm against the Saracen attack. As had so often happened, the almost mystical valor of the rugged Franks brought panic to the Saracen host. Fear swept through the ranks of the enemy, and joyfully the Crusaders slashed them to pieces. Thousands of Moslems were slain. It was grizzled Raymond's finest moment.

He could not hope to storm walled Tripoli with only 300 men, no matter how valiant they might be. Toward the end of 1103, Raymond built a vast castle on a hill overlooking the city and began what amounted to a permanent siege of Tripoli. He kept the city isolated by land; but he lacked naval power and could not prevent the Arabs from bringing provisions to Tripoli by sea. In the summer of 1104, a Saracen army raided Raymond's castle and set fire to the outlying buildings; they were driven off, but the old warrior himself was injured when a burning roof collapsed on him. He died six months later, Tripoli still unconquered, none of his grand dreams realized.

His lands in Toulouse were inherited by his son Bertrand. Such territory as Raymond had held in the East went to his cousin, William-Jordan. William-Jordan was acting as regent for Raymond's infant son, Alfonso-Jordan, born only a few months before his father's death.

William-Jordan continued the blockade of Tripoli. Wisely allying himself with Byzantium, he obtained ships and supplies from Constantinople and was able to close Tripoli from the sea. Starvation threatened the besieged city; a pound of dates sold for a gold piece. Tancred, in Antioch now, saw a chance for some quick profit, and smuggled food to the Arabs of Tripoli through William-Jordan's lines.

Through 1106, 1107, and the spring of 1108, William-Jordan tightened the noose around Tripoli. The city's rulers sent to Baghdad for help from their Arab cousins of Iraq but with no results. In despair, they turned next to the Fatimid Arabs, who were of a different Moslem sect and regarded themselves as enemies of the Tripoli Arabs. The Fatimids obligingly broke through the Frankish blockade and brought food to Tripoli—and seized control of the city in the bargain.

William-Jordan was thwarted in his hope of taking Tripoli, and soon he had worse troubles. The two sons of Raymond had made an exchange of territory. Alfonso-Jordan, the child for whom William-Jordan was the regent, was going back to Toulouse, while Bertrand, a grown man, was coming to the East! Bertrand would have no need for a regent. And William-Jordan was cold to the idea of stepping aside in Bertrand's favor.

Next Tancred entered the picture. Already master of Antioch and, by proxy, Edessa, he announced his support of William-Jordan, no doubt with the thought of adding Tripoli to his land. Bertrand, needing some powerful ally himself, turned to King Baldwin. The King was eager to check Tancred's growing might. He arrived at Tripoli at the head of an army, and by sheer force of personality imposed his will on all the squabbling princes. The territory of Raymond of Toulouse was divided. Tancred's man, William-Jordan, would get Tortosa and another city, Arqa, that he had recently captured. Baldwin's vassal, Bertrand, would have Tripoli after it was taken. On the death of either Bertrand or William-Jordan, the other would inherit his possessions.

With that out of the way, the Franks went about the task of storming Tripoli. Under a joint effort that left the besieged city reeling in defeat, Tripoli fell in July, 1109, and King Baldwin turned it over to Bertrand. Raymond's son took the title of Count of Tripoli. Within a few weeks, William-Jordan died mysteriously, pierced by an arrow that struck him out of the blue. Tancred had been foiled; Bertrand took control of William-Jordan's lands, as had been agreed, and at last the son of Raymond of Toulouse was master of the rich principality that his father had hoped to win.

Now there were four Frankish states in the East: the Kingdom of Jerusalem, the Principality of Antioch, the County of Edessa, and the County of Tripoli. As of 1110, all but Antioch, which Tancred still held supposedly as regent for the dying Bohemond, were under King Baldwin's control.

Until 1108, Tancred had controlled Edessa too. The other Baldwin, Count of Edessa, had been a prisoner of the Turks since 1104, and no one had done much about ransoming him, not even his cousin, King Baldwin of Jerusalem, who was perpetually short of cash. Baldwin of Edessa had passed from Turk to Turk. His first captor was Jerkermish of Mosul. When Jekermish died in 1106, the

110

The Triumph of King Baldwin

Seljuk Sultan Kilij Arslan took Baldwin, but a war among the Turks cost the Sultan his life in the summer of 1107. Count Baldwin's new captor was a Turk named Jawali. Jawali was carrying on a private war against another Saracen, Mawdud. To raise money for this war, Jawali offered to sell Count Baldwin back to the Franks. A down payment was produced, and Jawali generously released Baldwin, who raised the rest of the money after he was free.

Count Baldwin returned to Edessa after an absence of four years. Tancred had governed there through his cousin, Richard of Salerno, and refused to surrender the city unless Count Baldwin swore allegiance to him. Baldwin refused, and it seemed for a while as if there would be open war among the Franks. Tancred was at last pressured into withdrawing peacefully. Baldwin resumed his power at Edessa.

King Baldwin of Jerusalem, relieved to see Tancred's influence shrink a little, moved now to finish the job of conquering the Moslem cities of the coast. He captured Beirut in May of 1110 with the help of Count Bertrand of Tripoli. In December, aided by Norwegian and Venetian Crusaders, King Baldwin took Sidon. But Tyre and Ascalon, the only remaining independent cities, resisted him. He encircled them and let them be, since other campaigns looked more attractive at the moment.

The King was tireless. Having secured most of the coast, he carried his armies inland, building fortresses along his desert frontier. With methodical diligence, King Baldwin was doing exactly what needed to be done to transform the precarious Kingdom of Jerusalem into a living, thriving state. It was a rare stroke of good fortune for the Franks that Baldwin I turned out to be so able a monarch.

The only threat to the kingdom lay in the ambitions

of Tancred. It was well known that Tancred looked only to the advantage of Tancred. He had conspired with Moslems at times, betrayed Bohemond, and coolly left Baldwin of Edessa to rot in prison. But for the strength of King Baldwin, he might well have swept Jerusalem too into his possession. But the King was able to contain and check Tancred.

In 1112, a change in the balance of power occurred that gave Tancred a momentary advantage. Bertrand of Tripoli died, and his young son Pons, the new Count, came under Tancred's influence. But he had little time to make use of Count Pons in his scheming. Tancred fell ill late in 1112 and died in December, only thirty-six years old. An energetic and courageous soldier, but an unscrupulous self-seeker, Tancred had few mourners. If he had lived longer, he might have wrecked the Frankish East.

On his deathbed, Tancred named his nephew Roger as his heir. But Tancred had no real claim to the throne of Antioch himself; he was only the regent for Bohemond. Bohemond was dead, but he had left children in Italy. With belated loyalty to Bohemond, Tancred forced Roger to swear that if the young Bohemond II ever came to the East, Roger would hand over Antioch to him.

Young men now ruled in Antioch and Tripoli. Of the original Crusaders, only the two Baldwins still remained. The Moslem leaders had changed, too: gone were such early foes as Kilij Arslan, Ridwan of Aleppo, Duqaq of Damascus, Kerbogha of Mosul. The Saracen princes who now ruled had lived with Franks in their midst for nearly a generation. They had come to accept the Crusaders as a permanent force in the East.

They did not enjoy having the "Christian dogs" amongst them, of course. They still dreamed of a day when the Franks would be driven into the sea. Their poets sadly bewailed the bloodshed the Christians had brought, as in these lines by an Arabic bard, Mosaffer Allah Werdis:

> We have mingled our blood and our tears.
> None of us remains who has strength enough
>   to beat off these oppressors.
> The sight of our weapons only brings sorrow to
>   us who must weep while the swords of war
>   spark off the all-consuming flames.
> Ah, sons of Mohammed, what battles still await
>   you, how many heroic heads must lie under
>   the horses' feet!

Patriotic Moslems dreamed and sang of triumph over the Franks. Yet the new generation of Saracen leaders often denounced the Franks for political reasons, to gain support in their home cities, while privately making deals with them. It was not uncommon for alliances to be made that crossed religious lines, as happened in 1108, when Jawali of Mosul made war on Ridwan of Aleppo. Ridwan sought and got help from Tancred. Jawali instantly turned to his former prisoner, Baldwin of Edessa, who loaned him several hundred knights in gratitude for the kind treatment he had received in his captivity. So Christian and Moslem fought against Christian and Moslem—not for the first time, nor the last.

Through all these tangled years, King Baldwin I steered a steady course. He knew that safety lay in keeping the Franks united and the Saracens at each other's throats. With Tancred dead, Baldwin's task was that much easier. So long as no Moslem hero emerged who could draw all the quarreling emirs under one banner, Jerusalem was safe.

Such a leader appeared to have arrived about 1115,

in the person of Mohammed, the last great Seljuk Sultan. From his base of power in Iraq and Iran, he sent out armies ordered to bring all of Moslem Syria under one rule. After that, Sultan Mohammed planned to drive out the Franks.

Both the Moslems of Syria and the Franks were disturbed by the Seljuk Sultan's ambition. The immediate response was something that would have been unthinkable fifteen years before: an alliance of Crusaders and Saracens. Two Moslem princes, Toghtekin of Damascus and Ilghazi of Mardin, made a pact with Roger of Antioch. Count Pons of Tripoli and King Baldwin of Jerusalem also supplied troops, and the combined army swept down on the Seljuks from a hill called Tel-Danith in Syria. The invading Turks were caught unawares and thrown into disorder; few of them survived the rout.

Obviously things were changing in the East. Religious zeal had become a secondary motive. The Crusaders had become local princes. Though their numbers were few, their strength was great, and their place in Eastern life was assured.

For a few thousand knights to have won such a domain was remarkable enough. To have maintained it and made it endure was a far more difficult achievement. The credit for it belongs chiefly to one man who was of relatively little importance in the early campaigns of the Crusade—Baldwin I, King of Jerusalem.

viii

Tbe ÖeATb
OF princes

HERE were strange omens in the year
1117. The chronicle of Fulcher of Chartres
declares that in May, "grasshoppers de-
voured the vineyards, corn, trees of all
kinds, eating all green things and the bark,
going forth in bands like an army, some on
foot, some flying. In the following month,
June, the moon on the thirteenth day of
her age was all red and afterward black, and two hours
together lost her light. In July happened an earthquake. In
December, the whole heaven was fiery like blood, in some
places shining white."

To the men of the twelfth century, such mysterious
events could only mean that unsettled times were coming.
And indeed 1118 proved to be a year of the death of
princes. In January, Pope Paschal died in Rome. In April,
the Seljuk Sultan Mohammed went to his grave. On the
sixth of August died the Caliph of Baghdad, Mustazhir,
leader of half the Arab world. Nine days later, Emperor
Alexius died at Constantinople after a successful reign of
thirty-seven years.

115

The Crusaders in their camp

King Baldwin I was another victim of that dread year. In March of 1118, he had set out on the boldest expedition since the conquest of Jerusalem nineteen years before. He led a small but sturdy army across the Sinai Peninsula into Egypt, intending to strike at the Fatimids in their own land.

The army reached the fabled Nile. Camping by the side of the vast river, Baldwin planned his offensive. Fulcher of Chartres writes that "some of the knights skillfully speared a few young fish with their lances, took them to their lodging, and began to eat them. Suddenly the King felt ill inside, because the pains of an ancient wound started again with great violence."

Baldwin was dying. There was no question of continuing the invasion. Carrying the monarch on a litter, the Crusaders sadly retreated toward Jerusalem. He blazed

with fever. At the frontier town of el-Arish, Baldwin slipped into death on April 2, 1118, and five days later he was buried beside his brother Godfrey in the Church of the Holy Sepulchre, Jerusalem.

He had ruled long and well, and even the Saracens were moved by his death. All Palestine had fallen to him. Only the coastal cities of Tyre and Ascalon had eluded him. He had won the respect, if not the affection, of all. But he had failed in one royal duty: like Godfrey, he had not named a successor to the throne. And he had left no children.

King Baldwin's closest survivor was his elder brother, Eustace of Boulogne. Eustace had long since returned to France. Messengers were sent to him by some of the Crusaders, offering him the crown of Baldwin. He hesitated to accept, and by the time he finally brought himself to set out for Jerusalem, it was too late. Without waiting for Eustace, another man had taken the throne, probably to Eustace's relief. The Count of Boulogne turned around and went home.

The new monarch was the late King's cousin, Count Baldwin of Edessa, the last surviving prince of the first group of Crusaders. His claim to the throne was nearly as good as Eustace's from the point of view of family ties, and it was far better in other ways. Count Baldwin had been in the East for twenty years; he had fought well and ruled well, had experienced captivity, had won many friends. And, perhaps not by coincidence, he had made a pilgrimage from Edessa to Jerusalem that spring, and he happened to arrive in the Holy City on the very day of King Baldwin's funeral.

So for the second time a Count Baldwin of Edessa became King of Jerusalem. Baldwin II was crowned on Easter Sunday, April 14, 1118. Pious and dignified, he lacked the awesome majesty of the first Baldwin. He was a genial, friendly person who did not carry himself in an excessively kinglike way. He was restrained and calculating where the first Baldwin had been bold and swashbuckling, but he was a man who could be respected and admired.

He named his cousin, Joscelin of Courtenay, as the new Count of Edessa. Pons of Tripoli and Roger of Antioch paid homage to the new King, recognizing him as their overlord. There was little break in the smooth continuity of the government.

From the Saracens came an instant challenge to Baldwin II's rule. The Egyptians, angered that Baldwin I had dared to invade their soil, assembled a great army and brought it as far north as the town of Ashdod. Baldwin II, summoning reinforcements from Antioch and Tripoli, led the army of Jerusalem down to meet them. For three months the armies confronted each other, but neither side attacked. As Fulcher of Chartres wrote, "Everyone liked better to live than to die." At last both armies simply went home.

A more serious battle occurred the next year when Saracens clashed with the army of Antioch and slew all but a few men. Roger of Antioch was among the fallen, and the Franks gave the battlefield the name of *Ager Sanguinis*, "the Field of Blood." The heir to Roger's title was Bohemond II, then a boy of ten living in Italy. Baldwin II resolved to take over the rule of Antioch himself until young Bohemond should come of age.

There were other battles, endless battles, for the Moslem princes were ambitious, and their way of gaining prestige was to attack the Franks. Warfare had been a way of life for the Crusaders for nearly a quarter of a century. They met each test in a steadfast way.

During the early years of Baldwin II's reign, there was a significant development that changed the balance of power in the East: the rise of the military orders, the Hospitallers and the Templars. These organizations began as simple monkish orders, but before long they were political forces in their own right, often sinister and unscrupulous in their pursuit of their private goals.

The Hospitallers were founded first. Their roots went back before the Crusades, to the 1070's, when the Holy Land was under Egyptian rule. Pilgrims from Europe were still able to reach Jerusalem at that time, and many of them arrived ill and exhausted from their journeys. A knight named Gerard Tenque of the Italian city of Amalfi persuaded the Egyptians to allow him to establish a hospital in Jerusalem to care for these pilgrims. It was staffed

A *Templar*

by monks of the Benedictine order who took the usual
monkish vows of poverty and chastity. During the Crusade,
Gerard, the Grand Master of these Hospitallers, was banished from Jerusalem, but after the Frankish conquest he
returned and the hospital was reopened. The monks were
given money and land to support their work; they cared
not only for the sick but for the elderly, the poor, and the

hungry. Often they had as many as two thousand patients a day.

About the time that Baldwin II came to the throne, Gerard died. The new Grand Master of the Hospitallers, Raymond of Le Puy, transformed the order by giving it new purposes. No longer would the Hospitallers concern themselves only with caring for pilgrims; they would become a military organization dedicated to fighting to keep the routes of pilgrimage open. The Knights Hospitaller were established—a body of fighting men who took the usual monkish vows, but who were by no means men of peace. Their distinctive badge was a white cross that they wore on the tunics over their armor.

The second military order, the Knights Templar, had its beginning in that same critical year, 1118. Nine knights led by a certain Hugh of Payens banded themselves together to assume the duty of keeping the road to Jerusalem free of brigands. Before long, the group had evolved into another order of warrior-monks, bound by holy vows but free to take lives in the service of the Lord. The badge of the Knights Templar was a red cross worn on a white tunic.

The Hospitallers and the Templars were a strange mixture of the pious and the pitiless. They lived austerely, at least at first, forbidden to amass wealth, to drink and carouse, or to hunt any beast except the lion. They had to observe all religious fast days scrupulously and pray at the proper hours of the day. Their military discipline was equally harsh: their vows forbade them to flee in battle or break ranks. They were devoted soldiers who fought to the death against the most hopeless odds.

The military orders represented something new in the Frankish East: two permanent, well-trained armies, owing

121

allegiance not to the King of Jerusalem but merely to their own Grand Masters and to the Pope. Other Crusaders might come and go between Jerusalem and Europe as the mood took them, but the Templars and the Hospitallers were bound by their oaths to remain in the East. Though they continued to perform their charitable duties—particularly the Hospitallers—the two military orders rapidly became more military than religious. They built a network of fortresses through the East, and involved themselves in adventures everywhere.

Although their members were individually bound to vows of poverty, the orders themselves grew rich. They received contributions from faithful Christians in many parts of the world, invested the money wisely, and amassed great wealth. The Templars became the bankers of the Eastern world and did business with Franks and Moslems alike, to their great profit. From their originally religious base, the two orders turned into aristocratic brotherhoods whose members were arrogant, self-willed, and independent of all other authority. They were respected for their military prowess, but hated by the other Franks for their sly political intrigues, their great power, and their cold-blooded haughtiness. One Grand Master of the Templars who lived late in the twelfth century, Odo of Saint-Amand, was described by a chronicler as "an evil man, proud and insolent, breathing fury, and without fear of God or respect for any man." In time the arrogance of the Templars would bring destruction to the Frankish states of the Holy Land. But Baldwin II had no inkling of that as he allowed the two charitable orders to get footholds in Jerusalem. To him, they represented merely the badly needed permanent regular army that the Frankish East was lacking, and he gave them his full support.

Soon the Frankish states were in a shaky position indeed, bereft of their leaders. Roger of Antioch had been slain in 1119, leaving that state without a Prince until Bohemond II grew up. In 1122, Count Joscelin of Edessa was captured by a new Turkish leader named Balak, who offered to free him if Joscelin would turn Edessa over to him. The Count refused and became a prisoner in the remote castle of Kharpurt.

King Baldwin II, already administering Jerusalem and Antioch, had to take over the rule of Edessa as well. But he did not bear the triple burden long. In the spring of 1123, Baldwin led a small army northeast to scout the territory where Joscelin had been captured. Camping one April morning, Baldwin was amusing himself with his trained falcon, when, in the midst of the royal hunt, the soldiers of Balak appeared from ambush. The King was taken prisoner and sent to join Joscelin at Kharpurt.

It was the second time that Baldwin II and Joscelin had been prisoners together. During Baldwin's long captivity from 1104 to 1108, his cousin Joscelin had been imprisoned with him. Then Baldwin had been Count of Edessa; now he was King of Jerusalem, the mainspring of the Frankish government, and his loss was a severe blow. Nevertheless, the government survived. Count Pons of Tripoli was the only ruler of the four states who remained in control; in the other three states, temporary administrators were appointed by the patriarchs of the Church.

Joscelin was popular among his Armenian Christian subjects of Edessa, and they laid plans to rescue him and the King. Fifty Armenian soldiers came to Kharpurt disguised as merchants and monks, and gained entry under the pretense of wishing to place a petition before the fortress's Turkish governor. Once inside, they drew their swords and overpowered the garrison.

But Kharpurt was in the midst of Turkish-held territory. How were Baldwin and Joscelin to return to Frankish lands? They decided that Baldwin would remain, defending the fortress against possible Turkish attack, while Joscelin slipped away to bring help.

Fulcher of Chartres, the indefatigable chronicler of the First Crusade, tells the story: "The Lord Joscelin declared himself ready to face the danger of almost certain death. So, commending himself to the Creator, he left the castle with three of his servants and succeeded with the help of the moonlight, though as full of fear as he was of courage, in passing through the enemy host. Once safe, he immediately sent back to the King one of his servants, telling him to give his ring to Baldwin as a sign that he had made his escape from the Turks who were besieging the castle. Thereafter, fleeing or hiding by turns, and marching mostly at night, he came to the river Euphrates barefoot and weary."

Count Joscelin could not swim. But his two companions had brought skins along as water-vessels. Blowing these skins full of air, Joscelin stretched out on them and floated across the river. Half dead with fatigue, they stumbled on for days, hiding in the underbrush when anyone approached. But they were discovered by a peasant, who recognized him as Count Joscelin and fell at his feet in awe. Joscelin explained his plight, and the peasant agreed to help the count reach his castle of Turbessel. Joscelin would disguise himself as a fellow peasant. Says Fulcher: "So this peasant went away and returned with his family and his animals. Count Joscelin got on the peasant's donkey and took the peasant's baby girl in his arms, and carried her in front of him with as much care as if she were a daughter of his own blood." The motley procession went unchallenged on the road, and in time Joscelin reached

Turbessel, where he rewarded the faithful peasant with two yoke of oxen. Hurrying on to Antioch and then to Jerusalem, Joscelin assembled an army to rescue the King. The troops set out for Kharpurt.

But the Turk, Balak, had already reached that fortress upon hearing of the uprising there. Laying siege to it, he offered to release King Baldwin in return for a peaceful surrender of the castle. Baldwin did not trust Balak's offer and decided to wait for his rescuers to arrive. By way of reply, Balak had his engineers mine the wall of the castle. It collapsed and the Turks broke in. They slew the Armenians who had captured it, and put to death all the captive Franks except King Baldwin, who was removed to an even more remote castle for safekeeping.

Joscelin knew that it was useless to risk a rescue attempt at that distant fortress. King Baldwin would have to remain a prisoner a while longer. In May, 1124, Balak invaded Syria and defeated an army led by Joscelin; but just as he seemed to threaten the entire Frankish land, Balak was killed by a stray arrow. The King passed into the custody of another Turkish emir, Timurtash, who did not care to play host to so important a prisoner. Timurtash opened negotiations immediately for Baldwin's ransom.

Meanwhile the Franks were making a determined effort to capture Tyre, one of the two coastal cities that remained in Saracen possession. A formidable Venetian fleet had arrived at Acre in the spring of 1123, looking for gold and glory. After shattering the Egyptian navy and capturing ten richly-laden Fatimid merchant vessels, the Venetians offered their services to the Crusaders. They would help besiege either Tyre or Ascalon, as the Crusaders chose, but they demanded a stiff price for their aid. Always concerned with furthering the business ambitions of

Venice, they insisted on being granted a street of their own in every town of the kingdom, where they could open shops and a church. They were to be excused from all tolls and customs duties throughout the kingdom, and they would receive annual royalties in cash besides. They also demanded that the kingdom not be allowed to give merchants of other cities the same privileges without Venetian consent. In this way, they hoped to gain heavily on their traditional rivals in commerce, Pisa and Genoa.

With King Baldwin a prisoner, Patriarch Gormond of Jerusalem agreed in his name to the Venetian terms, and in February, 1124, the siege of Tyre began. The ancient Phoenician city was officially subject to the Egyptian Fatimids, but actually it was ruled and defended by the Turks. The city lay off shore, joined to the mainland by a narrow passage built by Alexander the Great fourteen hundred years earlier. Tyre's water supply reached it through an aqueduct running from land, and the first act of the besiegers was to cut the aqueduct.

Tyre had plenty of water stored in cisterns, but eventually it would run low. The Venetian ships blockaded the harbor, and the Frankish soldiers settled down on the mainland to wait until thirst compelled Tyre to surrender. They bombarded the walls with stone-throwing catapults, the equivalent of cannons in those days before gunpowder. The defenders of Tyre answered back with stones of their own and cascades of Greek fire. The Turks asked Egypt to send a fleet in Tyre's defense, but the Egyptians had already experienced the skill of the Venetian navy, and no fleet came. In July, 1124, food and water began to give out in Tyre. The city offered to surrender, provided there would be no looting and any Moslem who wished to leave would be allowed to go in peace. These terms were accepted, much to the annoyance of the common soldiers, who were looking forward to a glorious session of plunder in the wealthy city. Tyre passed into Frankish control; its Moslem citizens departed; and the Venetians sailed away pleased with the concessions they had gained.

The ransom of King Baldwin had now been negotiated. Timurtash demanded 80,000 gold dinars and five minor towns that had been held by the Franks. A down payment of 20,000 dinars was required; Baldwin would then be released, provided he surrender his four-year-old daughter Joveta as a hostage, along with Joscelin's eleven-year-old son and ten other children of the nobility. The hostages were produced and King Baldwin was released.

He raised the missing 60,000 dinars by defeating a Moslem army in Syria and seizing its belongings, and the children were redeemed. Jerusalem once more had its King. Soon after, in 1126, Baldwin was able to give up the administration of Antioch, for Bohemond II, now eighteen, arrived to claim his inheritance. He had his father's height and magnificent bearing, but also an air of refinement that he owed to his mother, the daughter of the King of France. He had the promise of greatness, but it was never to be fulfilled, for by 1130 he was dead, slain by the same Danishmend Turks who had once ambushed and captured his father.

After welcoming Bohemond II to Antioch, King Baldwin next set about doing what neither Godfrey nor Baldwin I had done: he provided for a successor to his own throne. By this time it was understood that the Kingdom of Jerusalem would remain in the family of the Baldwins, although the crown was not quite hereditary; the high council of knights and clergy had the right to decide on the actual successor. Baldwin II had four daughters but no sons, and arrangements were made to give the throne next to the husband of the eldest daughter, Melisende.

Melisende was still unmarried, though her younger sister Alice had become the bride of Bohemond II of Antioch. The Franks decided to choose a husband from the ranks of the French nobility. They wrote to King Louis VI of France for suggestions. He put forth Fulk, the Count of Anjou, one of the wealthiest and most powerful French barons.

Fulk of Anjou was about forty years old. His first wife was dead and his son, Geoffrey, had reached manhood. Geoffrey had recently made a splendid marriage to Matilda, the daughter of King Henry I of England, and was destined to be the ancestor of a long line of English kings. Fulk himself, weary of Europe, had resolved to make Geoffrey the ruler of Anjou and take the Cross himself. He had already made a pilgrimage to Jerusalem once, in 1120, and had left a good impression with Baldwin and the other Crusaders.

So it was arranged. Fulk would marry Melisende and become the heir to the throne of Jerusalem. They were married in 1129, to the satisfaction of everyone, except perhaps Melisende, who was young and fair, and not overly delighted by her middle-aged bridegroom. Royal princesses must marry as politics dictates, though, and Melisende accepted her fate.

With Fulk at his side, Baldwin II launched an ambitious project, the conquest of the rich Syrian city of Damascus. But the city withstood siege easily, and heavy winter rains turned the plain into an ocean of mud, forcing the King to withdraw. At the same time, both Joscelin and Bohemond II raided the equally great city of Aleppo, but they attacked separately, refusing to cooperate, and Aleppo remained Saracen.

The Death of Princes

The death of Bohemond II in 1130 provided new problems for King Baldwin. The young Prince of Antioch had left only one heir, a girl of two, Constance. Her mother, Princess Alice, was the daughter of Baldwin II. She at once named herself as regent for Princess Constance, without waiting to consult King Baldwin.

It was not unusual for a woman to rule in the lands of the Crusaders. Women had been present on the Crusades from the beginning, staying close to the battle lines, bringing water to the soldiers and encouraging them. A girl like Alice, born in the East, had known warfare all her life and felt strong enough to rule. But Baldwin objected to his daughter's ambitions. He sent word to Alice that she was to yield Antioch to Joscelin of Edessa.

Alice refused and dispatched a messenger to the Turks at Aleppo, offering to pay homage to them as overlords if they would defend her rights to Antioch. The messenger was captured by Baldwin's troops, and the King promptly hanged him when he learned of the message. Then he moved on toward Antioch. Alice slammed the gates of the city shut against her father and prepared to resist a siege.

The Frankish knights of Antioch decided that things had gone far enough. They opened the gates; Baldwin, Fulk, and Joscelin entered. Alice fled to a tower and emerged only under a promise that her life would be spared. She came before the King, kneeling in humiliation and shame. With royal generosity, Baldwin pardoned her, but banished her to northern Syria and named Count Joscelin as the guardian of Antioch until the child-princess was old enough to marry.

Thirty-five years had passed since Baldwin II had come to the East. He was well along in years, and by the standard of his own time he was extremely old. The strain of government had worn him out. He had fought many wars, had suffered twice in captivity, had endured the desert heat and the winter's chill too long. In the summer of 1131, his health began to fail, and by August death was near. He called to his side Fulk and Melisende and their one-year-old son, named Baldwin for his grandfather. The dying King entrusted the throne to Fulk and himself assumed the robe of a monk. Soon after the ceremony King Baldwin II was dead. He was interred beside Godfrey and Baldwin I at the Church of the Holy Sepulchre.

His cousin and comrade in captivity, Joscelin of Edessa, soon followed him. While besieging a castle near Aleppo, Joscelin was wounded when a wall collapsed on him. As he lay close to death, word came that the Danishmend Turks were attacking one of the fortresses of Edessa. Joscelin ordered his young son to go to the defense, but Joscelin II refused, saying the army was too small to attempt an engagement with the Danishmends. In anger, the dying Joscelin struggled to his feet and had himself carried in a litter to do battle with the Turks. The Danishmends had thought he was already dead, and they were disturbed to find him marching against them. Hastily, they lifted their siege and retreated. Joscelin uttered a prayer of thanksgiving when he was brought the news, and then life left him.

None of the old Crusaders remained, now. The new generation was in full control, most of them born in the Frankish East, speaking Arabic as well as they did French, tanned from childhood by the fierce sun. They were very different from their fathers and mothers in their way of thinking and their way of life. Even those who had been born in Europe were able to blend into the unique Frankish civilization.

The Death of Princes

Fulcher of Chartres sums up what had occurred during the first four decades of Frankish life in the East:

"We who were Westerners find ourselves transformed into Orientals. The man who had been an Italian or a Frenchman, transplanted here, has become a Galilean or a Palestinian. A man from Rheims or Chartres has turned into a citizen of Tyre or Antioch. We have already forgotten our native lands. To most of us they have become territories unknown, or places never heard mentioned any more. Now we possess houses and servants in this country which belong to us as if they came by right of age-long inheritance. Some men have already taken as wives Syrian or Armenian women, or even Saracens who have been baptized Christians. Through them we are involved in a whole network of family relations with the native people. We speak many tongues, and races utterly unlike each other live together in trust. He who was once a stranger has become a native, the immigrant has become an inhabitant."

The Franks had come to call their Eastern states by the collective name of *Outremer*, "Beyond-the-sea." The civilization of Outremer was unlike that of Europe in almost every way. The Franks of Outremer still spoke French, still observed Christian rituals, still maintained the structure of the European feudal system. But otherwise they had become as Eastern by nature as the Arabs and Turks. In Europe, the noblemen lived in cold stone palaces, the peasants in crude huts. Men wore coarse woolen clothing, rarely bathed, and ate dreary and tasteless food. Furniture was crude, carpets and jewelry and decoration unknown. In Outremer, a touch of Oriental splendor had entered. The Franks dwelled in handsome and airy mansions, ornamented with all that the superb craftsmanship of the East could provide: silken draperies, richly ornamented carpets, tables handsomely carved and inlaid with precious metals, dinnerware of gold and silver, vessels of porcelain imported from China. The knights, when they were not in armor, dressed in silk robes, Saracen-style, and shielded their heads from the sun with turbans. The women too dressed as the Moslem women did, in robes embroidered with gold thread or jewels. They even veiled their faces—not out of modesty, as did the Moslems, but merely to protect their complexions from the sun.

It was a life of luxury and opulence. The Franks had clear consciences about adopting Oriental magnificence, for in other ways their existence was unenviable. They never knew when they would be called upon to defend their cities against the Saracens, or to march into the bleak desert on some campaign of war. With life so uncertain, they comforted themselves with the delights that the Orient had to offer.

When new Crusaders came East from chilly Europe, they could not understand the ways of the men and women of Outremer. They looked upon them almost as Saracens. In the years ahead, conflicts grew between the Franks of Outremer and the newcomers from Europe. In their clumsy way, the new arrivals helped to shatter the delicate balance of relationships that had sprung up between Frank and Moslem in the Holy Land, and they brought disaster upon the Kingdom of Jerusalem.

ThE FALL
OF EDESSA

KING Fulk ruled at Jerusalem. He ruled well, but he was not as majestic as Baldwin I, nor as well known and respected as Baldwin II. There were serious challenges to his authority from the other Frankish princes.

Pons of Tripoli, though still a young man, was now the senior ruler of the Frankish states. He had never been happy to acknowledge the King of Jerusalem as his overlord, but he had done so out of fear of Baldwin II. Under King Fulk, Pons asserted that the King of Jerusalem was simply the first among equals and had no claim to regard the other rulers of Outremer as his vassals. It was an important point, for under the feudal system, vassals were required to supply troops when requested to do so by their overlord. Bertrand, the first Count of Tripoli, had submitted to Baldwin I as a vassal in order to protect himself against Tancred. But his son Pons did not feel himself bound by an agreement of a quarter of a century before.

In Antioch, both Roger and Bohemond II had recog-

133

nized Baldwin II as their overlord, but Princess Alice, the fiery daughter of Baldwin II, had claimed that they were wrong to do so. Baldwin II had forced her aside and named Joscelin as the guardian of Antioch, but now both Baldwin and Joscelin were dead. Backed by Pons of Tripoli, Alice attempted to take control of Antioch in the name of her young daughter, the rightful heir, Princess Constance. The new Count of Edessa, Joscelin II, was young and weak and also came under the sway of Alice.

King Fulk saw all three of the Frankish states threatening to break away from the Kingdom of Jerusalem. He set out with an army, but Pons refused to let him cross the territory of Tripoli. Traveling up the coast by sea instead, Fulk came to Antioch and defeated the rebellious army of his sister-in-law Alice. Then he forgave the rebels, and got an apology from Pons. The dissension in Outremer was not ended, but as least all was made smooth on the surface.

It was basically a family quarrel, since the nobles of Outremer were by this time interrelated by marriage. But a new enemy from without suddenly forced the bickering Franks to unite.

He was Imad ad-din Zengi, a Seljuk Turk whose rise to power had been rapid and impressive. In 1126, the Caliph of Baghdad, a Seljuk puppet, led an uprising against his Turkish masters. The Seljuk Sultan, Mahmud, sent an army to Baghdad commanded by a young captain who put down the revolt quickly and efficiently. The captain was Zengi. He won promotion as a result of his admirable work at Baghdad, and was placed in command of the important Iraqi town of Mosul. By 1128, Zengi had moved on to Syria and was ruling Aleppo. Within two years, he had gained control of Moslem Syria as far south as the town of Homs.

The Fall of Edessa

Zengi had plans for an eventual attack on the Frankish states, but first he had to consolidate his position. The eternal feuding among the Moslems delayed his progress. In 1132, Zengi was called back to Iraq to restore order there, leaving his Syrian territory to a lieutenant, Sawar. Sawar began to wreak havoc among the northern outposts of the Frankish states. Taking advantage of the weakness of the lazy, luxury-loving Joscelin II of Edessa, Sawar raided the city of Turbessel, which belonged to that state. Next he ambushed Pons of Tripoli and penned him up in a besieged fortress, which he left guarded by a small force while he prepared to attack Antioch.

King Fulk came to the rescue of the princes who had spurned him earlier. He freed Pons, then drove Sawar away from Antioch. But the next year Zengi was back. While Sawar menaced Edessa, Zengi invaded the outlying fortresses of the Principality of Antioch and captured four of them. Now the territory between Antioch and Edessa was in Saracen control, and a wedge had been driven between the two northernmost Frankish states.

At this critical moment Princess Alice of Antioch stirred up new trouble. She saw that Zengi represented a menace to her city, and she did not like the idea of turning to King Fulk as a protector. Instead, she sent a message to the Byzantine Emperor, John Comnenus. Alice offered the hand of her nine-year-old daughter Constance to the Emperor's younger son, Manuel. Manuel would thus become the new Prince of Antioch, and Byzantium would protect the principality against Zengi.

The other Franks were horrified at the prospect of handing over Antioch, a prize that the Byzantines had desired ever since the first Bohemond had conquered the city in 1098. King Fulk decided that Constance's marriage to Manuel had to be avoided at all costs—and the best way to avoid it was to find another husband for little Constance at once.

A husband was imported from France: Raymond of Poitiers, the younger son of the Duke of Aquitaine. Raymond was thirty-seven years old, handsome, dashing, of high birth, and eligible for marriage. He arrived at Antioch in April, 1136. How could his presence there be explained to Princess Alice, though? Radulph, the Patriarch of Antioch, had a scheme. Radulph told Alice that Raymond had arrived to marry not Constance but Constance's mother —Alice herself, who had been a widow for six years and who was still less than thirty. While Princess Alice rejoiced in her good fortune at gaining so romantic a husband, little Constance was spirited away and sped to the Cathedral, where the Patriarch married her to Raymond. Alice was defeated, and Antioch had a new Prince, loyal to King Fulk.

Raymond of Antioch set about strengthening his state's defenses against Zengi. Meanwhile, another Turkish commander, Bazawash, invaded the County of Tripoli and slew Count Pons. His victory inspired Zengi to attack the outer reaches of Antioch's territory once more. He laid siege to the important frontier castle of Montferrand. At Raymond's request, King Fulk came to the defense of Montferrand, causing the Turks to retreat. It was only a feigned retreat, however: they closed in again swiftly, and the King, taking refuge in the castle, found himself trapped.

Fulk was penned up in Montferrand for days with supplies running low and Zengi's siege engines hammering at the walls. At last he sent a herald out, asking for Zengi's terms. To his surprise, Zengi was generous. He would release the King and the other Franks, he said, in return for

The wedding of Constance and Raymond

Montferrand. Fulk accepted, glad to be let off so lightly. But Montferrand, with its key position in Syria, passed to the Saracens. The situation of the Franks was weakening steadily.

Byzantium took advantage of that weakness. The Emperor Alexius had never ceased to resent the failure of the original Crusaders to honor their oaths to him. When his vigorous son John succeeded him in 1118, it was with the hope of bringing the Franks to their knees eventually. Now, in the spring of 1137, a powerful Byzantine army led by Emperor John himself appeared at the walls of Antioch. Byzantine siege engines were moved into position. The attack that had been feared for almost forty years had at last arrived.

Raymond of Antioch was in no mood to fight Byzantium. He sent a message to Emperor John, asking for terms. John demanded unconditional surrender. Troubled, Raymond wrote to King Fulk for advice and received a cool reply. "Everyone knows," Fulk told him, "that in years gone by Antioch was part of the Empire of Constantinople, until it was taken by the Turks. The Emperor's claims are just. Can we deny the truth and oppose what is right?" In other words, Fulk did not want to risk his prestige and endanger his kingdom by a costly and futile war against Byzantium. He had tried to keep Antioch out of Byzantine hands by thwarting Princess Alice and bringing in Raymond, but that policy had failed. Now he advised surrender.

Raymond yielded. The banner of Byzantium was raised over the citadel of Antioch. In victory, the Emperor was kindly. He allowed Raymond to remain as Prince of Antioch—but only after making him swear a full oath of allegiance to Byzantium. And it was understood that if the Byzantines and Franks, fighting together, could conquer Aleppo and its neighboring Syrian towns, Raymond would give Antioch to the Emperor and become Prince of Aleppo instead.

But Aleppo, which had never fallen to the Crusaders, resisted even Byzantium. Emperor John abandoned the attempt to conquer it, and turned to nearby Shaizar. Now it was Raymond who showed little enthusiasm. He was afraid that if Shaizar fell, he would be forced to take it in exchange for Antioch, a poor trade indeed. So the Franks fought badly, and Shaizar held out. In the end, John let the town buy its freedom with a large ransom and had the Emir of Shaizar swear allegiance to him. Then the Byzantine monarch returned to Constantinople, satisfied at least by his triumph over Antioch. John's death five years later, in 1143, put an end to Byzantine claims to Antioch once more, however. A dispute between two of John's sons over the succession to the imperial throne weakened Byzantium and forced the Empire to refrain from adventures in Asia for a while.

The years from 1138 to 1143 were relatively peaceful ones in Outremer. The Byzantines had gone home, and the dreaded Zengi was occupied in fighting against other Saracens. Though things had been grim for the Franks for a while, the pressure relaxed, thanks to the tendency of the Moslems to make war on one another just when they could have successfully driven out the Crusaders.

Some of the Moslem writers of this period give us an idea of the relations between the Franks and Saracens during the reign of King Fulk: Within the four Frankish states were many Moslem peasants who cheerfully accepted the rule of the Christian newcomers. An Arab traveler, Ibn Jubayr, toured the Holy Land and reported that the

Moslem farmers "live in great prosperity under the Franks —may Allah preserve us from such temptation!" Their taxes were fairly light, and the Franks were just and righteous compared with the former Turkish governors, who customarily bled a province for all its wealth. Ibn Jubayr observed, "The Moslems are masters in their own dwellings and order their affairs as they think best. . . . It is sad that in Moslem countries our people must complain of the injustices of their rulers, whereas they have nothing but praise for the conduct of the Franks, on whose justice they can always rely."

The Franks allowed freedom of religion, too. Even in Jerusalem, the Holy City, Moslems were permitted to pray in their own mosques. This was only fair, since in the days when the Arabs had held the city they had generally tolerated the presence of Christian pilgrims. The new Crusaders who constantly came to Outremer, full of Christian zeal and hatred for Saracens, could never understand why the earlier Crusaders were so liberal toward Moslems. An anecdote dating from about 1140 shows clearly this conflict of attitudes. It comes from the memoirs of Usama ibn Munquidh, an Arab of the minor royal house that ruled the city of Shaizar. While visiting Jerusalem on a diplomatic mission, Usama went into the Mosque al-Aqsa to pray. Beside it was a smaller mosque, which the Franks had turned into a church. As he entered the bigger mosque, Usama found it occupied by Templars, who recognized him and told him that it would be all right for him to use the smaller mosque for his prayers, if he wished. Usama describes these Templars as "friends of mine," a good sidelight on the role they were already playing as go-betweens in Outremer.

He went into the small mosque and began to pray.

Then, he writes, "I was deep in prayer when one of the Franks fell upon me, laid hold of me, and turned my face to the east, saying, 'That is the way to pray!' A band of Templars came forward, took him, and forced him to leave. I started to pray again. The same Frank, breaking loose from them, fell upon me again, turning my face to the east once more and shouting, 'That is the way to pray!' Once again the Templars seized him and thrust him out; then they apologized to me, and said, 'He is a foreigner, who arrived a few days ago from the country of the Franks. He has never seen anyone pray without turning to the east.' I answered, 'I have prayed enough for today.' And I left, amazed at what a twisted face that devil had, how he shook with rage, and what an impression it had made on him to see someone pray facing Mecca."

Usama had little love even for the native Franks of Outremer, of course. He was a cultured, highly civilized man, as skilled in poetry as he was in the arts of war, with a heritage of generations of Arab scholarship and science behind him. To Usama even the second-generation Crusaders were scarcely more than barbarians. His verdict on the entire race of Franks was that "they are creatures who are superior in courage and valor in battle, but in nothing else, just as animals are superior in strength and aggression."

King Fulk's policy of tolerance toward the Moslems within his own kingdom brought a few years of peace to Jerusalem. He kept his defenses strong, but he was willing to make alliances with local Moslem princes where he thought it would help. In the north, in Joscelin of Edessa's territory, the situation was not quite so tranquil. Joscelin II was a poor ruler, and it was inevitable that the Turks would turn against him as soon as they were through with their current round of civil wars.

In the autumn of 1143, taking advantage of the relaxed state of affairs, the royal court of Jerusalem paid a visit to the city of Acre. Queen Melisende suggested a picnic, and on November 7 the royal party rode out into the countryside. Suddenly a rabbit leaped from the underbrush and scampered into the open. King Fulk spurred his horse and galloped forward in pursuit. The horse stumbled and the King was thrown to the ground. He died of his injuries three days later.

He had left two sons: Baldwin, who was thirteen, and Amalric, seven years old. Young Baldwin was obviously not old enough to rule alone in Jerusalem. Queen Melisende persuaded the council of barons to name her as regent, with the understanding that her elder son would be crowned as Baldwin III in due time.

It was the best arrangement that could be devised under the circumstances, but it was not really very satisfactory. The royal authority was divided between a woman and a boy. The princes of the northern states, who had never been inclined to accept Fulk as their overlord, were hardly likely to respect the wishes of Melisende. Raymond of Antioch had been quarrelling with Joscelin II of Edessa, and King Fulk had done his best to keep them from open warfare. Now there was no Fulk to serve as peacemaker.

The situation was exactly what Zengi had been waiting for. He had finished with his long series of campaigns against other Saracen leaders and was ready to turn against the Franks in their moment of greatest weakness. Late in 1144, Zengi attacked Kara Arslan of Diarbekir, a Turk who had formed an alliance with Joscelin II. Bound by his treaty, Joscelin II marched out of Edessa to intercept Zengi's army. Zengi at once cut short his attack on Kara Arslan and laid siege to Edessa itself.

Count Joscelin was far from his city when the attack came. Instead of returning to Edessa, he retired to his second city, Turbessel. He felt that Edessa's fortifications would hold out against Zengi and that by occupying Turbessel he could keep reinforcements from reaching Zengi's army. Joscelin planned to wait until Jerusalem and Antioch could come to his aid.

Antioch was closer; but Count Raymond, quite content to see his enemy Joscelin vanquished by Zengi, offered no help. Queen Melisende of Jerusalem did raise an army for Joscelin, but by the time it made the long trek from Palestine to the Armenian borders, it was too late. On Christmas Eve, 1144, the siege machines of the Turks broke through Edessa's walls. The citizens were thrown into confusion as sword-wielding Saracens burst into their city. Thousands were trampled to death in the panic; thousands more were slain by Zengi's men. Zengi ordered all the Franks in the city to be executed, but he spared the Armenian Christians who made up the bulk of the population.

Edessa had fallen! The news stunned Franks everywhere. Never before, in the long years of constant war between Frank and Saracen, had the Moslems taken any major city from the Crusaders. The tide of victory had always gone the other way, from the early days of Nicaea and Antioch onward. More than that, Edessa was a strategic city, the last outpost of the Frankish world, a buffer zone lying between the Saracen countries of the East and Crusader-held Syria.

Fresh from triumph at Edessa, Zengi moved on in

January, 1145, to capture Saruj, another of Count Joscelin's cities. He turned next to nearby Birejik, but halted his offensive long enough to return to Mosul, put down a rebellion against his authority, and accept the congratulations of his Turkish supporters.

Joscelin remained at Turbessel, half his lands now lopped away by Zengi. At Antioch, Raymond began to consider his own danger and traveled to Constantinople to ask help from the Emperor in case of a Turkish attack. Emperor John's youngest son Manuel had emerged in control of Byzantium. He received Raymond amiably, but offered no aid. The Byzantines were busy with military adventures of their own in a different part of Asia Minor.

Zengi could have finished off Count Joscelin and what remained of the County of Edessa, or he could have attacked Antioch. He did neither. He had never lost his old ambition to possess the Arab-held city of Damascus, and he turned away from the Frankish states to lay siege there. It was his last campaign. In September, 1146, while besieging Damascus, Zengi angrily rebuked one of his servants for drinking wine from his master's glass. The servant, enraged by Zengi's insulting words, crept upon him in his sleep and murdered him.

The sudden death of Zengi threw the Saracen world into chaos once more. Zengi's sons, Saif ed-Din and Nur ed-Din, both proclaimed themselves his successor, one seizing control of Mosul and the other taking Aleppo. The other Turkish leaders promptly made their own bids for power. The Franks took heart. Raymond of Antioch led a raiding party to the walls of Aleppo, and the weakling Joscelin II began to plan the reconquest of Edessa.

Nur ed-Din, Zengi's twenty-nine-year-old son, drove Raymond away from Aleppo and pushed him all the way

144

The Fall of Edessa

back to Antioch. Then Joscelin attacked Edessa with a
small army. Nur ed-Din stopped fighting Raymond, hurried to Edessa, and bottled up Joscelin's army, nearly destroying it. Joscelin was wounded, but managed to escape;
the other Franks were put to death. The native Armenian
Christians of Edessa were forced to leave their city and
go into exile.

Zengi was gone, but Nur ed-Din had emerged as an
able successor. Islam had finally produced a man, it
seemed, who could thrust the infidel Franks into oblivion.
In the months that followed, Nur ed-Din demonstrated
that he had the ability to undo all the achievements of the
Crusaders.

In Europe, there was fresh stirring of zeal. The Holy
Land was threatened.

The time had come for a Second Crusade.

THE SECONd
CRUSADE

CRUSADERS had come to Outremer in a small but steady flow ever since the original conquests. The first Crusaders, those who had left Europe in 1096, were followed by others in 1100 and 1101, and after that it was a common thing to take the Cross and join the Franks overseas. And so, when we speak of a Second Crusade, a Third Crusade, a Fourth and a Fifth and so on, it must be remembered that the Crusades were actually a continuous movement lasting two hundred years, and not a series of separate operations.

But the Second Crusade received its name because it marked a rebirth of the whole Crusading idea. Instead of random parties of landless younger sons and adventurous knights coming to the East, what now took shape was an entire new army, led by the greatest kings of Europe, a venture conceived in grandeur and destined to end in chaos.

It had its beginning in 1144, just after the fall of Edessa. Queen Melisende and Raymond of Antioch decided to send a messenger to the Pope asking for assistance in the form of a new Crusade. A bishop was dispatched, but he did not reach the Pope until the fall of 1145. A new Pope, Eugenius III, had been elected only a few months before. He was sympathetic to the idea and wrote to King Louis VII of France, a devout and virtuous man, asking him to organize the Crusading army.

Louis VII was the logical choice. Most of the Frankish knights in Outremer were of French descent, though the Normans and Italians and Germans there were loosely classed as "Franks." King Louis was surely the man to save this largely French kingdom in the East. He was eager and willing to take the Cross in this time of danger and need.

In fact, Louis proposed to do what no reigning monarch yet had done: he would go to the Holy Land in person at the head of the Crusading army. At Christmastime, 1145, he called the chief lords of France together and told them of his intention.

They were cool to the idea. Not only did they have little interest in taking the Cross themselves, they opposed letting Louis leave his kingdom to go Crusading. Only one man, the Bishop of Langres, supported the proposal. But King Louis was determined to fight in the Holy Land. He was a man driven by a powerful streak of religious mysticism; even his own wife, Eleanor of Aquitaine, would mock him in time by saying, "I have married a monk, not a king!" And Louis felt that he was responsible for the deaths of thirteen hundred innocent people who had perished when his soldiers set fire to a town while putting down a local uprising in France. His Crusade would be in the nature of a penance.

Unable to generate any enthusiasm himself, King

147

Louis invited a famous religious leader, Bernard, the Abbot of Clairvaux, now known as Saint Bernard, to stir up fervor for him. Bernard was then the most famous man in France. He had the gift of preaching, and he spoke with an inner fire, a blaze of conviction, that drew the attention of the entire Christian world. He was a celebrity in almost exactly the same way that movie stars and athletes are celebrities today. When Saint Bernard neared a town as he traveled, bells were rung, and thousands of curiosity-seekers came out to meet him, crushing so close that he was often in danger of being smothered. He was credited with working miracles. A German chronicle tells us solemnly that on a single day, "eleven blind men received their sight by the laying on of his hands, ten maimed men were restored, and eighteen lame ones made straight-limbed."

Though he was never elected Pope, Bernard was the most powerful churchman in Europe, so much so that when a monk from his own abbey became Pope Eugenius III in 1145, Bernard could tell him truthfully, "I am said to be more Pope than you." To this man King Louis VII entrusted the task of firing the imagination of Europe as Pope Urban II had done fifty years before.

On March 31, 1146, Saint Bernard addressed a vast gathering at the French town of Vézelay. His words have not been preserved, but he asked for a new Crusade and promised that all who joined it would be forgiven their sins. His huge audience listened spellbound as this master orator told them of the urgent need to save Jerusalem once more from the infidel Moslem. Before he had finished, men were crying out in ecstasy and excitement, "Crosses! Give us crosses!" Saint Bernard flung off his own robe to be cut up. King Louis was the first to take the Cross, and the barons who had been so cool to a Crusade before now found themselves caught in the frenzy of the moment. Long after sunset Saint Bernard and his helpers worked to stitch Crosses to the garments of the volunteers.

Hundreds of knights and thousands of common people yielded to Saint Bernard's persuasion as he toured France preaching the Crusade. Within a few days he was able to write to the Pope, "You ordered; I obeyed. . . . I opened my mouth; I spoke; and at once the Crusaders have multiplied to infinity. Villages and towns are now deserted. You will scarcely find one man for every seven women."

As the vast army gathered, its leaders offered its command to Bernard himself. But the saint had no taste for warfare. When it seemed as though the barons were going to insist, Bernard became frightened, and wrote to the Pope, exclaiming, "Who am I, that I should set camps in order, or should march before armed men?" He beseeched the Pope to defend him against the will of those who would make him a general.

Placing command of the French soldiers in King Louis's hands, Bernard visited Germany and enrolled thousands of new Crusaders. They were to be led by King Conrad himself. The Germans had played a small part in the Crusades thus far, leaving the care of the Holy Land to the Frenchmen and Italians. But now King Conrad found himself almost against his will enrolled in the project.

The Second Crusade began with the same high ideals that had ennobled the first. Its leaders, Louis of France and Conrad of Germany, were monarchs of majesty and intelligence. Its chief spiritual mover, Saint Bernard, was ablaze with piety and zeal. Certainly such men as these would repeat the exploits of Godfrey and the first Baldwin, drive out the troublesome Saracens, and strengthen the position of Christianity in the East.

But it did not work that way. The huge armies that Louis and Conrad assembled, though led by knights, were made up mostly of rabble. The Pope had agreed to pardon any criminals who took the Cross, and thousands left the jails to become Crusaders. Petty bandits and hardened murderers mingled with simple peasants in the new armies. The ranks were swollen by pilgrims who could not and would not fight, men and women who simply wished to see the Holy Land and attached themselves to the armed forces. What came together was an unwieldy, unruly, unmilitary assortment of humanity, lacking the skills of warfare, and in particular lacking any knowledge of how to cope with the unique conditions of warfare in Outremer.

King Conrad set out with his turbulent troops in the spring of 1147. He was past fifty, in poor health, no longer able to assert much command. His nephew and heir, Frederick, Duke of Swabia, was the real leader of the expedition. Many other German nobles went along, and their personal rivalries threatened to create the same sort of bickering among the Crusaders that had weakened the First Crusade.

They took the familiar route of Crusaders through Hungary into Byzantium. Once more, Byzantine escorts met them politely, offering assistance and food in the hope of preventing a general pillage of the countryside. But the Germans's discipline broke down in Bulgaria, and there was rioting and even open combat between the Crusaders and the local villagers. It looked for a while as though the Byzantine Emperor Manuel would call out his army to suppress the disorders, but finally King Conrad and Duke Frederick restored peace and the army arrived at Constantinople in September.

The Second Crusade

The French army under King Louis had left for the East in June. Louis was only twenty-six, a pious man but not a strong leader, and he had had no experience in large-scale war. Following the route of the Germans, the French were better behaved, but found the townspeople hostile because of the criminal acts of King Conrad's soldiers. A French chronicler, Odo of Deuil, told of the shameful things the German crusaders had done as they passed through Byzantine territory, setting fire to houses and looting farms.

"Even our own men," wrote Odo, "could not bear those Germans. On one occasion some of our people, eager to avoid the discomfort of the crowd pressing round King Louis, went on ahead and took lodging near the Germans. All of them went to the market, but the Germans would not let our people buy anything until they had served themselves. As a result a brawl broke out, and it made appalling noise; for since neither side could hear the other, they shouted at the tops of their voices and talked without being able to make themselves understood. . . . In such ways the Germans, marching ahead, spread trouble everywhere."

With the men of the two armies brawling even before they had reached Constantinople, the outlook for a successful Crusade was not bright. Prospects grew even dimmer as soon as the Crusaders crossed into Asia Minor. Ignoring Emperor Manuel's advice, King Conrad decided to follow the path of the first Crusaders across the heart of the peninsula instead of taking the coast road through territory held by Byzantium. By October 15, 1147, the Germans were at Nicaea, which had been Byzantine since its surrender half a century before. Then the Crusaders struck out into Turkish-held land. On October 25 they camped near Dorylaeum, where Bohemond, Raymond of Toulouse, and Godfrey had won such a great victory during the First Crusade. Turkish horsemen arrived just as the tired Germans were dismounting to rest their horses. A massacre resulted. The weary, heavily-laden Crusaders were no match for the fast-moving Turks. Nine-tenths of the German troops were wiped out. King Conrad, his Crusade at an end before it had even begun, fled back to Nicaea with the survivors.

The French army had stayed behind at Constantinople a few extra weeks. Arriving at Nicaea in November, King Louis met the remnants of the German force and learned of the disaster. Rather than risk the same fate, he chose to take the coast route south. The Frenchmen and the surviving Germans marched together, but without friendliness, for the French taunted the Germans for their defeat, and the Germans replied with angry curses. Further brawling between the two groups was prevented by the presence of Turkish raiders whose sallies were a constant menace. As winter closed in, the Crusading army turned into a ragged mob of stragglers without discipline or order. Their numbers dwindled from day to day as Turkish archers picked them off from the distance. Illness, cold, fatigue all took tolls. The battered, harried Crusaders sent messages to Constantinople, begging for food and medicine and military support.

Emperor Manuel gave some aid, but not very much. He had little fondness for these Crusaders after their conduct while passing through his own domain. Still, they were Christians, and he sent them a little food. It was not in the interest of Byzantium to get involved in a war with the Turks of Asia Minor at that moment. The Crusaders darkly suspected that the Emperor had allied himself with the Turks, and they denounced his "treachery." In fact, there was no alliance, but the Emperor had made a truce with the Seljuk Sultan in the spring of 1147, and he intended to keep that truce now. The Crusaders were never able to understand the Emperor's motives. They could not bring themselves to realize that Byzantium had many enemies on many sides—such as the always troublesome Normans of Sicily—and was trying to avoid a war with the Turks if at all possible.

At last, in March of 1148, the Second Crusade limped into Antioch. It was far from being the triumphant force of rescuers that the Franks of Outremer had asked the Pope to send. Seeing the haggard, half-starved survivors, the rulers of Antioch knew that no great achievements were likely to be forthcoming. But hopes remained high, all the same, in a kind of desperate optimism.

Raymond of Antioch, the handsome, dashing Frankish Prince, was now the leader of the settlers in Outremer. The King of Jerusalem, Baldwin III, was eighteen years old and still had not been formally crowned; he was locked in a struggle with his mother, Queen Melisende, for control of the kingdom. King Louis proposed to go on to Jerusalem at once, to visit the holy shrines and discuss strategy with King Baldwin. But Raymond of Antioch, knowing the unstable situation in Jerusalem, advised against it. Before the French army wearied itself marching all the way to Jerusalem, said Raymond, it should join the forces of Antioch in an attack on the city of Aleppo, stronghold of the Saracen leader Nur ed-Din.

King Louis refused to listen. He argued that his vows compelled him to go at once to Jerusalem. He had a personal reason, too. His wife, Queen Eleanor, had come along on the Crusade, but it was well known that she did not love the King. At Antioch, Eleanor began to flirt with the gallant, romantic Prince Raymond. King Louis was motivated mainly by jealousy as he gave the order for his forces to march on Jerusalem.

King Conrad, with the remnant of the German troops, had gone by sea from Asia Minor to Acre and had already arrived at Jerusalem, where King Baldwin and his mother provided a royal reception. King Louis arrived a month later. A great assembly was held late in June. Every high Frankish noble and prelate was there—with two exceptions. Raymond of Antioch, angry that King Louis had ignored his advice, stayed home. And Joscelin of Edessa, who had already lost much of his territory to the Turks, remained at Turbessel guarding against further attacks.

King Louis stood among the leading men of the Kingdom of Jerusalem in a glittering host of barons and clergymen. The Patriarch of Jerusalem was there, and the Grand Masters of the Templars and Hospitallers, and dozens of knights and lords. There was a long debate on the course the new Crusade should take. At length, after much discussion, the assembled dignitaries voted to attack Damascus.

A poorer choice could not have been made. Damascus was a rich Moslem city, and would indeed have been a fine prize to capture. But it was one of the few Saracen cities still independent of Nur ed-Din. The rulers of Damascus feared Nur ed-Din as much as did the Franks, and they would gladly have allied themselves with the Crusaders against Zengi's all-conquering son. But the barons of Jerusalem, hungry for the wealth of Damascus, foolishly voted to invade that city instead of striking at the real enemy, Aleppo, the city of Nur ed-Din.

A huge army, one of the largest that the Crusaders

had ever put in the field, headed for Damascus. Three kings were at its head: Conrad of Germany, Louis of France, Baldwin III of Jerusalem. On July 24, this impressive force of men camped in an orchard outside Damascus.

Unur, the Emir of Damascus, could hardly believe his eyes. He had known of the new Crusade, but he had never imagined it would begin by besieging Damascus, of all unlikely places. He instantly sent a messenger to Aleppo asking help from Nur ed-Din. Thus, by their bungling, the Crusaders had created an alliance between Damascus and Aleppo, two powerful Moslem cities that until then had been in separate camps.

For three days, the Crusaders fought successfully, reaching the walls of Damascus. Then the Saracen reinforcements arrived, and the Franks were driven back. The trees of the orchards where the Franks were camped provided ideal hiding-places for Saracen guerillas, whose raids cost heavily. On July 27, the Crusaders decided to evacuate the orchards and take up a new position on the plain to the east where the raiders could not approach them so easily.

It was another enormous blunder. The Crusaders were abandoning shelter and moving to an exposed, unprotected spot that lacked a good water supply. It was so clumsy a move that the Frankish soldiers muttered that their leaders must have been bribed by Damascus. Soon came word that more Saracens were on their way from Aleppo, this time, a mighty army headed by Nur ed-Din himself.

Frightened now, the Franks conferred and discussed their predicament. King Louis and King Conrad wanted to storm Damascus at once, enter the city, and defy Nur ed-Din. But the Palestinian barons were more realistic.

Taking Damascus would be a tough proposition. Most likely, they would be repelled and left exposed in the plain, where Nur ed-Din's army would destroy them. Nur ed-Din might then go on to conquer Damascus himself, thereby becoming so powerful that no Frankish army could withstand him. The barons of Palestine insisted on an immediate retreat. Better to get out of the way of certain defeat, they argued, than to stand still and be annihilated.

Exasperated, King Conrad gave in to their wishes and left for home. King Louis returned to Jerusalem, still hoping to lead Christian armies in a successful Crusade, but soon word came from Paris that he had better go back and attend to the problems of France. He left in the summer of 1149. Upon his homecoming, he quarrelled with Queen Eleanor and divorced her. Almost immediately she married the young prince who was soon to become King Henry II of England.

The Second Crusade had been a total disaster—as complete a failure as the mad People's Crusade led by Peter the Hermit long before. The new Crusaders had lost every important battle they had fought. Their one major campaign, against Damascus, had been a mistake from start to finish. Thousands of men had perished, absolutely nothing had been gained, and it had all been a tremendous waste of energy and money.

The Franks of Outremer, bewildered by the folly of the Second Crusade, knew now that they could not depend on Europe to save them from Nur ed-Din. If they were going to survive at all, it would be through their own efforts alone.

The hopes of survival did not appear very great. While the leaders of the Second Crusade were still planning their ill-fated attack on Damascus, Raymond of Antioch was

156

under ambush by an army of Nur ed-Din. On June 29, 1149, Raymond and a small band of men were surrounded in the desert far from Antioch. As they tried to fight their way out, the wind blew sand into their eyes, and the Moslems charged. The Franks were wiped out. An officer named Shirkuh personally slew Prince Raymond. Antioch was left without a lord, and the strongest figure in Outremer was gone.

Joscelin II of Edessa, who was not a strong figure at all, still remained in his fortress at Turbessel. He had negotiated a temporary truce with the Moslems. Late in 1149, the truce ended, and the following spring Count Joscelin was captured by Nur ed-Din. He was blinded and sent to Aleppo as a prisoner. He remained in his dungeon until his death, nine years later.

Young King Baldwin III led a party of knights north from Jerusalem and prevented Nur ed-Din from seizing leaderless Antioch. He could not save what was left of the County of Edessa. Joscelin's wife, Countess Beatrice, sold her six remaining cities to Emperor Manuel of Byzantium. Within a year, Nur ed-Din and the Seljuk Sultan Mas'ud surged into the region and divided it between them. With the fall of Turbessel in July of 1151, the County of Edessa was extinguished. The first of the Frankish states to be formed was also the first to be obliterated by the Saracens.

Antioch, once again, was without a grown heir to the throne. Princess Constance, who had been a child of two when her father, Bohemond II, was killed, now had four small children of her own. The heir, Bohemond III, was only five. King Baldwin III of Jerusalem, who was hardly more than nineteen years old himself, undertook to act as regent until Bohemond III came of age or until Princess

Constance could find a new husband. Baldwin suggested several possibilities, but Constance rejected them and invited Emperor Manuel of Byzantium to send her a member of his family to wed. Nothing came of that, though. Princess Constance remained a widow.

King Baldwin, now reaching manhood, was restless at his mother's continued power in Jerusalem. In 1152, when he was twenty-two, the King insisted that his long-postponed coronation take place. Queen Melisende attempted to see to it that she was named joint ruler at the ceremony, but Baldwin outwitted her. He gathered an escort of knights and came to the Church of the Holy Sepulchre on a Tuesday, when no one expected any ceremony to take place. The Patriarch was taken by surprise, and, surrounded by a ring of cold-eyed warriors, was forced to crown Baldwin in his mother's absence. With the general support of the younger barons, Baldwin III began to replace his mother's friends with his own in the government.

The new strength of King Baldwin was matched by sudden new weakness among the Fatimid rulers of Egypt. Family intrigue and a series of assassinations and civil conflicts left Egypt in the hands of incapable leaders. King Baldwin III took advantage of the situation by fortifying Gaza, a town at the edge of Egyptian territory, and then turned his attention to Ascalon.

Ascalon was the only coastal city of the East that had never fallen to the Crusaders. Its walls, arranged in a semicircle flanking the harbor, were lofty and in good repair, and the Egyptians had supplied the city's garrison with provisions against a long siege. In January, 1153, Baldwin III collected every available soldier of the kingdom, marshalling all his siege engines and even bringing along the relic of the True Cross. A grueling siege that lasted many

The siege tower at Ascalon

months failed to weaken the city. Then, late in July, the Franks had a stroke of luck. They had dragged an enormous wooden tower against the walls of Ascalon. It was so tall that it overtopped the walls, allowing the Crusaders to fire flaming arrows and hurl stones into the city. One night, the Egyptian defenders stole forth and set fire to the tower. It blazed so fiercely that the heat caused a section of the masonry to collapse along the wall.

Forty Templars rushed into Ascalon. The Egyptians began to panic; but the Templars were so hungry for glory that they posted a guard to keep other Franks from following them in. Suddenly the Egyptians recovered their courage and slew the invaders. The breach in the wall was repaired, but the incident had thrown fear into the defending garrison, and the surrender of the city soon followed. The Franks entered in triumph while an almost endless stream of Moslem refugees departed, carrying whatever possessions they could manage to pack. Baldwin III made his younger brother Amalric the lord of the city. The great mosque was renamed the Cathedral of Saint Paul.

It was a marvelous victory. Ascalon was a prize that had eluded many great warriors of the past generations, and Baldwin III was understandably proud of his achievement. Yet it was the last such moment a King of Jerusalem would ever know. From then on, the story of the kingdom would be one of steady losses and growing weakness.

xi

pERiL
OUT OF EGYPT

WHILE Baldwin III was conquering Ascalon, the Turkish general Nur ed-Din was registering a triumph of his own. He arrived with an army at Damascus and laid siege; traitors within the city opened its gates, and Nur ed-Din captured it almost without a skirmish. In April, 1154, Nur ed-Din found himself the master of a territory that stretched down the entire eastern border of the Frankish states from Edessa to the deserts beyond the Jordan River. No one Moslem leader had ever had such power in that part of the world before.

He did not hurry to attack the Franks, who still held the whole coastline from Syria to the Egyptian border. Instead he made a two-year truce with King Baldwin, and turned north to make war on the Seljuk Turks of Asia Minor. The campaign kept him busy for more than a year, and in 1156 destructive earthquakes ravaged Syria and left both Moslems and Franks so occupied with rebuilding that they had no time to think of war. Late in 1157, Nur ed-Din fell ill and came close to death. Though he recovered, something of the spark of leadership was gone from him, and he was never the same afterward. His brilliant career had seen him unify much of the Moslem East under a single rule, but he had reached the peak of his accomplishments. It would remain for a younger man to complete the Saracen victory over the hated Franks.

The battle of Ascalon had demonstrated that the youthful Baldwin III had potential greatness. In time, men said, he might match the daring deeds of the two earlier royal Baldwins. What would tell the tale was his handling of the tangled domestic problems of the Frankish states.

One source of trouble was Constance, the widowed Princess of Antioch. Baldwin's attempts at finding a new husband for her had failed. Now Constance found one herself. Her choice made few people in the Frankish world happy. He was Reynald of Chatillon, a newcomer to the East and a man whose complete lack of honor would one day help to bring the Kingdom of Jerusalem crashing into ruin.

Reynald, the younger son of a French nobleman, had come to the Holy Land with the army of King Louis. After the disastrous ending of the Second Crusade, Reynald had remained behind, looking for opportunities to win wealth and power among the Franks. First taking service under King Baldwin, he journeyed to Antioch in 1151, and by 1153 had won the heart of Princess Constance. The great families of Outremer were offended. He did not seem a fitting match for a princess. They disliked Reynald for his coarse ways and his uncontrollable greed. And, since Reynald was new to Outremer, he seemed crude and barbaric to the Franks of long residence. He was not part of their culture in any way.

Peril Out of Egypt

But he was the husband of Constance. And he had been shrewd enough to ally himself with the Templars. Those haughty knights appreciated Reynald's cruelty and callousness. He was a man who thought the way they did, and they supported and encouraged him. Before long, Reynald's arrogance knew no bounds. When the elderly Patriarch of Antioch denounced the marriage, Reynald cast him into prison. He was beaten cruelly, and honey was smeared on his wounds; then the old prelate was left chained all day in the sunshine on the roof of a building while insects crawled over him. Reynald extorted a huge ransom from the Patriarch before agreeing to free him. Then he used the money to finance an expedition of piracy against the wealthy island of Cyprus, a Byzantine possession in the Mediterranean. King Baldwin tried to warn the Cypriotes, but it was too late; Reynald and his men sacked and plundered the hapless island, butchering the people, stealing treasure, and carrying off the leading citizens to Antioch as prisoners to be held for ransom.

King Baldwin III knew that this wild man had to be brought under control. The best tactic, he decided, was to obtain the aid of the Byzantine Emperor, Manuel. Baldwin was on good terms with Manuel; in 1157 he had asked for the hand of a Byzantine princess, and the following year Baldwin was granted the niece of the Emperor, thirteen-year-old Theodora, who became his Queen in September, 1158. Manuel was determined to crush Reynald after the savage raid on Cyprus. He assembled an enormous army and set out through Asia Minor from Constantinople.

Reynald was terror-stricken as this great force neared Antioch. He sent envoys to Manuel, offering to submit. Manuel sent for him. Reynald entered the great tent of the Emperor barefoot and bareheaded, to ask forgiveness. He knelt in the dust before Manuel, who simply ignored him for many minutes. Finally, Manuel dictated his terms. Reynald was to recognize Manuel as his overlord and to carry out no more raids on Cyprus or other Byzantine territory.

Reynald was humbled, just as Manuel's grandfather Alexius had humbled the equally proud Bohemond long before. For eight days Manuel remained in Antioch, accepting the homage of the Frankish knights and taking part in a tournament of horsemen. Then the mighty Byzantine army left the city and headed eastward toward the frontier of Nur ed-Din's dominion. The Franks, looking to Manuel as their champion, hoped that he would attack and crush the Turk. But Manuel had no such intention. He did not care to fight a war this far from his main base of supply at Constantinople. Besides, Manuel did not regard Nur ed-Din as a real enemy. Instead he wanted to conserve his power for war with the Turks of Asia Minor, who posed a much more immediate threat to Byzantium. So when Nur ed-Din proposed a truce, Manuel gladly accepted. The Franks were furious, and once more there was talk of Byzantine treachery.

Manuel next took his army into Asia Minor. In several successful campaigns, he brought the Seljuks to heel. Sultan Kilij Arslan II was defeated and sued for peace. He gave back all the cities of Asia Minor that the Seljuks had seized from Byzantium in recent years and even swore an oath of allegiance to Manuel. The Emperor had good reason to feel satisfied. He had shattered the pride of Reynald of Chatillon, made peace with Nur ed-Din, and defeated the Seljuks of Asia Minor, all within two years.

King Baldwin, shining in Manuel's reflected glory,

was in a strong position. He did not have to fear Nur ed-Din for the moment, because that general was at war with the Danishmend Turks somewhere east of Edessa. Reynald of Chatillon ceased to be a problem, for he had been rash enough to lead a raiding party into Turkish territory in November of 1160, and was captured by the brother of Nur ed-Din. Reynald was taken to Aleppo, and thrust into a dungeon. There he remained for sixteen years. None of the Franks felt any need to ransom him. The throne of Antioch went to Reynald's stepson, Princess Constance's eldest child, Bohemond III.

During 1161, Baldwin was busy strengthening the defenses of the kingdom. The former boy-king was at the height of his manhood now, thirty-two years old, a tall, powerfully-built man with ruddy complexion and a thick golden beard. While visiting Tripoli late in 1161, the King fell ill, and he died at Beirut the following February. There were dark whispers that he had been poisoned by an Arab physician whom the Count of Tripoli had sent him, but probably his death was caused by disease. Sanitation was poor, and life was short in Outremer.

The King and his young Byzantine wife, Queen Theodora, had had no children. Unexpectedly, then, Baldwin's younger brother Amalric found himself on the throne. He was twenty-five years old, as tall and sturdy as his brother had been, with the thick golden beard and fair complexion that ran in his family. Amalric was a man of few words, possibly because he was afflicted with a stammer. At unpredictable moments, though, he would explode in sudden startling laughter. When he became King, he was not regarded as his brother's equal as a statesman.

Amalric soon showed his ability. There were riots and disturbances in Antioch as Princess Constance tried to

165

push aside her son, Bohemond III. Amalric saw to it that the bothersome Constance went into exile, leaving young Bohemond a clear path in Antioch. It was a forceful start for the new King.

Egypt beckoned to Amalric. The troubled situation that had led Baldwin III to attack Ascalon in 1153 was no less troubled in 1162. Amalric planned to fulfill his dead brother's dream of conquering Egypt. It is hard to say why the Crusaders looked toward Egypt when Nur ed-Din still menaced them on their eastern flank. But Egypt was rich, and at the moment Egypt was weak. The temptation was too powerful to resist.

Fatimid power was crumbling there. The young Caliph al-Zafir had been murdered by his own closest friend, a young man named Nasr. Nasr had been encouraged to the deed by his father, Abbas, the Caliph's vizier or chief minister. Accusing the dead Caliph's brothers of the murder, Abbas put them to death also, and brought to the throne the Caliph's young son, a sickly five-year-old boy. Soon after, the remaining members of the Fatimid family discovered the truth. In 1154 Abbas and Nasr were forced to flee from Egypt, and they were slain as they escaped. The boy-Caliph died in 1160 and was succeeded by his nine-year-old cousin. The real power in the country was in the hands of the vizier, but within the space of two years, two viziers were assassinated and a third was driven from the country.

In September, 1163, King Amalric decided to attack the Egyptians while they were still in a state of chaos. He chose the wrong season. The Nile was at its annual flood tide, and the Egyptian vizier simply opened a couple of dykes and sent the Franks back in the face of a torrent of water.

166

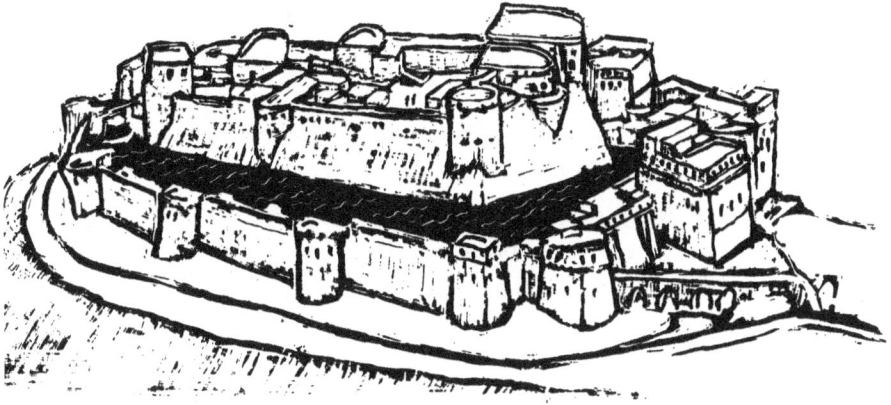

Krak des Chevaliers

While Amalric was involved in this adventure, Nur
ed-Din stirred and made an assault on Frankish Syria. His
target was Tripoli, the weakest of the Crusader states. Nur
ed-Din marched against Krak des Chevaliers, the finest
of all the fortresses of the Crusaders. Rising high on the
summit of a hill above a plain, Krak commanded the entire district between the strong towns of Homs and Hama.
If it fell, Nur ed-Din could sweep into the territory of the
Franks.

Krak was an awesome citadel, covering five acres, en-
closed by a double ring of walls. It had its own wells and
cisterns, windmills for grinding corn and sugar, and a huge
chamber for food storage. It could house two thousand
warriors, but only a skeleton garrison guarded the fortress
when Nur ed-Din appeared. The rest of the Crusaders
were off in Egypt with Amalric.

It seemed as though Krak must certainly fall and,

with it, all of Syria. But the citadel held out. One day in the full blaze of noon a band of Crusaders left the besieged fortress and fell upon the Turks, who were not expecting an attack in such heat. Nur ed-Din's forces panicked and scattered, and Nur ed-Din himself beat a hasty retreat. Against heavy odds, the defenders had triumphed.

Now began a complicated tangle of intrigue and counter-intrigue. While Nur ed-Din sulked at his court and brooded over his defeat, there came to him an Egyptian named Shawar who had been Egypt's vizier for eight months in 1163. Shawar had been driven out by a rival, and he wanted Nur ed-Din's help. If Nur ed-Din would send an army to restore Shawar to power, the ex-vizier would pay a yearly tribute of immense size and recognize Nur ed-Din as his overlord.

Nur ed-Din mulled this offer for many months. Finally he agreed. He chose his most trusted lieutenant, Shirkuh, to lead an army into Egypt on Shawar's behalf. Shirkuh's second-in-command was his nephew, a young officer named Saladin. Saladin was twenty-seven years old and had spent most of his life in Damascus.

The army of Shirkuh and Saladin quickly defeated the Egyptians and gave Shawar back his post as vizier. Shirkuh remained in Cairo, much to the annoyance of the vizier Shawar. Shirkuh levied tributes from the Egyptians, ignored Shawar's wishes, and generally acted as though Egypt were his private property. Shawar looked around for help. Where did this Arab vizier seek aid? Why, from King Amalric of Jerusalem, of course!

The year before, Amalric had invaded Egypt and was forced to retreat. Now, in the summer of 1164, he found that the Egyptians under Shawar wished to hire him to throw Shirkuh out of their country. Amalric named a stiff price for his services and marched south. Shirkuh, besieged by Amalric in a Egyptian town called Bilbeis, agreed to withdraw. The Syrian army marched out of Egypt, and so did the Franks. Shawar was left in control of Egypt, thanks to Amalric's help. Thus did a King of Jerusalem take sides in a struggle between two Saracen powers.

For the next two years, Nur ed-Din raided the Frankish lands without accomplishing much. It irked him to think that Amalric had been able to force Shirkuh out of Egypt so easily, while the mere mention of Shawar's name caused him to explode in wrath. Early in 1167, Nur ed-Din decided to conquer Egypt and avenge himself on Shawar. Once more, Shirkuh and Saladin led Syrian forces toward Egypt. And, for the second time, Shawar asked King Amalric for help.

Shirkuh was not eager to face Amalric again. With one of the lightning-fast diplomatic reversals that marks the whole history of the Crusades, Shirkuh wrote to Shawar proposing a deal. "I am ready to leave Egypt," Shirkuh declared, "and I swear to you that I will never return here and that I will never attack you again, if you will join forces with me against the Franks. Now, the enemy is in the heart of the kingdom. He is cut off from all help; it will be difficult for him to escape. Let us unite and overwhelm him. We may never have so good a chance again, so let us exterminate this nation."

All would have been over for Amalric and the Kingdom of Jerusalem if Shawar had listened. But Shawar feared a trick. He turned the letter over to Amalric, and put Shirkuh's envoy to death. When he learned of this, Shirkuh bit his fingers in dismay. "If Shawar had only believed me," he said, "there would not be a single Frank alive."

Shawar and Amalric proceeded to negotiate a formal treaty. The King sent two Arabic-speaking knights to Cairo to deal with Shawar and the young Caliph. The Frankish ambassadors, Hugh of Caesarea and a Templar named Geoffrey, found themselves in a setting out of *The Thousand and One Nights*. The chronicle of William of Tyre describes the splendor of the Caliph's palace at Cairo as the two knights arrived:

"They saw fountains of marble filled with clearest water, and flocks of birds unknown in our world were heard. . . . There were galleries to walk in, lined with marble columns sheathed in gold and adorned with carvings. The floors were made of various materials and all the surroundings of these galleries were truly worthy of the royal power." An official of the court led them into the palace, "and they passed through other buildings still more elegant than those they had already seen. There was a most astonishing variety of animals. The hand of an artist would have delighted to paint them; poetry alone could have described them, or the imagination of a sleeping man might have invented them in his dreams at night. Yet such creatures really exist in these lands, although the West knows nothing about them."

The Caliph awaited them. The dazzled envoys were taken into the throne room. "Curtains of cloth of gold, adorned with an infinite variety of precious stones, were hanging in the middle of the room, enclosing the throne. They were drawn apart with amazing swiftness, and the Caliph came into view, showing his face to all beholders."

He was a young man, "extremely dark, tall, with a beautiful face, and a very generous disposition." He sat "on a golden throne, clad in garments more magnificent than those of kings." The Vizier Shawar, approaching

King Amalric's ambassadors before the Caliph

meekly, kissed the feet of the sovereign on his throne. He explained the reason for the presence of the ambassadors and reported the nature of the treaties he had concluded.

All that remained was for the Caliph to give his approval. He was still the ruler, at least in name, and Shawar's treaty would not be binding without the Caliph's word. Hugh of Caesarea, maintaining a cool mind even amid all this pomp and glitter, insisted that the Caliph show his agreement by shaking hands. It took some while before the young monarch understood what Hugh meant, for in Egypt it was unheard of for anyone to touch the Caliph's body, least of all a Christian. Hugh was stubborn, and at length "the Caliph stretched out his hand with great reluctance and presented it covered with a veil."

That did not satisfy the Frankish knight. He declared boldly, "My Lord, good faith is straightforward. It is necessary that everything be laid bare in making the contracts which bind one prince to another. Unless you offer your hand uncovered, I shall be obliged to think that you are holding something back and are less sincere than I should like." Forcing himself to smile, the not very amused Caliph pulled aside the veil and put his bare hand in that of Hugh of Caesarea as he swore his oath.

The treaty bound Egypt to pay a tribute of one hundred thousand gold pieces a year to the King of Jerusalem. For his part, Amalric solemnly swore to remain in Egypt until Shirkuh had been defeated. The joint Frankish-Egyptian army pursued the Syrian forces under Shirkuh and Saladin and chased them southward up the Nile. At Ashmunein, well to the south of Cairo, the two armies met.

Amalric had more men, but most of them were foot soldiers. Shirkuh's smaller army was made up chiefly of fast-moving Turkish cavalrymen. Both sides hesitated to do battle. But Amalric, who wore a fragment of the True Cross on a chain round his neck, was visited in his sleep by Saint Bernard. The voice of the vision commanded the King to attack, "as a good Christian should." Rashly, Amalric obeyed. On the next morning, March 18, 1167, the Frankish knights charged the center of the Syrian line.

An Arab historian, Ibn al-Athir, tells us what happened:

"Saladin was in command of the center, and his uncle Shirkuh said to him: 'The Franks will probably think that I am in the center and will attack it. You will put up little resistance and will quickly flee. When he stops pursuing you, you will retrace your steps.' Shirkuh chose the bravest of his men, particularly those known for their audacity and coolness, and took up his position with them on the right wing. When the fighting began, the Franks, as he had predicted, attacked the center; Saladin put up a feeble resistance and began to yield ground, but without breaking his ranks and always pursued by the enemy. Then Shirkuh flung himself on the troops opposing him and caused great carnage among them. When the Christians who had chased Saladin came back, they found their brothers slain or routed and they too took flight. Shirkuh only needed one or two thousand horsemen to triumph over the Franks and the Egyptians."

Amalric and a handful of soldiers escaped and made their way in chagrin back to Cairo. His losses had been heavy, with many deaths and a number of knights such as Hugh of Caesarea taken prisoner.

Shirkuh did not choose to attack the Egyptian capital. Bypassing it, he marched to the port city of Alexandria to gather strength for a new campaign. Amalric and Shawar

immediately blockaded the city. After a month, with starvation threatening the Syrian army, Shirkuh managed to
escape from Alexandria, leaving Saladin in command. Saladin held out a month longer, but when it became clear
that his uncle could not rescue him, he began to discuss
surrender terms.

After much haggling, a simple solution was reached.
Shirkuh suggested that both he and Amalric take their
armies out of Egypt, leaving the country to Shawar. King
Amalric, who was getting impatient to return to his own
land, agreed. The siege of Alexandria was lifted and Saladin and his men were freed. During the negotiations,
Amalric and Saladin held frequent discussions. The King
began to see that of all the Saracens, the young officer was
by far the most honorable and trustworthy, and perhaps
he was sorry to have allied himself with Shawar instead
of with Saladin.

In the fall of 1167, Amalric returned to Jerusalem
after his long campaign in Egypt. He found that Nur
ed-Din was still making menacing gestures and that the
country was in a poor position to defend itself if the emir
finally attacked. Frankish manpower was low, and not
many new men were coming from Europe to swell the
ranks. In order to provide for the defense of his kingdom,
Amalric found it necessary to hand more and more power
to the Templars and the Hospitallers, those sinister knights
who owed him no allegiance. The Templars in particular
took control of a great stretch of territory north of the
Kingdom of Jerusalem.

Amalric also strengthened his alliance with Byzantium. Like his brother Baldwin, he married a Byzantine
princess, Maria, the grand-niece of Emperor Manuel.
Amalric began to plan an attack on his one-time ally,

Shawar, with Byzantine help. Shawar was showing himself to be a poor ruler, and Amalric had never forgotten his desire to conquer Egypt.

A Frankish army gathered at Ascalon in October, 1168, and marched once more into Egypt. Shawar was outraged. He had not suspected that Amalric would turn on him so callously. Amalric let it be known that he might withdraw from Egypt for a price, say, two million gold pieces, but Shawar refused to deal with him and offered resistance. An Egyptian fortress fell to Amalric in the battle that followed, and the prisoners included Shawar's son.

But when he reached Cairo, Amalric found that he was in an awkward position. He could not take the great city, and knew it. Once more, he invited Shawar to buy him off. Shawar began to bargain with Amalric over the price, but did not hurry, for possible rescue was on the way.

Another bizarre shift of alliances had taken place. In the past, Amalric had leagued himself with Shawar to defeat Shirkuh. Now Shirkuh was coming to defend Shawar against Amalric!

Calling in Shirkuh had not been Shawar's idea. One of his sons had taken the step, offering Nur ed-Din a third of Egypt's land in return for the services of Shirkuh. Eight thousand Syrian troops, led once again by Shirkuh and Saladin, entered Egypt, circled through the desert, and took up a position south of Amalric's army. It was Amalric's turn to be astonished by the course of events. He could do nothing but retreat, leaving Cairo to Shirkuh.

On January 8, 1169, Shirkuh entered Cairo. Making the best of the situation, Shawar greeted him warmly, and they began to discuss arrangements for sharing power in Egypt. Saladin had other ideas. He warned Shirkuh that Shawar was a dangerous, treacherous man who was best removed from the scene. In short order Shawar was taken prisoner and the order for his execution was carried out. Shirkuh replaced him as vizier. Nur ed-Din could not have been more satisfied.

Shirkuh did not enjoy his new rank for long. Within two months he was dead, a victim of overeating at a feast. Power passed to Saladin. The young officer—he was only thirty-one—had stood to the side while his uncle conquered Egypt. Now he reaped the reward of Shirkuh's accomplishment.

Officially, Saladin was the representative of Nur ed-Din. But Nur ed-Din was far away in Syria, and he was old and ailing besides. Many years before, it had seemed as though Nur ed-Din was the man marked to overthrow the Franks. That destiny had never quite been attained. Now Saladin had his opportunity, and he would not waste the chance. Here, at last, was the man to drive the Crusaders from the Holy Land.

The Might
of Saladin

ONCE more the balance of power had changed. Amalric's dream of conquering Egypt was ended, and now he found himself hemmed in between two strong foes, Nur ed-Din to the east and his vassal Saladin to the south. A pincer movement could easily crush the Kingdom of Jerusalem.

Amalric sent ambassadors to Europe, calling for a new Crusade. Such monarchs as Henry II of England and Louis VII of France were invited to save the Holy Land, but Europe was torn by political struggles; none of its leaders had time for Jerusalem. The only ally that Amalric could find was his wife's relative, Emperor Manuel of Byzantium.

Saladin bided his time, consolidating his new position in Egypt. He had many enemies, both among the Egyptian royal family and in the ranks of Shirkuh's officers, who regarded him as a young upstart of low birth. Slowly, patiently, he added to his power and isolated his rivals.

The attack on Damietta

The Might of Saladin

Late in October, 1169, Amalric made his move. Supported by the Byzantine navy, he invaded the important Egyptian city of Damietta. Damietta, the powerful fortress that commanded the entrance to the main branch of the Nile, was the gateway to Cairo. When the Crusaders appeared, Saladin ordered a great chain to be flung across the river to keep the Greek ships from sailing upstream to the capital. The city held out well against the besiegers, and there were wide areas of disagreement between the Franks and the Greeks on matters of strategy. By the end of the year, the invaders withdrew in failure.

It was Amalric's last invasion of Egypt. For the next few years his battles were waged in the north. In the spring of 1174, Amalric saw a fine opportunity to remove one of the threats that hung over the Kingdom of Jerusalem. Nur ed-Din and Saladin had begun to quarrel, for the older man had started to fear the power of his vassal. Nur ed-Din was actually planning a military expedition to Egypt to bring Saladin under tighter control, but in May, the old warrior fell ill and died. His heir was his son, Malik as-Salih Ismail, a boy of eleven. At once, Nur ed-Din's Syrian empire began to fall apart.

Amalric met with the Turkish regent, Ibn al-Muqaddam, and began to negotiate a treaty of alliance against Saladin. A pact was signed. It seemed as though the growing strength of Saladin would be checked. But while the negotiations were going on, King Amalric came down with an attack of dysentery. As he lay weak and fevered at Jerusalem, his doctor treated him in the approved manner of the day, by opening his veins to allow the disease to bleed away. What bled away was the King's life. He died in July, 1174, at the age of thirty-eight. With him died the last hope for the survival of the Kingdom of Jerusalem.

The heir to the throne was a boy of thirteen, Baldwin IV. Young Baldwin, Amalric's only son, was brave, intelligent, everything that a prince ought to be, but he was afflicted with a dread disease that was certain to cut short his life within a few years, throwing the Kingdom of Jerusalem into new chaos. His tutor, William of Tyre, had made the discovery when Baldwin was nine. He tells of it in his chronicle:

"We took as much care in training his character as we did in teaching him literature. He was always playing with the young nobles who were his companions, and they often pinched each other on the arms or hands as children of that age do when they are together. The others cried out when this hurt them, but the young Baldwin bore these games with unusual patience, as if the pain meant nothing to him. . . . I thought at first that this showed courage on his part, and not a lack of feeling. Then I called him to me . . . and I found that he could feel nothing in his right arm or hand. . . . It was the first symptom of a much more serious and quite incurable disease. By the time he had begun to reach manhood we realized, and we weep as we speak of it, that the young man was a victim of leprosy."

A doomed boy ruled at Jerusalem. An even younger boy was the heir to Nur ed-Din's power. The situation was made to order for Saladin. He was already in full command in Egypt; the last Fatimid Caliph had died, and Saladin had packed the royal relatives off into comfortable exile. He was free now to invade Syria and then the territories of the Franks.

The Franks were suffering from a bitter family feud—one which would grow steadily worse as the years passed. King Amalric had been married twice. His first wife, Agnes of Courtenay, was the sister of Count Joscelin II of Edessa. She was the mother of Baldwin IV and of a young girl, Sibylla. But Agnes was a vicious, scheming woman, and when Amalric had become King of Jerusalem the barons had forced him to divorce her. They felt she was unworthy to be Queen. Amalric's second wife, the Byzantine princess, Maria Comnena, had given birth to a child named Isabella. With Amalric dead, there was immediate rivalry between his two widows and the factions of nobles that gathered around them.

On one side in the feud was the regent, Count Raymond III of Tripoli. A dark-skinned, hawk-nosed man of thirty-four, he was a cousin of the late King Amalric, and he served as the ruler of Jerusalem while the new King Baldwin IV was growing up. Count Raymond belonged to the faction of Queen Maria.

On the other side gathered a group of hate-filled, ambitious nobles, surrounding the fierce Agnes of Courtenay. They included Agnes's nephew, Count Joscelin III of Edessa, a count without a territory to rule. Another figure in this group was Gerard of Ridfort, the Grand Master of the Templars, who hated Count Raymond of Tripoli because Raymond had failed to arrange Gerard's marriage to a certain wealthy heiress. Another of Agnes's supporters was Reynald of Chatillon, the wild man who had so cruelly invaded Cyprus many years before.

Reynald had been a Moslem prisoner in Aleppo for sixteen years, and none had missed him. But in 1174, Saladin's army invaded Syria and threatened Aleppo. Count Raymond of Tripoli took the field because he was unwilling to see Aleppo fall into Saladin's hands. Saladin retreated. In gratitude, the local Turkish ruler of Aleppo agreed to free all the Frankish prisoners in his dungeons, and in an evil moment Reynald of Chatillon was turned loose. Count Raymond was thus indirectly responsible for restoring the liberty of Reynald, something he would later have keen reason to regret.

The youthful Baldwin IV, guided by his able regent Count Raymond, attempted to steer his way through the poisonous atmosphere of hatred that enveloped Outremer. No feuds are as ugly as family feuds, and by now the Frankish nobles were intricately related to one another, thanks to three generations of intermarriage. The split in the nobility grew wider all the time, and tempers were hot.

Saladin was thriving on the disunity. There was no real leadership to oppose him, either in the Frankish states or in Moslem Syria. He made himself the master of one Syrian city after another, proclaiming himself King of Egypt and Syria. Of the major Saracen-ruled cities, only Aleppo was able to withstand him. He was obviously gathering strength for an eventual attack on the Frankish states. Saladin, a deeply religious Moslem, had no intention of allowing Christians to remain in control of so much of the East.

King Baldwin IV was aware of this, and aware, too, of the disease that was literally devouring his body. His death could not be many years away, and a successor to the throne had to be found. When Baldwin was fourteen, in 1175, he arranged a marriage for his older sister, fifteen-year-old Sibylla. The husband was William Long-Sword, a cousin of King Louis VII of France, who left Europe to marry Sibylla. It was understood that William would become King of Jerusalem after Baldwin's death. But William himself died first, in 1177. He had given Sibylla a baby boy, who could be considered the heir to the throne, but a full-grown heir was needed at once. Envoys of Baldwin went searching for a new husband for Sibylla.

The Might of Saladin

In this troubled time, the only ally Jerusalem could count on was Byzantium. Suddenly that prop was removed. The truce between Byzantium and the Seljuks of Asia Minor had broken down, and Emperor Manuel, in a moment of ambition, decided to invade Asia Minor and shatter the Seljuks forever. In September, 1176, the Byzantine army was ambushed at a place called Myriocephalum, and the Turks dealt Manuel a devastating defeat. The power of Byzantium, built up so shrewdly by Manuel's grandfather Alexius and his father John, was broken in a single day.

When he heard of the overwhelming Byzantine defeat, Saladin felt that the time had come to move against the divided Franks, who now were without their only support. He led an army of 30,000 troops out of Egypt, up the coast into Palestine.

His purpose was to capture Jerusalem and deprive the Christians of their capital. With one stroke he hoped to destroy the Crusaders for all time.

Though in the agonizing grasp of illness, King Baldwin hurried down to the fortress of Ascalon, which controlled the Egyptian border. Saladin's huge army swarmed up to it and surrounded it. Leaving a small force to keep the King bottled up in Ascalon, Saladin set out toward Jerusalem. The Saracens were in high spirits, confident and cheerful. Jerusalem would fall easily, Saladin believed.

Baldwin managed to get a message to a band of Templars at the nearby fortress of Gaza. They rushed to Ascalon and helped the King break free. Then Baldwin and the Templars sped after the Egyptian army. On November 25, 1177, the Egyptians were crossing a ravine near the castle of Montisgard, not far from the town of Ramleh, when the Franks unexepectedly swooped down on them.

The rout was total. The valiant young King Baldwin,

183

with 500 knights of his own, eighty Templars, and about 2,000 infantrymen, annihilated the surprised Saracens by the thousands. Baldwin himself fought in the front lines. The Egyptians took to their heels, even throwing their weapons aside so they could run more swiftly. They retreated in disgrace across the forbidding Sinai desert into Egypt. Saladin had suffered the worst defeat of his career. Afraid of a rebellion in Cairo when news of the disaster reached Egypt, Saladin sent a message ahead by carrier pigeon to let the Egyptians know that he was still alive and was returning to punish anyone who attempted a revolt against him.

The great victory at Montisgard cheered the Franks immeasurably, but it did not really change anything. They still were few in number, divided against themselves, and soon to lose their King. Neither Europe nor Byzantium was able to come to their aid. Against them was arrayed the might of Saladin, master of Egypt and most of Syria. The next time he attacked he would be more cautious.

A new husband had finally been found for King Baldwin's sister Sibylla. He was Guy of Lusignan, a young French nobleman who came out to Palestine in 1180 for the exact purpose of marrying Sibylla. Guy was young and handsome, but he was also vain and foolish, a flighty weakling with no mind of his own. Sibylla, though she was a widow and a mother, was only in her late teens. She was charmed by Guy, and insisted on marrying him.

King Baldwin and most of the barons were deeply disturbed. If he married Sibylla, Guy would become the heir to the crown of Jerusalem. The thought of the spineless stranger leading the Franks against Saladin was horrifying. But Agnes, the mother both of Sibylla and King Baldwin, pressed the issue, and Baldwin wearily gave his consent. The marriage took place in the spring of 1180. Guy took his place with Reynald of Chatillon, Joscelin III of Edessa, Gerard of Ridfort, and the other trouble-making satellites of Agnes of Courtenay.

It was Reynald, that dark and brutal individual, who pushed the weakening Franks on to their downfall. Saladin and King Baldwin had made a truce in 1180 after a terrible drought had left both Moslems and Franks short of food. The Franks had more to gain from the truce than did the Saracens, and Baldwin knew it. But Reynald of Chatillon was thinking only of himself. He deliberately broke the truce and provoked Saladin's wrath.

The treaty provided that Christian and Moslem merchants could pass unharmed through each other's territory. Reynald was now lord of Oultrejourdain, a desert domain east of the River Jordan. Before his long imprisonment he had been Prince of Antioch, but his first wife Constance had died years before and the throne of Antioch was in the hands of her son, Bohemond III. Reynald, after leaving his dungeon, had married the widow of the recently-murdered lord of Oultrejourdain.

It irked Reynald to see Moslem caravans loaded with rich goods passing unmolested through Oultrejourdain on their way to Arabia. In the summer of 1181, he attacked a caravan and seized its merchandise. Saladin demanded the return of the goods. King Baldwin was unable to make Reynald obey, and the truce came to an end. The angry Saladin left Egypt in May of 1182 to wage war against the Franks.

He probed the Frankish strength at several points without any real battles on either side. Then Saladin postponed his campaign against the Christians long enough to take possession of Aleppo, whose young Moslem ruler had just died. By the summer of 1183 Saladin was the master of the greatest Saracen empire in centuries. All of Egypt was his. He held much of Syria. His lieutenants ruled loyally in his name in Iraq. The Seljuks of Asia Minor feared him. Only the bothersome Franks still defied him. They held most of Palestine and nearly all the coastal cities. They were infidels to Saladin, and he saw their continued presence as shameful to him.

Of all the Franks, Saladin hated only Reynald of Chatillon personally. He had nothing but admiration for the courageous King Baldwin IV and for some of the other Frankish barons. Saladin respected valor, regardless of a man's religion. But Reynald he despised. The breaking of the truce in 1181 had been followed by a worse outrage the next year. With a band of piratical comrades, Reynold sailed down the African coast of the Red Sea, raiding ports and sinking a ship laden with pilgrims bound for the Moslem shrines at Mecca. It seems his intention was to attack the Holy City of Islam itself and carry off its treasures. An Egyptian fleet drove him away, but Saladin vowed that Reynald would pay with his life for the expedition.

Late in 1183, Saladin once more began to invade Frankish lands. King Baldwin's leprosy was so far advanced that he was unable to govern the country. He was nearly blind, and he had lost the use of his arms and legs. His mother Agnes and his sister Sibylla persuaded the tragic young King to name his brother-in-law Guy of Lusignan as regent. When Guy led an army against Saladin, he behaved with such stupidity and hesitation that the other barons were shocked. Only luck saved the Franks from defeat. King Baldwin removed Guy as regent and attempted to govern the country himself once again. At the same time, he named his nephew Baldwin as his heir in place of Guy. He was Sibylla's six-year-old son by her first marriage.

The Might of Saladin

There was another royal marriage later in 1183. King Baldwin's half-sister, Isabella, was now eleven years old. She had been betrothed to Humphrey of Toron, a gentle, good-looking boy of seventeen. King Baldwin had hoped to bring together the quarreling factions of his family by this union. Humphrey was Reynald of Chatillon's stepson, and Isabella was the daughter of Queen Maria, the enemy of Reynald and Agnes. The wedding proved nightmarish, though. Members of both factions were present, glaring at each other and plotting dire things, and in the midst of the ceremony held at Reynald's castle in Oultrejourdain, Saladin's army appeared and began to bombard the walls. The child bride and her young groom were helpless pawns, caught in conflicts they could barely understand.

Saladin failed to take the fortress, and the wedding guests went home when the siege was lifted, but nothing had been accomplished toward uniting the Franks. The feud remained as bitter as ever. King Baldwin was on his deathbed.

Early in 1185, the dying King called the barons together and made them swear to recognize his little nephew as King Baldwin V. Guy of Lusignan and Reynald of Chatillon were not present. By the wish of King Baldwin, Count Raymond of Tripoli would govern the country until the young King reached manhood. If the boy died without an heir, the throne would pass to one or the other of the royal princesses, Sibylla and Isabella. King Baldwin provided that the four great European rulers, the Pope, the Holy Roman Emperor, the King of France, and the King of England, would decide whether to give the throne to Isabella's husband or Sibylla's.

In March of 1185, death at last came to King Baldwin IV. He was twenty-four years old. Despite his terrible affliction, he had done well in preserving the kingdom. If he had been healthy and granted a normal span of years, he might have achieved greatness as a ruler, but his early death delivered Jerusalem over to chaos. Within eighteen months, King Baldwin V was also dead, less than nine years old, and the long-awaited showdown between the two feuding parties was at hand.

Who would be the new King of Jerusalem?

By Baldwin IV's will, the monarchs of Europe were supposed to decide between the claims of Isabella and Sibylla. Raymond of Tripoli, the regent, called his supporters together to decide what to do. But Raymond's enemies moved swiftly. Joscelin III of Edessa seized Acre and sent troops to occupy Tyre and Beirut. Reynald of Chatillon hurried out from his desert castle to join Sibylla and her husband Guy at Ascalon. The seacoast now was in the hands of the supporters of Sibylla and her ambitious mother Agnes. Reynald and Joscelin proclaimed Sibylla to be Queen of Jerusalem, and invited Raymond of Tripoli and the other nobles to attend her coronation.

Sibylla had a good claim. Her brother Baldwin IV had been King, and so had her son, Baldwin V. But if Sibylla became Queen, Guy of Lusignan would be King, and Guy was not capable of ruling. Raymond objected, but there was nothing he could do. In Jerusalem, the Templars seized the city. Their Grand Master, Gerard of Ridfort, hated Raymond and would do anything to thwart him. The gates of the Holy City were locked. Reynald, Gerard, Guy, and Sybilla went to the Church of the Holy Sepulchre, where the Patriarch of Jerusalem was waiting. A chronicler of the time describes what followed:

"They took out two crowns and carried them to the Patriarch. The Patriarch put one of them on the altar of the Holy Sepulchre and with the other crowned Princess

188

Sibylla. When the lady was crowned Queen, the Patriarch said to her: 'Your Majesty, you are a woman. It is proper that you should have a man to help you govern your kingdom. Here is a crown. Take it and give it to such a man as can help you govern your kingdom and knows how to govern.' Sibylla came and took the crown and called her husband Guy of Lusignan who was before her and said to him, 'Sire, come, receive this crown, for I could not use it better.' He knelt down before her and she put the crown on his head."

So the foolish weakling Guy of Lusignan became King of Jerusalem on a Friday in the early fall of 1186. "I will wager that he will be King for less than a year," said one of Guy's enemies when he heard of what had been done.

THE HORNS
OF HATTIN

GUY and his backers had moved fast, out-witting Raymond of Tripoli, but Raymond felt that he had the strength of the kingdom on his side. Most of the barons despised Guy. Only a few malcontents such as Reynald, Joscelin, and the Templar Grand Master Gerard supported him. Count Raymond believed that all was not lost, and that Guy could be pushed from the throne for which he was so poorly fitted.

Raymond's plan hinged on Humphrey of Toron, the husband of young Princess Isabella. Isabella, as the daughter of King Amalric, had as good a claim to the throne as did Sibylla, her half-sister. Count Raymond planned to crown Humphrey as King of Jerusalem and bring him to the capital. The barons would, if necessary, fight a civil war to replace King Guy with King Humphrey. Since a truce with Saladin once again existed, there was no danger of an attack by the Saracens during this time of disunity. Saladin was, after all, an honorable man who would keep his word.

190

The Horns of Hattin

There was just one hitch. Humphrey, who was fond of poetry and conversation, had no taste for being King. He panicked and slipped away from Raymond, riding by night to Jerusalem. Begging to see Guy and Sibylla, Humphrey came before them sheepishly, "like a naughty child caught red-handed," as a chronicler remarked. He pledged allegiance to them and assured them that he had no wish to challenge their right to rule.

Raymond was furious. Blocked in his plan to put Humphrey on the throne, he could do nothing but withdraw, vowing never to pay homage to King Guy. When the new monarch called an assembly of barons, Raymond did not attend. The others coolly acknowledged that Guy was indeed their King.

Guy ruled in Jerusalem. Before long, Reynald of Chatillon committed another dastardly deed, breaking the new truce as he had broken the old, and disaster enveloped both King and kingdom as a result. The chronicler tells it:

"A spy came to Prince Reynald and told him that a great caravan was coming from Cairo to Damascus and would pass by the land of Kerak. Reynald instantly mounted his horse, rode to Kerak, gathered as many men as he could, and went and seized this caravan and with it the sister of Saladin who was with it. When Saladin heard that Prince Reynald had seized his caravan and his sister, he was sorely vexed and grieved. He at once sent envoys to King Guy, demanding the caravan and his sister, and saying that he did not want to break the truce that he had made in the time of the little King [Baldwin V]. King Guy ordered Prince Reynald to give back to Saladin the caravan he had taken, and his sister. He replied that he would not give them back, that he was lord of his land, as the King was of his, and that he had made no truce with the Saracens. The taking of this caravan led to the loss of the Kingdom of Jerusalem."

For many years Saladin had eyed the Frankish states, invading in a halfhearted way, then withdrawing and accepting a truce. Now he would show no mercy. Reynald of Chatillon, who had pillaged caravans, who had showed no respect for Saladin's sister, who had blasphemously sworn to enter Arabia and dig up the sacred bones of Mohammed, would have to die.

Many of the Frankish princes were as outraged by Reynald's acts as Saladin. Raymond of Tripoli, wanting no part of this war of revenge, quickly made a truce with Saladin. So did Bohemond III of Antioch. Reynald and his pitiful friend King Guy would have to stand alone against the mighty Saracen.

King Guy knew that without the support of the powerful Count Raymond he could never withstand Saladin. His first thought was to besiege Raymond in his town of Tiberias and force him to submit. Encouraged by the treacherous Gerard of Ridfort, head of the Templars, Guy called his vassals together and marched against Raymond. The King was met by a neutral baron, Balian of Ibelin, who pointed out that if the King did battle against Raymond, Raymond would surely win. Balian urged Guy to send ambassadors to Raymond to work out a peaceful settlement of their quarrel. "If you lose the help and counsel of Count Raymond, you are finished," Balian warned.

Guy named Gerard of Ridfort, the Archbishop of Tyre, and Roger, the Grand Master of the Hospitallers, to go with Balian and negotiate peace with Raymond. They set out from Jerusalem on April 29, 1187.

While Balian's plan was being considered, Count

The Horns of Hattin

Raymond was receiving another group of envoys—from al-Afdal, the son of Saladin. Saladin's son was on a routine mission of military reconnaissance in his father's Palestinian lands. It was necessary for him to cross Count Raymond's territory with his soldiers. Since a truce existed between Raymond and Saladin, al-Afdal requested permission to enter and pass through Raymond's domain. Raymond had no reason to refuse. He simply made the conditions that the Saracens come and go between sunrise and sunset and do no harm to the villages through which they traveled.

Raymond then sent a message to the ambassadors of King Guy, who were journeying toward him, to warn them that there would be Saracens in his country the next day. Raymond hoped in that way to avoid an accidental clash between al-Afdal's men and the envoys from Guy. But Gerard of Ridfort saw a chance to take the Saracens by surprise and slaughter them in a merciless ambush. He at once called together all the Templars and Hospitallers in the area, about 130 knights altogether. The little army trailed the Saracen host and came upon it near Nazareth.

The Moslems, suspecting none of this perfidy, were peacefully watering their horses at a place called the Springs of Cresson. As the knights came over the hill, they saw thousands of Saracen soldiers below. Roger, the Grand Master of the Hospitallers, advised a quick retreat in view of the unexpectedly great number of Moslems. A high-ranking Templar, James of Mailly, also argued against what would surely be a suicidal attack.

Gerard, though, was not merely vicious and evil; he was foolish as well. As a chronicler comments, "The Master of the Templars was a bold knight, very sure of himself, and, like those who are overbearing, he despised all other people." Scornfully he taunted James of Mailly, declaring, "You love your blond head too well to want to lose it."

"I shall die in battle like a brave man," James retorted. "It is you that will flee as a traitor."

Gerard's mockery had its effect. The knights charged down the hill, and the amazed Saracens seized their weapons and cut them down with ease. The Grand Master of the Hospitallers was beheaded, as were James of Mailly and eighty-six other Templars. Only four Franks escaped, Gerard of Ridfort and three fellow Templars. The unnecessary massacre left Gerard more determined than ever to stir up war against Saladin.

King Guy's ambassadors had made their way to Count Raymond by this time. They conferred, and Raymond let himself be persuaded against his better judgment to support Guy. He agreed to break his truce with Saladin and present a united front against the impending Moslem attack. Saladin was assembling a vast army on his side of the frontier, and on the first of July he crossed the Jordan into Frankish-held land.

The first town to be surrounded was Tiberias, which belonged to Count Raymond. Raymond had gone to join King Guy at Acre, where the army of Jerusalem was assembled. His wife, Countess Eschiva, remained in Tiberias and herself led the defense of the besieged town.

The Franks held a council of war. Count Raymond was the first to speak. It was the height of summer, he pointed out, and any attempt to march into the desert to battle Saladin would be foolhardy. In the fierce heat, no attack would last long. The wisest policy was to go on the defensive and wait for Saladin to move. Saladin could not maintain such a huge army for long in the parched desert, and he would be forced to withdraw. Also, Raymond

194

noted, reinforcements were coming from Antioch, and it made no sense to launch an attack against the Saracens until they arrived.

He was followed by Reynald of Chatillon and the Grand Master Gerard. Hotly, bitingly, they called Raymond a coward and accused him of being in the pay of the Saracens. They insisted on an immediate attack. The ringing words of the two fierce men, both of them hungry for warfare at any risk, cowed King Guy. Over Raymond's objections, he gave the order to march toward Tiberias.

The next afternoon, the Franks camped at Sephoria, a place with a good water supply and ample pasturage for the horses. Raymond once again argued that they should remain there and let Saladin come to them, instead of venturing into the desert. Guy reminded Raymond that his wife was at Tiberias and should be rescued.

Raymond replied, "Sire, know that any damage done to Tiberias is my affair and falls on me and no other. My wife and my children are there, and I would not have harm come to them. But I would rather lose Tiberias and all within it than let the kingdom be lost. Let us wait at Acre so as to be near our fortresses. Saladin is so proud that he will not leave until he has joined battle with you, and if he comes to fight you before Acre we can call on the other cities nearby to help us. And if God gives us the victory, so that we may defeat him before he has regained his own territory, we shall have so vanquished and broken him that he will never be able to recover."

"I spy treason!" shouted Gerard of Ridfort.

Guy, swayed once again, agreed for the moment to follow Raymond's advice. But Gerard continued to hammer away. "Sire, will you trust a known traitor?" he demanded. King Guy changed his mind several times during the night and finally sent heralds through the camp to announce that the army would set out at daybreak for Tiberias.

Raymond clenched his fists in despair. But he had agreed to obey King Guy, and so when morning came he led the procession away from grassy, fertile Sephoria into the barren wastes of the desert. There was no water to be had as the Franks marched. The sun, a ball of flame that seemed to fill half the sky, was brutal. In the cloudless sky vultures wheeled and circled as if they knew what lay ahead.

All day the Franks plodded on through the oven-hot wastes. By late afternoon, they came to a plateau called the Horns of Hattin, where two rocky peaks rose about a hundred feet above the scrub-covered slopes. Beyond lay a lake and an inviting green valley. Up onto this exposed plateau the Franks filed, carrying before them their most sacred relic, the True Cross, a bit of wood encased in gold and studded with precious gems. The exhausted men looked down into the valley. Some of the Templars sent word to the King that they were too tired to go on, and wished to make camp here for the night. Guy himself was willing to halt, and gave the signal to make camp.

It was the worst of all possible places to halt. There was no water on the hillside. The camp was without shade. The Saracens could easily surround it and sweep to victory. When Count Raymond heard of Guy's decision, he flung himself wearily to the ground, muttering, "Ah, Lord God, the war is over. We are dead men. The kingdom is finished."

The Moslems were astonished that the Franks should camp in such an insane place, but they were quick to take advantage of Guy's folly. They moved their camp into the

The Horns of Hattin

valley below the Horns of Hattin, pitching their tents so close to the Franks that, as a chronicler said, "if a cat had escaped from the army of the Christians, it could not have got away without the Saracens taking it."

The night brought terror to the Franks. The dry heat made their throats rage with thirst, but there was no water in the camp. From below came the sound of joyful Moslem voices raised in prayers and battle-songs. Now and then, a Christian would steal down the hillside hoping to find water, only to be caught and killed by the Saracens. Toward morning, the Moslems set fire to the dry brush that covered the hill, sending gusts of hot smoke over the camp of the Crusaders. Behind the cover of smoke, Saladin moved his men inward and took up a position of attack. But he did not begin the battle until after sunrise. He wanted the hot sun to do its work on the already thirst-ravaged Franks.

Smoke and flames engulfed the tormented men on the hill. Wildly, the Christian soldiers came down the slope, hoping to reach the mocking lake that gleamed like

197

a mirage beyond. But the Moslems by the thousands stood between the Franks and the water. The Christians were cut down easily. Many, their mouths swollen with thirst, croaked out the words of surrender. It was a one-sided rout.

The horsemen still remained on the hill. Seeing his infantry cut to shreds, King Guy asked Count Raymond to lead a cavalry charge that might break the Moslem lines. Raymond and his knights mounted their horses and spurred them forward in an all-or-nothing attack. The Moslem response was shrewd. The Saracens simply gave way, letting the knights ride past, and formed their line again after they had gone. Raymond found himself on the far side of the Moslem host, unable to return. Cut off from the Horns of Hattin by a surging sea of Saracens, Raymond left the battlefield and rode off in dejection to Tripoli.

Atop the Horns of Hattin only a few hundred knights remained, gathered about the red tent of King Guy at the highest point of the hill. The Crusaders formed themselves into a close ring, wielding their swords in a furious and futile defense as the Saracens closed in.

Saladin and his son al-Afdal stood below, watching the battle. At one point, the Crusaders rallied and forced the Moslems back to the bottom of the hill. Saladin tugged at his beard, scowled in anguish, rushed forward to encourage his men. The Saracens charged to the summit of the hill.

"We have routed them!" al-Afdal cried. "They flee!"

But the Franks found new strength, and drove the attackers off once again. A second time the Saracens charged, and a second time the Franks fell back, and a second time al-Afdal shouted, "They flee! We have routed them!"

Saladin turned to him coldly and said, "Be quiet. We

have not beaten them so long as that tent still stands." Hardly had the words left his lips when King Guy's tent collapsed under a horde of Saracens. Saladin dropped to the ground and gave thanks to God, weeping tears of joy.

The surviving Christians were taken prisoner. They included King Guy, Grand Master Gerard, Reynald of Chatillon, and many others. An Arab chronicler, Ibn al-Athir, declared that "when one saw how many were dead, one could not believe there were any prisoners; and when one saw the prisoners, one could not believe there were any dead. Never since their invasion of Palestine had the Franks suffered such a defeat."

The exhausted prisoners were brought to Saladin's tent. In his moment of victory, Saladin was generous and gracious. He seated King Guy beside him; then, seeing that the King was suffering pangs of thirst, Saladin offered Guy a goblet of rosewater, chilled with ice from a distant mountain. Guy drank, and handed the goblet to Reynald of Chatillon, who was beside him.

Saladin sprang forward in anger. By the Arab laws of hospitality, to give food or drink to a captive is to guarantee the safety of his life. Saladin snapped to his interpreter, "Tell King Guy that he, and not I, gave drink to that man!"

Then, turning to his old enemy Reynald, Saladin named his many crimes. Reynald answered with a few sneering words that cast scorn both on Saladin and on Mohammed. Saladin seized his sword and in a moment of fury cut off Reynald's head. The bloody corpse fell practically at the feet of cowardly King Guy, who huddled in a trembling heap, fearing that he would be the next to die.

But Saladin had no hatred for poor Guy. He handed the reddened sword to one of his men and said gently,

"Have no fear. A king does not kill a king." Guy and the other barons were to be made prisoners, but Saladin ordered that they be treated with courtesy and lodged in comfort. Only for the Templars was there no mercy. Two hundred thirty of the proud, ambitious knights had been captured. They were led forth, and, one at a time, they were asked if they would become Moslems if their lives were spared. Each man in turn refused, and was put to death. But the demonic Gerard of Ridfort was spared. Perhaps Saladin knew that this man's vaulting arrogance had helped to lead the Crusaders into their disaster, and that so long as Gerard lived he would continue to weaken and divide the Franks. Gerard went free. He bought his liberty by giving Saladin the fortress of Gaza, which was Templar property, in violation of his oath. There were those who said that he had also agreed to accept Islam to save his life.

The strength of the Franks had been smashed at the Horns of Hattin. Saladin journeyed to Damascus and rode through its streets with the True Cross tied to his horse's tail and dragging in the dust. The captured knights went to their comfortable dungeons. The captured infantrymen were sold into slavery; there were so many of them that the price of slaves fell to nearly nothing.

All that remained for Saladin was to complete his conquest by taking possession of the Kingdom of Jerusalem. Tiberias surrendered two days after the battle. Saladin allowed Countess Eschiva to go free and join her husband Count Raymond at Tripoli. He moved his troops to Acre, where Joscelin III surrendered with shameful haste. Saladin's brother laid siege to Jaffa and took it. An attack on well-fortified Tyre failed, but of the other coastal cities, Sidon, Beirut, and Jebail yielded quickly. Ascalon fell after a short siege. The Templars at Gaza, though infuriated with Gerard for giving the castle to Saladin, nevertheless obeyed their oaths to their vile Grand Master and surrendered to the Saracens.

By September, 1187, nothing remained to the Christians south of Tripoli except a few outlying castles and the cities of Tyre and Jerusalem. The only baron of Jerusalem still at liberty was Balian of Ibelin, who had managed to escape from the disaster at Hattin, and he led the defense of the city when Saladin appeared on September 20. There were few able-bodied soldiers in Jerusalem. For every man there were fifty women and children. Saladin's great siege machines began to batter at the walls near the place where Godfrey of Bouillon had broken into Jerusalem eighty-eight years before.

A Saracen witness, Ibn al-Athir, wrote, "the Franks at first showed great bravery. On both sides this war was regarded as a religious matter. The soldiers needed no commands from their leaders to rouse their ardor; all defended their positions fearlessly; all attacked without looking behind them." The wall was breached on the twenty-ninth of September; the next day, to avoid the inevitable massacre, Balian of Ibelin went to Saladin's camp to surrender.

When the Crusaders first had taken Jerusalem in 1099, they had been guilty of an outrageous slaughter of innocent people. Saladin was more merciful. He accepted a cash ransom and saw to it that there was no looting and no murdering. On Friday, October 2, the Saracens entered the city, and long lines of Christian refugees began to stream through its gates, heading for Tyre, Tripoli, or Antioch. Crosses were taken down, and churches were turned into mosques. Saladin let it be known that in the

Saladin lets the old men remain in Jerusalem

future Christian pilgrims would be allowed to enter the city on payment of a fee, but he insisted that all the Franks who had settled in Jerusalem go elsewhere.

There were two exceptions. An old man named Robert of Coudre was found, who had served in boyhood with Godfrey of Bouillon when Jerusalem first was taken. He was said to be more than a hundred years old. Another, Fulk Fiole, had been born in the Holy City just after its conquest by the Crusaders, and was close to ninety. They asked Saladin to let them remain and end their lives in Jerusalem, and he gladly agreed.

The Horns of Hattin

On October 9, Saladin and a great throng of Moslems entered Jerusalem's greatest mosque to give thanks for their triumph. The Kingdom of Jerusalem was no more, except for the lone city of Tyre. The weakness of Guy and the rashness of Reynald and Gerard had undone the work of nearly a century, and had delivered the land of Jesus once more to the Saracens.

THE THIRD CRUSADE

SALADIN still had some work to do. In 1188 he moved north to deal with the Principality of Antioch and the County of Tripoli. Count Raymond of Tripoli had died at the end of 1187, still grieving for the catastrophe he had not been able to head off. The Saracen swept through the territory of Tripoli, taking everything but the capital city itself. Then he lopped off most of the possessions of Prince Bohemond III of Antioch. But Saladin's soldiers were growing tired of campaigning, and when Bohemond suggested a truce, Saladin accepted, thinking he could finish off the rest at some later date.

Of the Principality of Antioch, nothing remained except the city of Antioch itself and the castle of Marqab. Of the County of Tripoli, only the towns of Tripoli and Tortosa and the isolated fortress, Krak des Chevaliers, were in Crusader hands. Of the Kingdom of Jerusalem, Tyre alone remained.

Tyre might have fallen if Saladin had pressed the attack in 1187, but he had passed by after a brief siege. It was a grave mistake, as time showed. Soon after the battle of Hattin, a ship from Constantinople arrived, carrying a rugged warrior named Conrad of Montferrat. Conrad was the brother of William Long-Sword, the first husband of Queen Sibylla. He had come to the Holy Land on a pilgrimage, knowing nothing of the fate that had befallen the Crusaders. He attempted first to land at the port of Acre, but was surprised to find Moslem officials in charge. Hurriedly departing, Conrad went to Tyre and learned the full story. He took command at once, and ordered that Tyre's walls be strengthened against another Saracen attack. When the Saracens returned a few months later, they discovered that Tyre was too strong to capture, and they let it remain. Tyre thus became the headquarters for the Crusaders who still harbored the glowing hope of defeating Saladin and winning the Holy Land a second time.

Conrad saw that the government of Outremer had fallen to him by default. He was a strong man who had arrived in the right place at a critical time. Raymond of Tripoli was dead; King Guy of Jerusalem and most of his nobles were prisoners. Bohemond III of Antioch had no wish to get involved in the struggles of the Kingdom of Jerusalem. Conrad sent word to Europe that Jerusalem had fallen and determined to hold the fort until a new army of Crusaders could be gathered.

Saladin chose to release many of his prisoners in the summer of 1188, including King Guy and Queen Sibylla. It was a generous move, but also a clever one. In defeat the barons of Jerusalem were even more quarrelsome than before. They blamed each other for the disaster at Hattin, and as soon as they were free they began to divide into factions again. The ones who had supported Raymond of

Tripoli now gave their allegiance to Conrad of Montferrat. The others, backing King Guy, went to Tripoli to plan their strategy.

King Guy led his men to Tyre for a confrontation with Conrad. Conrad slammed the gates of the city in their faces. He told Guy bluntly that by his foolishness at Hattin he had forfeited the crown and was no longer King. Guy crept back to Tripoli to brood after Conrad had told him and his Queen that "it was as much as their lives would be worth to set foot in Tyre."

By the summer of 1189, Guy had decided that the only way to assert his claim to the kingdom was to lead the Franks in a victorious campaign against Saladin. He put together a small army and marched it recklessly against well-defended Acre as the first step in a new war of reconquest. Saladin was suffering from malaria, and did not hurry to go to Acre's aid.

Guy camped outside Acre at the end of August and laid siege. Then reinforcements began to arrive from overseas, Crusaders from Denmark, Flanders, France, and Germany, who had heard of the fall of Jerusalem and had come to fight for its recapture. Worried by the presence of the newcomers, Saladin at last marched toward Acre. In early October, Saracens and Crusaders clashed outside the city. Each side inflicted heavy losses on the other, but Saladin could not drive the outnumbered Franks away. For the first time in two years, the Christians were actually holding their own in battle against Saladin's army.

Conrad was persuaded to join the attackers at Acre. On his side, Saladin began to call in auxiliaries from other parts of his territory. The siege was settling into a stalemate. Both the Franks and the Saracens maintained camps outside Acre, while the besieged city itself was supplied by sea, thanks to Moslem ships that slipped through the Crusaders' blockade.

Minor skirmishes continued on into 1190. The intention of the Franks was simply to hang on until more Crusaders arrived from Europe, for now it was definite that great new armies were being assembled. Saladin, troubled by his illness, did not seem to have the energy of old, and he made no real attempt to eliminate the Franks from their position. In one of the skirmishes, though, the sinister Gerard of Ridfort fell into Moslem hands, and this time the Grand Master of the Templars was put to death.

Guy and Conrad, now together in the same camp, patched up their disagreements. Conrad agreed to recognize Guy as King, and Guy agreed to leave Conrad in control of Tyre, as well as Beirut and Sidon if they could be recaptured. But in the summer of 1190 an event took place that changed the political situation. An epidemic of disease swept the Frankish camp, and one of those who died was Queen Sibylla.

The only real claim that Guy of Lusignan had to the throne of Jerusalem was that he was the husband of Sibylla, who was the daughter of King Amalric. Now that Sibylla was dead, did Guy have any right to the title? The barons of Jerusalem debated the point. Those who, like Balian of Ibelin, had always regarded Guy as a weak King now saw a chance to get rid of him. There was another royal princess, Sibylla's half-sister Isabella. Her husband was Humphrey of Toron, who had refused the crown in panic a few years back when Count Raymond of Tripoli had tried to give it to him. Balian now suggested that a new husband be found for Isabella—specifically, Conrad of Montferrat. As Isabella's husband, Conrad could be made King of Jerusalem in Guy's place.

There were a few complications. Isabella was already married. Conrad, too, had a wife back in Europe—some said he had two, one in Constantinople and another in Italy. But the barons dealt with these problems in a blunt way. Humphrey and Isabella were ordered to accept a divorce, for the sake of the kingdom. Conrad's other wives were conveniently forgotten. In November of 1190, the grim middle-aged warrior Conrad became the husband of eighteen-year-old Isabella.

The marriage did away with Guy's claim to the title, but he refused to admit the fact and clung to what he said were his rights. Since Guy still called himself King of Jerusalem, Conrad did not formally take the title until the matter could be settled, but so far as nearly everyone was concerned, Conrad was King in all but name.

The siege of Acre continued while Conrad and his bride began their married life at Tyre. The campaign stretched into the winter of 1190–91. Saladin had encircled the Frankish camp. It was closely surrounded; food supplies were hard to obtain. By February of 1191, famine was striking in full force: the Franks slaughtered their horses for food, ate grass, chewed bare bones, paid fantastic prices for eggs or beans. Then came the news that all Christians had been awaiting for nearly two years: the King of France and the King of England had led their armies to the East and would shortly be landing at Acre to join in the siege.

The Third Crusade had been a long time in starting. Messages had gone to Europe in 1187, immediately after the fall of Jerusalem, asking for help. King Henry II of England had taken the Cross, as had his relative and rival, King Philip II of France. But Henry and Philip were then at war, and could not leave their kingdoms until the conflict was settled. Henry's death in 1189 brought the war to an end, but further delayed the Crusade. The new English King was Henry's eldest son Richard, whom men called *Coeur-de-Lion*, "the Lion-hearted." He, too, had taken the Cross, but months would pass before King Richard could complete his plans for departure. It was July of 1190 before Richard and Philip at last set out for the Holy Land.

The Crusading fever had also swept through Germany. In the early months of 1188 the Holy Roman Emperor, Frederick Barbarossa, took the Cross at Mainz, and thousands of knights offered their swords in the war against Saladin. Frederick had been ruler of Germany for thirty-five years. As a young man, he had taken part in the catastrophic Second Crusade. Then, as Duke of Swabia, Frederick had been second-in-command to his uncle, King Conrad. Now, close to seventy years old, he was the mightiest monarch of Europe, a legend in his own lifetime, a powerfully-built man with flowing yellow hair and a bushy reddish beard. In May of 1189, Emperor Frederick departed for the East at the head of the largest single force yet to leave on a Crusade. The memory of the Second Crusade's total collapse burned fiercely in him, and he was determined to avenge that fiasco.

All went smoothly until the German troops had crossed Hungary into Byzantine territory. Byzantium was then in a state of chaos, because of a series of rapid changes of rulers, and the outlying provinces were in revolt. When Frederick's Crusaders marched through Serbia and Bulgaria, the rebels were on the rampage. At first there was conflict between the Crusaders and the rebels; then the local chieftains asked Frederick's help in overthrowing the Byzantine Emperor. The Emperor, Isaac Angelus, began to believe that Frederick was going to attack Constantinople, and arrested the German envoys at his court to hold as hostages. For a while it appeared that there would indeed be war between the two Emperors. Frederick restrained his fury, though, and the quarrel was patched up.

In the spring of 1190 Frederick led his army into Asia Minor. The Seljuks were in control of the inland regions, and the bones of Byzantine armies could be seen along the road as the Germans pressed forward. The Seljuks were awed by the size of Frederick's force, and made little attempt to resist. But calamity struck in June, as the Crusaders were approaching the city of Seleucia. It was necessary to cross a river. The aging Emperor Frederick, riding ahead of his troops, came to the waterside. Somehow he fell into the river; perhaps his horse threw him, or perhaps he was kneeling to take a cool drink and tumbled forward. Before his men could reach him, the Emperor had drowned.

The great leader was gone, and the Crusade fell apart. Many of the discouraged German princes returned to Europe at once. Frederick's son ordered the pitiful remnant of the giant army to continue on to Syria, and the Emperor's body, preserved in vinegar, was carried like a sacred relic. Turkish archers thinned the ranks of the Germans; bubonic plague struck; hunger and thirst bedeviled them. Only a handful of dazed, ailing men staggered into Antioch late in June. Frederick's decomposing body was hastily buried, except for a few bones that were removed and taken onward in the hope that they could be laid to rest in Jerusalem.

The Crusades led by Philip of France and Richard the Lion-hearted of England met better fates. Although Richard and Philip had little liking for one another, they had agreed to cooperate on the enterprise, and they set out together from France on July 4, 1190. Unlike the earlier Crusaders, they planned to make the trip to the East entirely by sea.

The contrast between the two monarchs was great. Richard was a handsome, swaggering man of thirty-three, with red-gold hair and a muscular frame. An Arab historian spoke of his "high soul and strong heart," and called him "famous for his many wars, of dauntless courage in battle." Hot-tempered, impulsive, he loved to fight, to drink, to sing lusty songs. But he was a poor administrator who did not have the patience to carry out his own plans. Since he had spent most of his life in France, he spoke hardly a word of English, the language of the country whose King he was. In fact, during the ten years that Richard was King of England, he spent only six months there—from August to December of 1189 and from March to May of 1194. The rest of the time he was off at war on foreign soil, or held prisoner by foreign monarchs.

King Philip of France, who was twenty-five years old when his Crusade set forth, was of a different stamp. Blind in one eye and not a courageous man, he disliked battle as much as Richard loved it. Where Richard was inexperienced as a ruler, Philip was a veteran, who had come to his throne more than ten years before. The French King was shrewd, calculating, a patient spinner of plots, who saw far ahead and cunningly worked toward his goals. The Crusaders much preferred the boisterous, outgoing Richard to the cold, unattractive Philip. But the fact was that Richard was a poor King who squandered his country's resources, while Philip served France well.

A trip by sea in those days was made in many cautious stages, the vessels keeping close to shore. The two fleets moved from port to port: Marseilles, Nice, Genoa, then to Messina in Sicily, where the English soldiers involved themselves in riots with the local people and the French, and then onward toward the Eastern lands. From Messina the French went straight to Tyre, arriving in the spring of 1191. But the English had a much more complicated journey ahead of them.

A storm struck the English fleet as it passed through the Greek islands. Several of the ships were lost, and three were carried toward the island of Cyprus. Richard himself found harbor in Crete, then went to Rhodes and spent ten days recovering from seasickness, for the valiant Lionheart was no sailor.

Of the ships that were driven to Cyprus, two were wrecked. The third, bearing Richard's sister Joanna and his fiancée Berengaria, came safely to a port. Cyprus had long been a Byzantine province, but in the recent time of troubles at Constantinople a local Greek prince named Isaac Ducas Comnenus had rebelled against the Byzantine Emperor and set himself up as an independent Emperor of Cyprus. It was a Christian island, Byzantine in its customs and population. Emperor Isaac invited Joanna and Berengaria to be his guests. But they were afraid of being imprisoned and held for ransom, and refused to go ashore. Isaac replied by withholding fresh water from the English ship, and otherwise treating its passengers discourteously.

A few days later, learning that his betrothed and his sister were at Cyprus, King Richard arrived with the rest of his fleet. He vowed vengeance against Isaac, and, with his usual impulsiveness, decided that it would be a good idea to conquer Cyprus as long as he was there. Soon afterward, several boatloads of Crusaders arrived: those who were opposed to Conrad of Montferrat. They included

The Third Crusade

King Guy and his brother Geoffrey, and many others, including Isabella's divorced husband, Humphrey of Toron. They had come to win Richard's support for their side in the dispute that divided the Franks. Richard made use of them in his conquest of Cyprus. Emperor Isaac surrendered and was bound with silver chains. All of Cyprus's wealth fell to Richard. The spendthrift monarch rejoiced, for he had already consumed much of the money that England had raised to pay the costs of his Crusade. With the casual conquest of Cyprus behind him, Richard at last went on to Acre and arrived on the eighth of June.

The siege had been going on for nearly two years, since August of 1189. The Franks and the Saracens had camped outside the city for so long that they had come to know each other as friends. The Arab historian Beha ed-Din, who was there, wrote that "when they were tired they laid down their arms and mingled together; they sang, danced, and gave themselves up to enjoyment; in a word, the two sides became friendly until, a moment later, the war started again."

The stalemated war had its moments of fierceness. The Franks built siege machines that they moved against the walls of Acre, an important port protected on two sides by great ramparts and on two sides by the sea. Beha ed-Din describes one such engine:

"The Christians had constructed a machine four stories high, of which the first was of wood, the second of lead, the third of iron and the fourth of bronze. This machine overtopped the ramparts of Acre and was already just a short distance from the walls. The garrison was in despair and thinking of yielding, when God allowed this machine to take fire. At this sight we gave ourselves up to joy and thanked God fervently."

From within the city the garrison hurled Greek fire against the attackers. The chronicler Ibn al-Athir tells of a man from Damascus who prepared and used it: "In order to deceive the Franks the man from Damascus first threw at one of the towers pots of naphtha and other substances not lit, which had no effect. The Christians, full of confidence, immediately climbed to the top of the tower with an air of triumph and mocked at the Moslems. In the meantime, the man from Damascus waited until the substance contained in the pots had spread over everything. Then he hurled a new pot all in flames. The fire at once spread everywhere, the tower was consumed, and the outbreak happened so swiftly that the Christians had no time to flee. Men, weapons, everything was burned. God willed it thus, so that the Christians might burn in the fire of this world before burning in the next."

Despite such incidents, the campaign was at a standstill. The Crusaders were unable to break into the city, and Saladin, ill and gripped by fatigue, was unable to drive them away. The arrival of King Philip in April gave new cheer to the Franks. Though Philip had no love for hand-to-hand combat, he enjoyed siege warfare, and put his men to work building machines of war. The French constructed a stone-catapult that they nicknamed the Evil Neighbor, and a grappling ladder called the Cat. They also assembled two mangonels—catapults that slung stones great distances from a spoon-shaped bar, using the force of twisted ropes. One of these was called God's Own Sling. Night and day these machines flung stones against the walls of Acre and into the city as well, killing many of the defenders. Philip's men mined the walls; they tunneled under the foundations and supported the wall with

Mangonels

wooden props so it would not fall on them as they dug, then set fire to the props and quickly withdrew. Sections of the wall began to collapse. Philip, though, preferred to supervise such operations from a safe distance. What the Crusaders needed was a brawny, sword-swinging, gallant leader who could command a victorious charge into the city. When Richard the Lion-hearted arrived in June, he filled the order perfectly.

But Richard fell ill almost as soon as he reached Acre. When he recovered, he bickered with King Philip about the division of spoils after the city fell, and there was no action while the rulers quarreled. Political matters caused trouble too: Richard and Philip argued over the inheritance of certain lands in Europe, and also over the problem of the throne of Jerusalem. Richard supported King Guy, while Philip wanted his cousin Conrad of Montferrat to have the crown.

Saladin, dug in behind fortifications opposite the Crusader camp, kept his distance and did not attack.

When Richard was ill, Saladin courteously sent fresh fruit and snow to cool his drinks to the English King's tent, a noble gesture from one monarch to another. Richard began to think of negotiating a truce. The skirmishes continued, however. An Arab chronicler wrote of his admiration for the Frankish armor, which was so useful in these little battles: "The soldiers were clothed in a kind of thick felt, and coats of mail as ample as they were strong, which protected them against arrows. I have seen soldiers with up to twenty-one arrows stuck on their bodies marching no less easily for that. They on the contrary pierced us with their spears, killing horse and rider at the same time."

Inside the town, the garrison began to lose hope. Saladin did not stir to aid them, and on July 12 Acre surrendered. Not until the treaty was signed did Saladin learn of it, but by then it was too late for him to take action. Always a man of honor, he accepted the arrangement and withdrew his forces. The Franks entered Acre in triumph.

But not in harmony. A German army had been on the scene, headed by Leopold, the Duke of Austria. He claimed a rank equal to that of Philip and Richard, and had his flag raised beside England's. An English soldier seized it and threw it in a ditch. A few days later, Leopold left for home, harboring a bitter hatred for Richard that would cost the English King dearly some years later.

Philip and Richard continued their personal dispute, too. After some discussion they managed to settle the question of the throne of Jerusalem. It was agreed that Guy would remain King until his death, and then the crown would pass to Conrad. Of course, Jerusalem itself still was held by the Saracens, and the Franks ruled only a narrow strip along the coast.

The Third Crusade

King Philip announced that he was going home. He had done his duty as a Christian by helping at the siege of Acre, and his frail health was breaking down in the heat of the East. He would leave most of his army behind to aid in the reconquest of Jerusalem. The English were angered by Philip's departure, calling it a cowardly desertion. Philip's own barons "were full of fury and anger," says the chronicler Ambroise, "but neither tears nor laments could make him agree to remain." Philip set sail for Europe in August.

King Richard remained, and took command of the army. Jerusalem was a logical goal. But Richard preferred first to gain control of the important trading cities of the coast and then to think about going inland to take the Holy City. The entire direction of the Crusades had changed, and it was the bankers of Europe, not the Pope, who were dictating the strategy. Commerce came first, even to a hero like Richard the Lion-hearted.

He headed southward. Saladin stayed ahead of him, laying waste to the land to hinder Richard's advance, but not giving open battle. The two armies clashed at Arsuf, where Saladin fought with some of his old fire. An Arab writer told of seeing him "galloping between the two armies, in the middle of a shower of arrows . . . inspiring the warriors and inflaming them with ardor. The air resounded with the noise of drums and trumpets and the cries of our soldiers exciting each other with the words: Allah is great! Allah is great!" Nevertheless, the Moslems were routed, and Richard continued his southward march, pausing to rest at Jaffa in July. Again, there was talk of a truce between Richard and Saladin. When the winter rains began, Richard headed for Jerusalem, coming within a dozen miles of the Holy City before the muddy going

218

forced him to retreat. Richard was starting to see that even if he took Jerusalem, he would not be able to defend it against the united strength of Islam led by Saladin. Perhaps a truce would be best, after all. Richard was growing bored with Crusading, and word had reached him that his brother, Prince John, was attempting to usurp power in England.

Despite the agreement of July, 1191, King Guy and Conrad were still at odds. Richard tried to settle the matter in April, 1192. He called all the knights and barons of Jerusalem together and told them that he would soon be leaving the Holy Land and wanted to leave it in peace. Which did they prefer: Guy as King, or Conrad? To Richard's surprise, no one spoke up for Guy. Guy was forced to step down, and plans were made for the long-postponed formal crowning of Conrad.

The ceremony never took place. On April 28, Conrad had dinner with his friend, the Bishop of Beauvais. As he strolled home through the streets of Tyre, two men approached him. One handed Conrad a letter to read, and as he studied it the other stabbed him to death. They were Moslems, members of a fanatical sect known as the Assassins, who had had a grudge against Conrad for a long time. Conrad's death left the Franks in confusion. He was a strong, ambitious man who would have been a capable ruler. Now they were leaderless. Would the throne fall once more to the foolish Guy of Lusignan?

That could not be allowed to happen. A young knight named Henry of Champagne had recently arrived in Tyre. He was handsome, brave, and well-liked, and he was the nephew of both the King of France and the King of England. To his own amazement, Henry found himself being thrust into prominence. He was invited to marry Isabella and become King of Jerusalem. A week after Conrad's murder, Isabella was married for the third time. She was only twenty-one years old.

For reasons that are not known today, Henry never was crowned. Possibly he was waiting until Jerusalem was retaken, or perhaps complicated political reasons prevented it. However, all the powers of the King of Jerusalem were his, and he became the leader of the Franks. He proved to be an able ruler, though, who drew together the various factions of feuding nobles.

King Richard, after hailing Henry as the new King, took care of the problem of former King Guy by sending him to Cyprus. Richard had run short on cash and sold the island to the Templars a short while before, but now he persuaded them to sell it in turn to Guy. A few weeks after the wedding of Henry and Isabella, Guy sailed for the island and gave himself the title of King of Cyprus.

After capturing Daron, Saladin's last fortress on the coast of Palestine, Richard toyed with the idea of marching toward Jerusalem again in June, but after some hesitation headed for Beirut instead. Saladin rose from his sickbed to lead an attack on Richard's base at Jaffa while Coeur-de-Lion was away. The Saracens took the city, but Richard hurried back to rescue it. With no more than a handful of knights, he launched an attack of such ferocity that the Moslems gave way. In the battle, Richard's horse was slain, and Saladin, in warm admiration of his foe, sent two fresh ones through the lines as a gift for him.

But Richard was tired and Saladin was a sick man. It was time to make peace. Richard too fell ill, and tossed in fever in his tent, while Saladin once again offered gifts of peaches and pears, and snow to cool his drinks. On September 2, 1192, a five-year treaty of peace was signed.

The Third Crusade

The coastal cities captured in the past three years would remain in the hands of the Franks, and Jerusalem would stay in Saracen control. Christian pilgrims would be allowed to visit the Holy City, and both Moslems and Christians might pass freely through each other's lands.

"I will return in time to conquer the Holy Land," Richard told Saladin.

The great Saracen replied, "If I must lose the Holy Land, there is no one to whom I would rather lose it than the English King."

The Third Crusade thus came to its end. Its main accomplishment was to have insured the continued survival of the shrunken Kingdom of Jerusalem. Richard set sail for his kingdom on October 9. He had fought bravely and had at least curbed the power of Saladin. His homeward journey was a difficult one. He was shipwrecked and forced to travel overland in disguise. At an inn near Vienna he was recognized and taken before Duke Leopold of Austria. Leopold had never forgiven Richard for the incident in which the Austrian flag had been thrown in a ditch at Acre. Richard was imprisoned on the charge that he had arranged the murder of Conrad of Montferrat, and he remained a captive for a year and a half, until freed by payment of a monumental ransom that nearly wrecked the English economy. The wandering monarch reached England in May, 1194, and remained only two months before setting off to do battle once more, this time in France. A stray arrow took his life five years later while he was besieging a castle, and his scheming brother John became King of England.

As for Saladin, he did not long survive his treaty with Richard. Twenty-five years of continuous warfare had worn away his strength. With peace reigning in Palestine, Saladin hoped to return to Egypt, and then to make a pilgrimage to the holy shrines of Mecca. But his health failed, and he spent the winter at Damascus. Gradually he sank toward death, knowing that the end was approaching, and at the beginning of March, 1193, the greatest Moslem leader of the Crusading era went to his grave.

The CRUSADE
That WENT ASTRAY

ERUSALEM was lost to the Saracens, but the Kingdom of Jerusalem itself still existed. Henry and Isabella ruled over a strip of land ten miles wide at its broadest, running down the Palestinian coast from Jaffa to Tyre. In the north, Bohemond III remained master of Antioch and a little land around it, while his son Bohemond had become Count of Tripoli, governing that city and its coastal neighbor of Tortosa.

With the death of Saladin, the empire of the Saracens dissolved. Saladin had left seventeen sons, and they immediately began to wage civil war among themselves. In short order the Moslem world was divided into fragmentary domains each headed by some son of Saladin. The situation gave the Franks a badly needed period of rest, allowing Henry of Champagne to restore order in what was left of the Kingdom of Jerusalem.

The death of Guy of Lusignan offered Henry a chance to end the old family feuds. Guy's older brother Amalric became King of Cyprus and came to a friendly agreement with Henry. The two kingdoms would cooperate from now on, and the alliance was sealed by the betrothal of Amalric's three sons to the three daughters of Isabella. Several years of tranquility followed.

Then, one September day in 1197, Henry came to the balcony of his palace in Acre to review a parade of troops in the street below. Losing his balance, he toppled to the pavement. His dwarf Scarlet, who had seized his robes in an attempt to save him, was pulled down with him, and both were killed. Isabella, at twenty-six, was a widow for the third time.

Her three daughters—one by Conrad and two by Henry—were small children. A new husband was needed to rule the kingdom. Isabella, accustomed now to being the plaything of political necessity, allowed the barons to choose her new mate. Amalric of Cyprus became Isabella's husband in January, 1198. A few days later he was crowned as King Amalric II of Jerusalem. Fate, by a strange series of twists, had given to Amalric what it had taken from his brother Guy.

Amalric was as forceful and prudent as Guy was weak and inept, and he ruled ably until his death in 1205, at the age of fifty. It was Amalric II who was on the throne of Jerusalem when the Fourth Crusade was organized. But this new Crusade did not return Jerusalem to Frankish control. It came nowhere near the Holy Land. It was the Crusade that went astray. The Fourth Crusade was fought not against Saracens but against Byzantine Christians. Its soldiers wrote a somber tale of greed, betrayal, and evil.

The Fourth Crusade began as had the first: with eloquent preachers and an idealistic Pope. A holy man named Fulk of Neuilly preached a new Crusade to the knights and barons of France, and they began to take the Cross. Their leader was Count Tibald of Champagne, brother of Isabella's late husband Henry. In 1199, word of their decision reached the newly-elected Pope Innocent III, and he called for a general Crusade to liberate Jerusalem.

Pope Innocent was forceful and direct, a reformer who was inflamed with Christian zeal. To him it was an eternal affront that Saracens should control the Holy City. "The pagans are crying, 'Where is your God?' " the Pope declared. "Words cannot answer their taunts, for they are only too true. There can be no answer but in deed; it is a matter of life and death for Christendom that Jerusalem should be regained."

He offered the usual promise of a spiritual reward: "All who shall take the Cross and serve God for one year in the army shall be pardoned for all the sins they have committed, provided that these have been duly confessed." The princes and knights were tempted by the offer. No man was without sin, though some had committed murder and others had merely eaten meat on days of fasting. Here was a chance for all to win a fresh slate together, doing battle for the Cross.

Plans for the Crusade were hampered by the early death of young Count Tibaldt, the prime mover of the enterprise. The barons spent a long time debating over his successor, and finally picked Boniface of Montferrat, the brother of Conrad. It was not a popular choice, and many Crusaders dropped out rather than serve under him.

The next problem was arranging for transportation. The old scheme that had suited the first Crusaders, marching across all of Europe and down through Asia Minor into Syria, did not appeal to these men. It would mean endless months of travel and bitter fighting through hundreds of miles of Turkish-held territory. The best way, they felt, was to go by sea, landing in a Palestinian port such as Acre and heading straight for the Holy City. So ships had to be hired. The great merchant-town of Venice, which had grown rich carrying the luxurious carpets, spices, jewelry, and porcelains of Asia to the markets of Europe, had the best navy. In 1202, the Crusaders sent envoys to Venice to ask for ships and sailors to transport them to the East.

The ruler of Venice, its Doge (Duke), was Enrico Dandolo, a crafty man of immense age. Some said he was more than ninety years old. Age had weakened his strength and robbed him of his sight, but his skill as a statesman was unimpaired. Dandolo let the Crusaders cool their heels in Venice for a week before he deigned to see them. Then the Doge informed them that he was willing to provide shipping for 4,500 knights with their horses, 9,000 squires or aides, and 20,000 infantrymen, along with provisions for nine months. He would also supply fifty armed galleys as a protective escort for this convoy. The price for the first part of the deal was 85,000 silver marks—something like $10,000,000 in today's money. For the armed convoy, Dandolo merely required that Venice was to receive "half of all that is conquered, whether in territory or in money, by land or by sea."

The Crusaders were stunned by the Doge's demands, but they agreed to the staggering terms without much hesitation. Perhaps they planned to cheat the Doge in some way, though they had no idea then how formidable a bargainer the old man was. The envoys returned to the other Crusaders and told them the price. Some were aghast and broke away to set sail from other ports. Those who remained under the banner of Boniface of Mont-

ferrat went forth with him in June, 1202, traveling overland through Italy to Venice.

They were greeted warmly by the Doge, whose blind
eyes wept with joy at the noble prospect of recapturing
Jerusalem from the infidels. Then he asked for the money.
The Crusaders were embarrassed to report that they were
still 34,000 silver marks short of paying the Doge's price.
Perhaps the Doge would kindly reduce the amount required?

The Doge had no such intention. He offered a suggestion to the Crusaders. Not far from Venice was the
little town of Zara, on an island in the Adriatic Sea. Until
recently Zara had belonged to Venice, but now it had rebelled and given its allegiance to the King of Hungary.
If the Crusaders cared to attack Zara and capture it for
Venice, they could pay the missing 34,000 silver marks out
of the spoils they took there.

It was a shocking suggestion. The Crusaders, who
were camped on the small island of St. Nicholas just across
the water from Venice, would not consider it at first. The
people of Zara were Christians, and the Crusaders had no
quarrel with them. The King of Hungary was a loyal sup-
porter of the Pope. It was criminal to force them to fight
a war against Christians on the behalf of Venice.

The Crusaders on St. Nicholas continued discussing
the situation, and each day Venetian boats brought them
food. One day the boats did not arrive. The Doge coolly
informed the Crusaders that he did not plan to lodge them
on St. Nicholas forever at his expense. If they were willing
to conquer Zara for him, they could proceed with the
Crusade. If not, they would unfortunately have to remain
on St. Nicholas and starve.

The leaders of the Crusade could feel the old man's

hand tightening around their throats. Scandalized as they were, they agreed to the terms and laid siege to Zara. On November 8, 1202, a splendid expedition set forth in Venetian ships. Geoffrey of Villehardouin, a French knight who took part in this Crusade and later wrote its history, declared, "The ships that the Venetians had fitted up were so rich and beautiful that never had any Christian seen any that were richer or more beautiful." The armada carried three hundred mangonels, and the gaudy banners of the Crusaders fluttered like rainbows above the decks.

The Crusaders arrive at Venice

The people of Zara hung Crosses on the walls of their city to remind the attackers that they were Christians. But they offered no real resistance, and on the fifth day the city fell and was plundered. The loot was divided equally between the Crusaders and the Venetians, and Dandolo agreed that he had been well paid for the services he was about to render to the Crusade.

Pope Innocent had forbidden the attack on Zara, threatening to excommunicate any Christian who attacked a Christian city. After the attack, the abashed Crusaders wrote to the Pope asking his pardon. They said that they had been helpless before Dandolo. If they had not accepted the Doge's terms, he would have starved them; besides, he had the ships they needed to get to Palestine, and they had no choice but to obey.

The Pope replied that the Crusaders all were excommunicated unless they gave back what they had taken from Zara. They agreed, but there is no record that anything was ever returned. The Venetians too were excommunicated, from the Doge downward, a fact that scarcely troubled Dandolo and his men.

Pope Innocent added a private message to the Crusaders that shows that he too was capable of devious scheming. He advised them to cooperate with the Venetians and permitted the Crusaders to sail with them to the land of the Saracens according to the contract, since the Venetians certainly would not refund the passage money that already had been paid. "But deal as little with them as possible," he suggested, with the comforting note, "even though the Doge has been excommunicated, you will not be touched by his excommunication when you are on board his ships, but will be excused in God's sight." In short, the Pope was saying, do business with the Venetians because you must, even though they are evil men. Jerusalem was to be regained at any price. The Pope even hinted that it might be permissible to murder the Venetians after the Crusaders had been safely delivered to the Holy Land.

Dandolo, meanwhile, had taken personal control of the Crusade. Merely renting his ships to the Crusaders was not enough. He called them together in the great Cathedral of Saint Mark. Mounting the pulpit, the wily Doge addressed the Crusaders in trembling, emotion-laden tones:

The Crusade That Went Astray

"My lords, you have with you the finest people in the world, and you are engaged on the highest enterprise that ever was undertaken. I am old and feeble, and need rest, and am weak in body, but I see that none can govern and guide you as I can. If you will permit me to take the Cross to lead you, and let my son stay here in my place and conduct the government, I will go to live or die with you, and with the pilgrims."

The Crusaders were moved by Dandolo's speech so much that they forgot his earlier trickery. They cheered their approval as the blind old man took the Cross. Dandolo had stolen the entire Crusade.

On Easter Monday, 1203, the Crusaders finally left Venice, sailing eastward aboard Dandolo's ships. It was a magnificent armada that might well strike terror into the hearts of the Saracens. But the Crusaders no longer were heading for Palestine. Dandolo had coaxed them into an adventure in Constantinople.

Nothing had gone well for Byzantium since the death of Emperor Manuel in 1180. He had been a great leader, but his disastrous war against the Seljuks of Asia Minor had left his empire badly weakened. His son Alexius II, who was only eleven, became Emperor. A family conspiracy followed; within two years the boy was murdered and his father's cousin Andronicus replaced him Andronicus was so cruel an Emperor that the people revolted against him. He was seized and torn to death by a maddened mob in 1185, and an elderly, bumbling member of the royal family named Isaac Angelus was pushed onto the throne. He ruled in a haphazard way for ten years. Then his brother dethroned him, blinded him, threw him into prison, and made himself Emperor Alexius III.

Isaac Angelus and his son Alexius remained prisoners.

But in 1201, young Alexius escaped and fled to Europe. Before long he was in Venice, begging the Crusaders and Doge Enrico to stop in Constantinople on their way to the Holy Land long enough to overthrow the usurper. He promised large sums of money to be paid out of the Byzantine treasury after his father was restored to the throne.

The clink of gold pieces always interested Enrico Dandolo. The Doge regarded Constantinople as Venice's chief rival for Mediterranean trade. It would be useful to place on the Byzantine throne an Emperor who owed a debt of gratitude to Venice. The Crusaders, too, had a reason for meddling in the situation. Byzantium had long considered itself independent politically and religiously from the Pope. The Greek Orthodox Church of Byzantium no longer paid attention to the decrees of Rome. Young Prince Alexius promised that in the future the Greek church would submit to the Pope's wishes. The attack on Byzantium became a kind of holy war between the two great factions of Christendom.

Pope Innocent did not care to have Byzantium returned to the fold in such a fashion. When he learned that the Crusaders had landed at Constantinople at the end of June, 1203, he sent a stern message: "Use your forces only to deliver the Holy Land and to avenge the sufferings of Him who was crucified. If you must look for spoils and conquest, seek them rather among the Saracens, your real enemies. By staying in the Greek Empire you run the risk of despoiling your own brothers."

There was no way for the message to arrive in time, and the Crusaders probably would have ignored it in any case. Dandolo was in command. The ancient Doge directed the capture of Scutari, Constantinople's suburb on the Asian side of the Bosporus. The entrance to the port at Constantinople was guarded by a great tower and blocked by a huge iron chain. Twenty Byzantine galleys stood by. The Venetian sailors leaped from their own ships to the decks of the galleys and threw the Greeks overboard while one Venetian vessel equipped with monstrous steel shears cut through the cable. The entire armada entered the port.

Never before had an invading force actually broken into Constantinople. Led by the superhuman Dandolo, the attackers swept over the ramparts. The defenders fled. That night, Alexius III made his escape from the city. The Doge brought blind Isaac Angelus from his dungeon, and put him on his throne. Then Isaac's son was formally crowned as the Emperor Alexius IV, to rule jointly with his father. To show his gratitude, Alexius IV invited the Crusaders to remain in Constantinople at his expense through the coming winter to prepare for their attack on the Holy Land in the spring.

It was a rash offer. Alexius IV had already promised the Crusaders 200,000 silver marks as the price of their aid. He was hard put to raise such an enormous sum, and the cost of providing rations for the Crusaders for many more months threatened to bankrupt Byzantium. Alexius IV's own courtiers tried to persuade him to break his agreements with the Franks. "You have paid them too much, sire," they told him. "Do not pay them any more. You have paid them so much you are quite ruined; make them depart and send them away from your lands."

Alexius was swayed. He told the Crusaders that there would be no more payments. Doge Enrico sent for the young Emperor and told him point-blank, "We have made you a lord and had you crowned Emperor. Are you going to keep your agreements with us?"

"No," replied Alexius. "I will not do more than I have done."

"No?" Dandolo asked. "You wicked youth! We pulled you out of the mire and we will cast you back into the mire! I defy you! From this time on we are enemies!"

While this dispute was going on, a fire was started in the city; no one knew how. It burned for eight days, and destroyed a vast section of Constantinople. The Byzantine people accused their Latin neighbors, Christian residents who were of Western European origin, of starting the fire. The Latins, some 15,000 of them, feared a massacre and fled from the city, taking refuge with the Crusaders across the harbor. Alexius IV declared that the Crusaders or the Venetians had started the fire. In revenge, he took seven decrepit ships, set fire to them, and let them drift into the Venetian fleet.

Hastily the Venetians went out with boat-hooks and dragged the blazing hulks away before they could ignite their ships. Open war threatened between Alexius and the Venetians and Franks who had put him on the throne. But in a moment of confusion the Byzantines themselves rose against Alexius, arguing that he was the agent of the Latins. They put him to death and put the son-in-law of the former Emperor Alexius III on the throne as Alexius V. Old Isaac Angelus died a few days later.

The Crusaders were faced with a strangely altered situation. They held a great council in April, 1204, and decided that they could not accept Alexius V as Emperor. He was a usurper, and the Franks used his rise to power as an excuse to invade Constantinople all over again. This time, it was agreed to seize the city. Its wealth would be divided equally between the Crusaders and their Venetian allies.

The attack began on April 8. The forces of Alexius V

held firm for three days, and the Venetian warships were unable to approach the towers of Constantinople. On the 12th, according to Geoffrey of Villehardouin, "Our Lord caused the north wind to arise, and this blew the ships closer to the shore than they had been before. Two ships which were lashed together, the one named the *Pilgrim* and the other the *Paradise*, approached a tower on either side, just as God and the wind brought them, so that the ladder of the *Pilgrim* was fixed to the tower; and at once a Venetian and a French knight scaled the tower, and others followed them, and the guardians of the tower were frightened and fled."

The Crusaders burst into the city. They set fire to one section. "This was the third fire in Constantinople since our arrival," wrote one chronicler, "and more houses had been burned in the city than could be found in any three of the greatest cities in France." Then they continued on to the heart of the city to plunder it. Alexius V fled into exile.

Constantinople was the richest city in Christendom. For centuries its Emperors had gathered treasure from every part of the world. The morning of April 13 revealed an incredible scene of pillage. Crusaders had broken into the magnificent Cathedral of Santa Sophia. They demolished the choir-stalls with their twelve columns of silver, and the holy altar, and seized forty chalices and an uncountable number of silver candelabra. Horses and mules ran through the building. A Russian traveler who had the misfortune to be in Constantinople at the time wrote, "They took the Gospel . . . and the sacred crosses with all the images, and the covering which was on the altar and forty incense burners of pure gold. And everything they could find in the way of gold and silver, and also of vases

235

of inestimable value, in the cupboards, on the walls, and in every place where they were shut up, in such quantities that it would be impossible to count them."

Men at that time reckoned that "two thirds of all the wealth of the world was in Constantinople," and it fell to the grasping hands of the conquerors. "Since the beginning of time," wrote Geoffrey of Villehardouin, "there was never so much taken in one town. Everyone took what he wanted, and there was enough. . . . And there was great joy for the victory which God had given them, since those who had been poor were rich and happy."

Boniface of Montferrat, the leader of the Crusaders, seized the Emperor's palace for himself. Robert of Clary, one of his knights, set down this eyewitness description:

"In this palace there were easily five hundred rooms, each one opening out of another, and they were all covered with golden mosaics. There were certainly thirty chapels, some big and some small. One of them was called the Holy Chapel and it was exceedingly rich and fine. There was no hinge nor ring in it made of iron; all were of silver. The columns were all made of jasper or porphyry, or of costly precious stones. The floor of the chapel was paved with a white marble so polished and so limpid that it seemed to be crystal."

Everyone took. Dandolo seized for Venice four great bronze horses that the Emperor Constantine had brought from Egypt nine hundred years before. They still can be seen in Dandolo's city, above the entrance to the Cathedral of Saint Mark. An abbot named Martin, scorning mere gold and silver, filled his treasure chest with holy relics. Constantinople abounded in relics: two big pieces of the True Cross, the head of the Holy Lance, the nails that had held Christ on the Cross, and many other such sacred objects. The fact that other cities also claimed to have the True Cross and the Holy Lance did not seem to matter.

The final act of the tragedy of Constantinople came a month after the sack of the city. The Crusaders and Venetians, swollen with their stolen riches, ceremoniously gathered to elect a new Emperor of Byzantium. He would not be a Byzantine. A Frank would be placed on the throne, the first Latin Emperor of the East.

Boniface of Montferrat offered himself for the honor. But the Venetians disapproved; he was too stubborn a man. They wanted someone more agreeable to their wishes. After a long parley, Count Baldwin of Flanders was chosen. On the sixteenth of May, he was taken into a chamber of the cathedral and garbed in rich robes decorated with golden buttons and precious stones. His outer garment was "a splendid mantle covered with jewels and embroidered with eagles," Robert of Clary informs us. "These were sewn on with jewels which glittered so that it seemed as if the mantle were on fire."

Count Baldwin was led before the altar. This minor baron knelt and removed his mantle to be anointed. The crown of Byzantium was placed upon his head, and he mounted a lofty throne clasping a scepter and a golden orb. After the celebration of the Mass, Emperor Baldwin climbed upon a white horse to ride from the cathedral to his palace. The Greeks unwillingly paid homage to him, and thus was born the Latin Empire of Constantinople, destined to survive only fifty-seven years. Emperor Baldwin's reign was short. The Empire began to split apart, and rebels in Greece and Bulgaria declared their independence. Ten months after his coronation, Baldwin led an army against the rebels, was captured by them, and was never seen again. His brother Henry succeeded him as Emperor.

Dandolo was not content simply to have a puppet on the imperial throne. He took control of the religious life of Constantinople also by electing a Venetian named Morosini as the new Patriarch of the Greek Orthodox Church. Morosini was not even a priest, and his election was against all the customs of Christendom, but he took office and obeyed Dandolo's orders.

In Rome, Pope Innocent was in a rage. "The Latins have given an example only of wickedness and the works of darkness," he wrote to his representative at Constantinople. "The Greeks may well detest us as dogs. These defenders of Christ [the Crusaders], who should have turned their swords only against the infidel, have waded through Christian blood. . . . They have presumed to lay hands on the Church's wealth. . . . They have been seen tearing away the silver plating of the altars, breaking them into fragments, violating sanctuaries, plundering relics. . . ."

But the Pope's own representative was under Dandolo's thumb. The Doge compelled him to issue a decree in Innocent's name forgiving the conquerors of Byzantium for all the crimes they had committed. Then came a second decree relieving the Crusaders of their vows to go to the Holy Land.

The Venetians went home heavy with the spoils of Constantinople. Many of the Crusaders returned to France and Germany richer by far than when they had set out. The rest remained in Byzantine territory, ruling over chunks of the former Empire. The Fourth Crusade had been fought, not for the greater glory of God, but for the greater profit of Enrico Dandolo's Venice. Constantinople was crushed, Venice was triumphant, and Jerusalem remained in the hands of the Saracens.

The Children's Crusade
And The Fifth Crusade

HE knights of Europe had sacked Constantinople instead of liberating Jerusalem. In the Holy Land, the Franks clung to the tiny remnant of their kingdom. King Amalric II had negotiated a treaty of peace with the most powerful of the Saracen leaders, Saladin's brother al-Adil. Neither side felt strong enough to break it. For more than ten years there was quiet in the East.

After Amalric's death in 1205, the throne passed to Maria of Montferrat, the daughter of Queen Isabella and Conrad. She was still a girl, and her uncle John of Ibelin ruled as regent for five years, until she was old enough to marry. Maria's husband was a sixty-year-old French knight, John of Brienne, penniless and obscure. He came to Palestine in 1210 and was crowned King of Jerusalem at Tyre that October. King John renewed the treaty with al-Adil for another five years. At the same time he wrote to the Pope, asking that a new Crusade be sent out when the truce had expired.

239

In the north, Bohemond III of Antioch had died in 1201. His nephew Bohemond, who was already Count of Tripoli, made himself Prince of Antioch as Bohemond IV. There were others who claimed the throne of Antioch, and a good deal of intrigue and even some fighting was necessary before Bohemond IV emerged in full control.

While these struggles were going on, the Crusading fever was sweeping Europe again. Pope Innocent III, distressed by the dismal record of the Fourth Crusade, called for a true war against the Saracens. Few knights were interested. When a response came, it was from a strange and unlikely quarter.

In May of 1212 King Philip of France was holding his court at Saint-Denis when a twelve-year-old shepherd boy came before him. The lad's name was Stephen, and he carried a letter for the King which he said had been given to him by Christ himself. The Savior had appeared to the boy while he was tending his sheep, telling him to gather Crusaders to march on Jerusalem. King Philip, a worldly man with little use for miracles, smiled and told the boy to go home. But Stephen persisted.

He began to travel through France, preaching a Crusade of children. The sea would dry up, Stephen declared, allowing the young Crusaders to walk on to Jerusalem as Moses had led his people across the Red Sea. The ragged shepherd boy was able to hold an audience spellbound in the way that Peter the Hermit had done more than a century before. Children began to gather at the town of Vendome, the meeting place for the new Crusade. Boys and girls, most of them peasant children but some of noble birth, ran away from home by the hundreds to flock to Stephen's banner. Some said that there were 30,000 of them, not one older than twelve.

The Children's Crusade and the Fifth Crusade

The older people did not know how to halt the Children's Crusade. Parents could not hold back children who glowed with such faith. Priests gave their blessings to the

The Children's Crusade

enterprise. Even Pope Innocent declared in admiration, "The very children put us to shame."

In June of 1212, the pathetic band of youthful Crusaders set out across France for Marseilles. Most went on foot, but Stephen, as their leader, rode in a gaily decorated cart, with a canopy shading him from the sun. The boy was regarded as a saint. People crowded the road to get a glimpse of the procession as it passed by, and perhaps to steal a shred of Stephen's garments or a lock of his hair. The Crusaders had taken no food supplies with them, and depended on charity as they went along. But a drought had afflicted France that year; crops had withered in the summer's heat. There was little food to spare. Many children fell by the side of the road and died. Others turned back and tried to find their way home. Stephen's cart rolled on toward Marseilles, though, and thousands of boys and girls still followed.

At Marseilles came calamity: the children rushed down to the harbor to see the waters open for them, and the waters did not divide. Stephen's promised miracle had failed to occur. Seeing they could not walk to the Holy Land after all, some tearfully denounced Stephen and left the Crusade. The rest waited, hoping each morning that the waters would at last give way.

In a few days, two merchants, Hugh the Iron and William the Pig, approached Stephen. They offered to provide seven ships, free of charge, to carry the Crusaders to Palestine. Stephen gladly accepted, thinking that the generous pair had been inspired by God to do an act of charity. The boys and girls of the Children's Crusade boarded the ships and headed out to sea. It was eighteen years before they were heard of again.

In 1230, a priest who arrived in France from the East

told the story of what had become of the Children's Crusade. He said that as a young man he had gone with Stephen to watch over the children. Two of the seven ships that put to sea at Marseilles were shipwrecked in a storm a few days out from harbor, and all aboard were drowned. The remaining five vessels turned southward across the Mediterranean and were met by a prearranged escort of Saracen ships who convoyed them to Algeria. Hugh the Iron and William the Pig had plotted to sell them all as slaves to the Moslems.

Some of the children were enslaved in Algeria. Others, including the young priest, were shipped to Egypt. One group was sent as far as Baghdad, where eighteen of them were put to death for refusing to become Moslems. Most of the children died during their captivity, the priest said; he himself had been lucky. Because he could read and write, he became the servant of the governor of Egypt, was treated well, and finally was released to return to France. The fate of the boy-preacher Stephen was never learned. He, like the rest of the 30,000 young Crusaders, disappeared forever into the slave markets of the Saracens.

No one knew, in 1212, of the grim fate that was in store for Stephen's Crusade. And so in that same year a second Children's Crusade was organized in Germany. A boy named Nicholas went through the land, telling as Stephen had done how the sea would part to let the children cross to Palestine. He went a step further, by declaring that when the Saracens saw this army of pious children approaching, they would be so moved that they would become Christians at once. Nicholas's Crusaders were a few years older than Stephen's, and they included a number of tough, undisciplined rascals—the juvenile delinquents of the thirteenth century.

One group of these Crusaders, numbering about 20,000, struggled over the Alps from Switzerland into Italy, their ranks thinning from day to day as hunger, desertion, and disease took their toll. When they reached the port of Genoa, the sea failed to open for them. A number simply settled in Genoa; the rest shuffled onward, their bodies sore and their feet bleeding, to some other place where the miracle of the waters might happen. They came to Pisa, where two ships were about to leave for Palestine. Several of the children went aboard, but their fate is unknown. The others, still led by Nicholas, continued to Rome. Pope Innocent greeted them in a kindly way and told them to go home and wait until they had grown up before they took the Cross.

The remnant of the marchers turned back, as did a second group that had been wandering down the east coast of Italy. Only a few hundred out of the many thousands ever returned safely to their homes. Nicholas was not among them, and what became of him was never told. The people of his village turned against Nicholas's father, accusing him of suggesting the vain Crusade that had cost the lives of so many children, and hanged him.

Children could not win back the Holy Land. But the grotesque Children's Crusades kept the dream of the Cross alive, and soon older men were talking of another attempt to defeat the Saracens.

The Crusading idea was on many minds. True, not all the proposed Crusades were directed against the infidels who ruled Jerusalem. Ever since the Fourth Crusade had fought Greek Christians instead of Moslems, it had become accepted to talk of Crusades against heretics and pagans of all sorts. Early in the thirteenth century, Crusades were launched within Europe, to wipe out certain Christian sects whose doctrines were disliked by the official Church of Rome. A typical viewpoint was that of the theologian Hostiensis, who declared in 1215, "Although public opinion looks favorably on the Crusade overseas, nevertheless to anyone who judges according to reason and common sense the Crusade on the home front seems more just and more rational."

Much energy was consumed exterminating heretics in France and Germany, but the call of Jerusalem was still strong. The truce between the Franks and Saracens was over, and in 1215 King John of Jerusalem asked Pope Innocent for an army. Plans were laid for a Fifth Crusade to depart on June 1, 1217. Among those who took the Cross was the Holy Roman Emperor, Frederick II, the most powerful ruler in Europe at that time.

Pope Innocent died in 1216. Emperor Frederick found excuses for sidestepping his vow and remained at home. After some delay and confusion, the Crusade left without him. By the spring of 1218, several hundred ships from Germany and France arrived at the port of Acre and were welcomed by King John.

The King had already planned the strategy of the war. The first target would be Egypt, the richest province of the Moslem world. If the Saracens could be driven out of Egypt, the Crusaders would be able to launch a two-pronged offensive on Jerusalem, going eastward from Acre and northward from Suez. And the way to take Egypt was to capture Damietta, the port that was the gateway to the Nile.

King Amalric I had tried to take Damietta in 1169. At that time Saladin had had a huge chain strung across the river as a barrier to naval attack, and the Franks had been forced to withdraw. Now the chain was drawn once again, anchored securely at each side of the river to a watchtower full of Moslem defenders. The Christians sent seventy ships up the river, protected by leather against Greek fire. They could not pass the chain, however, and the archers in the towers kept them from getting close enough to cut it. The Crusaders concentrated their attack on the towers. A contemporary account tells us:

"No day passed without some new assault. The stones flung by the Christians' machines were of a prodigious size; a single one weighed more than three hundred Egyptian pounds. The Franks were working at that time a kind of pontoon bridge called a maremme: it consisted of two or three ships placed together and joined with beams and planks so that they seemed to be a single ship. One of these was made of two ships; on top were four masts supporting a wooden lookout tower, which could be raised or lowered easily by means of straps and pulleys." The Franks advanced with this bridge of ships and maneuvered its pulleys to gain entrance to the Saracen tower. In moments, the defending tower was captured and the Saracens began to surrender.

It was August, 1218, when the Crusaders broke through the chain and proceeded up the Nile to the walls of Damietta, but not until November of the next year did the heavily-protected city fall to its attackers. During the long siege a curious incident took place. A Christian monk left the camp of the Crusaders and made his way to the Saracen lines. The Sultan of Egypt, Malik al-Kamil, Saladin's nephew, had given orders that any Christian who was captured would be beheaded on the spot. But this small, sweet-faced monk, accompanied only by another holy man, approached the Moslem guards and calmly said, "We are Christians. Lead us to your master."

Brother Francis and the Sultan of Egypt

He was Brother Francis of Assisi, later to be honored
with sainthood. This mild, unworldly man had followed
the Crusade to Egypt, and now he hoped to make peace.
The Saracens were startled by his inner confidence. Instead of beheading him they brought him to the Sultan.

Malik al-Kamil was delighted with Brother Francis's
saintly meekness and extraordinary courage. James of
Vitry, the Bishop of Acre, wrote an account of the meeting which declares that the Sultan "was turned gentle by
the aspect of the man of God, and listened with great

interest to the sermon on Christ which Brother Francis preached for several days to him and the other Saracens." He brought forth "gifts and treasures" to offer Brother Francis, but the little man, clad in his rough homespun robe, wanted no Saracen silks and satins. The Sultan insisted, saying, "Take them and give them to the churches and to the poor Christians." Brother Francis shook his head once more, replying that Divine Providence would look after the poor.

Then the monk made his proposal: he and a Saracen holy man would walk through fire together. If Brother Francis emerged unharmed, as he was certain would happen, it would prove that the religion of Christ was the only true faith, and he then would welcome the Saracens into Christianity.

The Sultan answered, "Friar, I do not think that any Saracen would wish to go through the fire for his faith." He began to realize that the piety of Francis might indeed win some converts among the Moslem ranks even without the ordeal by fire, and he decided that the time had come to send the monk back to the Crusaders. "Pray for me," al-Kamil said, "that God may choose to show me the law and the faith that are most pleasing to Him." That was in September, 1219. Two months later Damietta was in the possession of the Crusaders.

What happened next was one of the worst blunders in the long and blunder-filled history of the Crusades. The Pope had sent two Cardinals to the army at Damietta as his personal representatives: Robert of Courson, an Englishman, and Pelagius, who was from Portugal. "Cardinal Robert died and Cardinal Pelagius lived," a chronicler notes, "which was a great pity, for he did much evil."

With Damietta about to fall, al-Kamil decided to

offer peace terms. He knew that if the Crusaders took the city they would conquer all of Egypt next. So he suggested that the Crusaders call off their war and leave Egypt. In return, he would give back the True Cross that had been captured in Saladin's time, and he would hand over all of Palestine to the Franks, including Jerusalem!

It was an amazing offer. To trade Damietta for Jerusalem meant that the Crusaders would have accomplished their entire purpose in a single battle. King John and his barons were eager to accept. But Cardinal Pelagius interfered. This harsh, narrowminded man angrily denounced anyone who dared to negotiate with infidels. He wanted nothing less than unconditional surrender by the Sultan. Let the Saracens hand over Egypt and Syria as well as Palestine, or there would be no deal, Pelagius insisted.

Pelagius had some supporters. The Venetians opposed the trade, because they had no use for Jerusalem but wanted Damietta as a port for their merchant vessels. The Templars and Hospitallers were against the deal for complicated reasons involving their own political advantage.

King John of Jerusalem was unable to make headway against Cardinal Pelagius. The Pope's representative was a headstrong, tyrannical man who threatened to excommunicate anyone who disagreed with him. The Sultan's offer was refused curtly, and the hope of regaining Jerusalem died. When Damietta fell a few days later, Pelagius and John struggled for supreme authority, and the quarrel between them grew so violent that in February of 1220 John gave up and returned angrily to Acre.

Pelagius now ruled Damietta. He called for an all-out attack on Cairo, but the knights would not obey. They said they would fight only under King John, and King John had gone away. For a year and a half, the Crusaders remained in Damietta, harried by the Moslems. There was talk that Emperor Frederick II was at last setting out on his long-postponed Crusade, but the Emperor did not appear.

In the summer of 1221, King John let himself be persuaded to return to Damietta. He was gloomy about having to cooperate with Pelagius, but he did not want to be accused of ruining the Crusade. An army of 5,000 knights, 4,000 archers, and 40,000 infantrymen marched southward from Damietta, led by King John and the warlike Cardinal Pelagius. The Egyptian Sultan gathered all his forces to meet them. Worse, the Nile was about to begin its annual flood. It was no time to be fighting a war in Egypt, but Pelagius would not listen to advice.

The Crusaders won a few minor victories as they headed for Cairo. King John continued to plead with Pelagius to turn back toward Damietta before it was too late. The fiery Cardinal led them on and on. By July 24, the Crusaders found themselves face to face with the main body of the Sultan's army and discovered that a second Saracen force had circled behind them and lay between them and their base at Damietta. In a few weeks, they were cut off and surrounded. They carried food supplies for only twenty days. On August 26, without consulting Pelagius, the soldiers began to retreat. It was a chaotic scene. Rather than abandon their stores of wine, the Crusaders drank every bottle before they broke camp.

As the drunken soldiers lurched out of their camp, the Sultan ordered that one of the dikes holding back the rising river be cut. The path of the Crusaders became a huge lake of mud. The men staggered and stumbled through it, and thousands perished under the attack of the Turkish cavalry. Pelagius was able to reach his ship, and the floodwaters swept the vessel rapidly past the block-ading fleet to safety—but on board were the medical sup-plies of the army and most of its food, adding to the disaster.

Reaching Damietta two days later, Cardinal Pelagius knew that he was beaten. He asked the Sultan to name his terms for peace. Al-Kamil did not propose any trades, now. With the Crusaders at his mercy, he told Pelagius to with-draw from Damietta and observe an eight years' truce. But for the Cardinal's stubborn pride, the Fifth Crusade could have won Jerusalem at little cost. Now it had to abandon Damietta and retreat with nothing whatever gained. Pelagius reluctantly accepted, but he made one condition: he asked the Sultan to return the True Cross. In a moment of generosity, al-Kamil agreed. But when the time came to hand it over, the relic could not be found.

On September 8, 1221, the men of the Fifth Crusade left Damietta to the Saracens. The Crusade had failed. It was the old story: the barons of Outremer understood the Saracens and how to fight them, but lacked the strength to win. And the men of Europe, for all their strength, had no wisdom when it came to warfare in the East. King John had been too weak to lead, and Cardinal Pelagius had been too inflexible and intolerant to accept victory when it was handed to him. The result, once more, was catastrophe.

ThE EMPEROR
FREDERICK'S CRUSADE

MEN called him *Stupor Mundi,* "The Wonder of the World." He was Frederick II of Hohenstaufen, the Holy Roman Emperor, grandson of the almost legendary hero Frederick Barbarossa. No monarch of Europe in his day was Frederick II's equal in intelligence, cunning, or power.

In person he was unimpressive: a short, plump man whose red hair had begun to grow thin when he was young. His lips were full, his cold green eyes piercing but shortsighted. The Emperor spoke German, French, Italian, Latin, Greek, and Arabic fluently. He was learned in science and philosophy, able to hold his own in conversation with any scholar. He had studied the teachings of Mohammed as a matter of intellectual curiosity, though his fellow Europeans privately whispered that he was an atheist or even a Moslem. Certainly he was not known for his devotion to Christianity.

It was to this man, cruel and clever, selfish and sly, that all of Christendom now looked as the rescuer of Jerusalem. He set sail for the Holy Land from the Italian

252

port of Brindisi on June 28, 1228, beginning what is known as the Sixth Crusade. Even before he departed, he had received the title of King of Jerusalem. Yet no Crusade ever had a more curious beginning, for Frederick II was an outlaw in Christianity, an excommunicated man. Never before had a Crusade been launched against the wishes of the Pope.

Frederick had first taken the Cross in 1215, when it was a fashionable thing to do. But he was more concerned with extending his own power in Europe than in going to the Holy Land. He put off his vow from year to year while strengthening his position at home. In 1220, after the capture of Damietta, Frederick was expected to lead an army to Palestine, but he never showed up. Pope Honorius III, who had succeeded Pope Innocent, pleaded with Frederick to honor his pledge. The Holy Roman Emperors of the past had never paid much attention to the wishes of Popes, and Frederick upheld the tradition.

While Frederick tarried in Europe, reading books of philosophy and defeating the rival German barons who opposed him, King John of Jerusalem was taking steps to repair the damage done by Pelagius's actions at Damietta. The King was growing old, and knew that a successor had to be found, a husband for his daughter Isabella Yolanda. He journeyed to Rome to show the Pope why the Fifth Crusade had collapsed. The trouble, King John explained, was that Cardinal Pelagius had interfered with the authority of the King of Jerusalem. In any future Crusade the King would have to have a free hand.

Pope Honorius agreed. He went on to suggest that Emperor Frederick be given King John's daughter as his bride. Frederick's first wife had died a few months before. If the Emperor married young Princess Isabella Yolanda, he would become the heir to the throne of Jerusalem and thus the natural leader of the next Crusade. Both men saw it as an excellent scheme. For King John it meant an Emperor as a son-in-law and a strong man as the next King of Jerusalem. For Pope Honorius it represented one way of getting Frederick to begin his tardy Crusade.

The marriage was arranged without difficulty. Philip of Novara, a contemporary witness, writes that "the Emperor fitted out and armed twenty galleys to go to Syria and bring back the lady. . . . He ordered knights and servants to go in these galleys to accompany the said lady, and the Emperor sent costly presents to the lady and to her uncles and to her other relatives." Isabella Yolanda was only fourteen, but this was not the first time that a youthful princess had married a much older man for the sake of preserving the Kingdom of Jerusalem.

In August, 1225, Isabella Yolanda was brought to Tyre and married by proxy to Frederick, who had remained in Europe. After the ceremony, she was crowned as Queen of Jerusalem, but it was understood that her father King John would remain on his throne so long as he lived. In November, Isabella Yolanda joined Frederick and her father at Brindisi, and the marriage was celebrated a second time. Frederick was then thirty-one years old.

On the evening of the wedding Frederick showed his true character. He coldly told his father-in-law that he did not intend to honor any agreements between them. There was no written treaty concerning John's right to keep his crown, and Frederick announced that he was at this moment making himself King of Jerusalem. The astonished John of Brienne was forced to yield. He fled to the Pope, who found a new post for him. The Latin Empire at Constantinople was in turmoil, and a child had become

The Emperor Frederick's Crusade

Emperor as Baldwin II. A regent was needed, and John, though nearly eighty, accepted the assignment. Until his death nine years later he ruled over what was left of Byzantium.

The unhappy Queen Isabella Yolanda, who feared her Emperor-husband and yearned to go back to Syria, was sent to live in Sicily. A chronicler observes, "This lady lived only a short while in the Emperor's company. It came about that she had a son and his birth was so difficult that she died. And the child lived and was named Conrad." Isabella Yolanda was sixteen at the time of her death. She had served the Emperor Frederick well, though: she had given him an heir and she had brought him the crown of Jerusalem.

King and Emperor though he was, Frederick still did not rush to save the Holy Land. Just before his wedding in 1225, he had renewed his vows as a Crusader, taking an oath that he would depart for the East in August, 1227. In March of that year, Pope Honorius died. For more than a decade, he had waited patiently for Frederick to fulfill his vows. The new Pope, Gregory IX, was much less willing to coddle Frederick. In the summer of 1227, Frederick indeed assembled a fleet to sail to Acre. But he fell ill in September and let the ships leave without him. The stern, unyielding Pope Gregory decided that Frederick was stalling once more and excommunicated him for failing to keep his pledge.

An excommunicated man in the thirteenth century was an outcast before God. He could not enter any church nor receive any holy sacrament. Nor could an excommunicated man lawfully take part in a Crusade. Frederick ignored the Pope's action. When he recovered from his illness, he finished the preparations for his Crusade and took his leave—still excommunicated—on June 28, 1228.

His position as King of Jerusalem was extremely shaky. According to custom, the throne descended only in a direct line from the original ruling family. When Frederick's Queen Isabella Yolanda died in 1227, their newborn child Conrad officially became King of Jerusalem, and Frederick held power simply as the baby's guardian. The barons of Jerusalem could, if they wished, vote to make some other man the regent for their infant King. So Frederick set sail determined to show his strength at the outset.

His first stop was Cyprus. That kingdom also had a child as its King: Henry of Lusignan, the grandson of Henry of Champagne. The regent who was ruling the island was John of Ibelin, the lord of Beirut and the uncle of Frederick's dead wife Isabella Yolanda. John of Ibelin was the wealthiest and most powerful of the barons of Outremer, with family connections in every direction: he was related to the royal family of Jerusalem, to the royal family of Cyprus, and even to the overthrown royal family of Byzantium. The Franks of Syria and Cyprus looked to him as their leader.

When Frederick landed in Cyprus, he sent a messenger to John of Ibelin, "requesting him," according to Philip of Novara, "as his dear uncle to come and have a talk with him, and to bring the young King Henry of Cyprus, his own three children, and all his friends." John of Ibelin called his barons together and discussed the letter. Some of them warned him that Frederick had a reputation for treachery and that it was unwise to fall into his power. But John could not refuse such a cordial invitation from so mighty a man as Frederick. He did not want it said that John of Ibelin had harmed the Crusade by provoking a quarrel with the Emperor Frederick.

The Emperor Frederick's Crusade

John and his sons, accompanied by the other great lords of the kingdom, went to the castle where Frederick was staying. Frederick welcomed them warmly, giving them jewels and scarlet robes and providing a great feast for them. John of Ibelin sat beside Frederick in the banquet hall, and all was merry until the final course. Then, without warning, Frederick's soldiers appeared. He had hidden three thousand armed men in the stables and gardens of the castle.

Archers took up positions by the doors of the hall. The barons of Cyprus and Jerusalem struggled to remain calm. Frederick turned to John of Ibelin and said coolly, "I require two things of you. First, that you hand over the city of Beirut to me, for you have no right to hold it. Second, that you give me all the money raised by taxes in Cyprus for the past ten years, for such is my due according to the custom of Germany."

John was stunned. After a moment he blurted, "Sire, you must be having sport with me! You are not serious!"

Frederick's cold-blooded demand was no joke. He repeated his request more forcefully. John of Ibelin answered by stating his claim to Beirut: it was given to him by his half-sister, the much-married Queen Isabella, many years before. In detail he explained why Frederick could not possibly expect to receive from him either Beirut or the revenues of Cyprus, and that neither the threat of death nor the threat of imprisonment would make him submit.

"The Emperor was furiously angry," declares Philip of Novara, "and swore and threatened." Finally Frederick said openly, "All your wisdom and shrewdness and all your words will be useless against my strength."

Three thousand armed men backed up the Emperor's

demands. But John of Ibelin stood firm. Frederick saw that to impose his will he would have to slaughter most of the barons of Outremer, hardly a good beginning to his Crusade. So it was decided to appeal the whole question to the High Court of Jerusalem. Meanwhile, Frederick asked for and received John's two sons as hostages. They were chained and placed in a dungeon, and the remaining barons were allowed to leave.

Two of John's followers drew him aside and suggested that they go up to Frederick on pretense of parleying and strike him dead with daggers. John angrily refused. "The whole of Christendom would cry out, 'The traitors of Outremer have killed their Lord Emperor,' " he said. "He is my overlord. Let him do what he may, we shall keep our faith and our honor."

Frederick had shown the barons of Cyprus and Jerusalem that he was ruthless and unscrupulous in further-ing his ambitions. They had no choice but to recognize him as the regent for the infant King Conrad of Jerusalem. John of Ibelin also agreed to go to Palestine as a Crusader with Frederick.

Next the aging Bohemond IV, Prince of Antioch and Count of Tripoli, came to Cyprus to join the other barons. Frederick summoned him and insisted that Bo-hemond pay homage to him as overlord. This time the Emperor was outwitted. Philip of Novara writes, "The Prince imagined himself both dead and disinherited. So he pretended to be stricken both ill and dumb, and con-stantly cried out, 'Eh, ah, ah.' " Bohemond continued to feign insanity and deafness, and Frederick in disgust allowed him to return to his own land. "As soon as he arrived," says the chronicler with a touch of humor, "he made a remarkable recovery."

The Emperor Frederick's Crusade

After these preliminaries, Frederick headed for Acre to begin his Crusade. Word had gone ahead that the Pope had excommunicated him, and that fact presented difficulties. There was some doubt that an oath sworn to an excommunicated prince was binding. The Templars and the Hospitallers, who took orders only from the Pope, refused to serve under Frederick. The Pope went so far as to declare a Crusade against Frederick. He began to assemble forces to invade the Emperor's Italian lands and ordered the Templars and Hospitallers to attack Frederick in Palestine.

As usual, the Emperor was three steps ahead of everyone else. He mocked the Templars and the Hospitallers. He ignored the barons of Jerusalem. Frederick was not planning to do battle in the Holy Land at all. He had brought with him only a handful of knights. His was going to be a Crusade of diplomacy.

With his knowledge of Arabic and his deep interest in Moslem customs, Frederick had struck up a correspondence with the Sultan of Egypt, Malik al-Kamil. It is hard to imagine the first Kings of Jerusalem writing leisurely letters to Saracen princes, discussing matters of philosophy and literature, but that is what Frederick had been doing for the past several years. Of course, there had been some political discussions as well. Al-Kamil had quarreled with his brother al-Muazzam, the Sultan of Damascus, and it appeared that al-Muazzam was about to gather a fierce army of half-civilized Turks to invade Egypt. Al-Kamil expressed an interest in forming an alliance with Frederick against the Damascus Sultan.

Frederick had nearly outsmarted himself, though. While he had delayed coming to the East, al-Muazzam had died. The new Sultan of Damascus did not frighten al-Kamil nearly as much, and Egypt's interest in an alliance with Frederick had cooled by the time the Emperor reached Acre.

Even so, Frederick wrote a pleading letter to the Sultan of Egypt. He told al-Kamil: "I am your friend. Will you force me to go home with nothing gained? Jerusalem is the city that gave birth to the Christian religion. You Saracens destroyed her. She is now reduced to the lowest degradation. For pity's sake give her to me in the state in which she is, so that when I return I may hold up my head among the kings."

At the same time, the new Sultan of Damascus resolved to threaten Egypt, after all. That gave al-Kamil pause. When Frederick marched his small army along the coast, the Sultan decided to accept him as an ally as arranged earlier. On February 18, 1229, a treaty was signed at Jaffa giving Jerusalem back to the Christians.

Without striking a blow in battle, Frederick had won the Holy City. It had been in Saracen hands since Saladin's conquest more than forty years before. The Egyptians agreed to hand over the three holy places of Jerusalem, Bethlehem, and Nazareth, and a corridor running through Lydda and Ramleh to the sea at Jaffa, so that Jerusalem would have a port. It was also agreed that Moslem pilgrims would be allowed free entry into the Holy City. Those parts of Jerusalem particularly sacred to Moslems— the Mosque of Omar and the Mosque al-Aqsa quarters— would not be turned over to the Franks.

Frederick regarded the treaty as a great victory, a masterstroke of diplomacy. But no one else agreed. The Moslems were furious with the Sultan of Egypt for having handed Jerusalem away so lightly. Al-Kamil's own people spoke out harshly, while the Sultan of Damascus "ordered public mourning for the betrayal of Islam."

The Christians were equally incensed. Frederick's bloodless recapture of Jerusalem was met without enthusiasm, to say the least. The more fierce of the Crusaders cried that Jerusalem should have been taken by shedding the blood of Saracens, not in a tricky deal. The Templars were angered because the Treaty of Jaffa had given some of their property in Jerusalem to the Moslems. Cooler voices pointed out that it would be impossible to defend the Holy City against attack. Some Saracen prince who did not feel bound by al-Kamil's treaty could seize the city with ease.

When he announced that he intended to go to Jerusalem to be crowned its King, Frederick stirred new enmity. The barons argued that he was not the King, but simply the regent for his young son. The clergy declared that he was an excommunicated man and could not be legally crowned under any circumstances.

On March 17, 1229, Frederick entered the Holy City at the head of his army. There was no triumphal procession, no cheering throng. The barons of Jerusalem stayed away. The streets were empty and silent. On the next day, the Emperor went to attend Mass in the Church of the Holy Sepulchre. No priests were there. The Patriarch of Jerusalem had denounced Frederick. In the presence only of his own troops, Frederick went to the altar and had a royal crown placed upon it. A German knight read a statement praising the Emperor's accomplishments. Then Frederick lifted the crown and put it on his own head.

The Franks of the Holy Land had given Frederick a stony reception. He repaid them by showing every concern for the Moslems. The Sultan of Egypt had ordered the

261

mosques to close down while Frederick was in Jerusalem so that the Emperor would not be offended by hearing a "pagan" call to prayers. On the contrary, Frederick asked that the Moslems not change their customs because of him; he said that he had come to Jerusalem simply to hear the sound of the call of the muezzins, the officials who told Moslems when it was time to pray. The Emperor, still the keen student of Saracen ways, even visited a mosque himself. When a Christian priest followed him in, Frederick had him thrown roughly into the street and decreed that no Christian cleric should ever venture into a Moslem shrine without permission again on pain of death. Speaking to a group of Arabs in the mosque, Frederick referred scornfully to Christians as "the pigs," using a Saracen term of abuse. Frederick's actions simply shocked the Saracens. They could respect a faithful Christian, but they did not know what to make of an Emperor who did not seem to respect his own religion and who went out of the way to pay compliments to Mohammed.

A few days later Frederick traveled from Jerusalem to Acre. He found the city in turmoil and the Templars conspiring against him. Before he could take action against his opponents, news reached him that an army backed by the Pope and led by John of Brienne, his own father-in-law, was invading his territory in Italy. Frederick saw that the time had come to call an end to his Crusade and return. He did what he could to place barons of German origin in control of the kingdom, replacing the Frenchmen who had dominated it so long. Then, on May 1, 1229, he set sail from Acre. His leavetaking from the Holy Land was in keeping with his entire Crusade. Philip of Novara tells of it:

"Frederick's departure was a shabby affair. The Em-

Frederick II leaves the Holy Land

peror prepared in secret for his journey, and on the first day of May, without telling a soul, he set out before daybreak, going through the Butchers' Quarter to reach his ship. Now it happened that the butchers in these streets ran after him and pelted him shamefully with tripe and entrails. The lord of Beirut and Master Odo of Montbeliard heard the tumult, ran to the place, chased and arrested those who had assaulted him. Then from the shore they called out to him on his vessel, commending him to God. The Emperor replied in a low voice, and I do not know whether his words were good or ill. . . . And in this way the Emperor departed from Acre, hated, accursed, and reviled."

SAINT LOUIS AND
THE SEVENTH CRUSADE

NEVER had there been a Crusade like that one, nor a Crusader to compare with Frederick. After postponing his departure for the Holy Land for thirteen years, he had swept through Outremer like a hurricane, and when the dust settled Jerusalem belonged to the Franks again.

Frederick had done what every Crusader vowed to do: restore Christ's city to Christian rule. But in doing it, he had reaped a harvest of enemies and not built any lasting kingdom. It proved impossible to defend Jerusalem. The city's walls had been demolished by the Saracens, and Frederick's treaty with al-Kamil had not given the Franks the right to rebuild them. Only a few weeks after Frederick's hurried exit, a raiding party of fanatical Moslems attacked Jerusalem and forced its Christian residents to barricade themselves in a tower until knights from Acre could rescue them. The Moslems retreated, but it was obvious that Jerusalem could be taken at any time.

With Jerusalem's King Conrad a child in Europe,

leadership of the Franks went to John of Ibelin. But the always quarrelsome barons soon were at odds, and there was war between the Franks of Cyprus and those of the mainland of Palestine. After John's death in 1236, the situation became even more confused. In northern Syria, Antioch and Tripoli were now in the hands of another Bohemond, Bohemond V, but he was a weak leader who rapidly lost much of his remaining territory to the Saracens. A Crusade of French nobles set out in 1239 to restore some order and recovered the city of Ascalon, before collapsing from rash overconfidence as so many earlier Crusades had done. Finally, in 1244, a savage clan of Turkish horsemen, the Khwarismians, attacked Jerusalem and drove out its Christian population. The Holy City passed once more into Moslem hands, and this time it would be almost seven hundred years before a Christian army again occupied Jerusalem.

The work of Emperor Frederick had been undone. The Franks found themselves once more limited to the coastal strip. Frederick never returned to the Holy Land. Turmoil in Europe occupied him for the rest of his life; he was forgiven by Pope Gregory for his earlier misdeeds, then excommunicated again for fresh offences in 1239. A few years later he managed to obtain the election of one of his own supporters as Pope Innocent IV. Frederick quarrelled with him also, and by then had made so many enemies that he died in 1250 a broken man, stripped of most of his imperial powers.

A new hero had appeared as the champion of Christendom, a man very different in every way from Frederick. He was Louis IX, King of France, whose life was so virtuous that he was known even in his own day as Saint Louis. For a moment in the middle of the thirteenth century the original dream of the Crusades was born again. When Saint Louis took the Cross it was for the sake of God alone and not for political or commercial gain.

He came to the French throne in 1226, when he was eleven years old. His mother, Queen Blanche, served as regent, and for many years she ruled both France and her son with a hand of iron. While the saintly boy devoted himself to religion, Blanche ran the kingdom.

When he was nineteen, in 1234, a bride was brought for him: thirteen-year-old Marguerite of Provence. Queen Blanche allowed the marriage, indeed arranged it, for it was necessary to continue the royal line. But she made it clear that she would not cease to dominate Louis. Over the door of a chapel in France there can be seen the portraits in stone of Louis and Marguerite and the tyrannical Queen Mother Blanche, carved in 1238, four years after the marriage. Louis, at twenty-three, is a handsome young man with a strong chin, a prominent nose, and open, innocent eyes. His long hair falls in curls to his shoulders. Beside him is Marguerite, sweet and girlish. Blanche, who was fifty, is unmistakably regal. Her eyes blaze with authority, her lips are set in a tight, severe line.

In the year the portraits were carved, Louis had his first direct contact with the East. Baldwin II, the Latin Emperor of Constantinople, was in need of cash and offered to sell to Louis one of the holiest of Christian relics: the Crown of Thorns that had been placed on Christ's brow as he was taken to the Cross. Louis sent two monks to buy the treasure, but when they reached Constantinople they found that Baldwin had been unable to wait. He had pawned the Crown of Thorns to a Venetian businessman for 177,300 livres, some $5,000,000 in today's money. The monks redeemed the relic—the pawn ticket is still in the

French National Archives—and brought the Crown to Paris, where it was carried by King Louis to the Cathedral of Notre Dame. In the years that followed, the rest of Constantinople's holy treasures went the same route: the True Cross, the head of the Holy Lance, the Holy Sponge that had stopped Christ's bleeding, and others. Louis never hesitated at the price nor stopped to wonder if the relics were genuine. He would have bankrupted France to purchase them, if necessary. Most of them vanished during the French Revolution, but the Crown of Thorns is still at Notre Dame.

The piety of Saint Louis knew no bounds. To punish himself for what he considered his sins, he wore a prickly hair shirt beneath his royal robes, and each night was whipped by priests wielding a whip of flexible chain. He had himself awakened every few hours through the night to pray. Often he would enter a church and remain on his knees half the day, almost in a trance, finally rising to ask his knights, "Where am I?" He invited beggars to his palace, washed their feet, served them meat and bread. He deprived himself of the luxuries a king might enjoy. Like his great-grandfather, the Crusader King Louis VII, he was accused of being more a monk than a king. He replied, "You surely speak true. I am unworthy to be King. But if it had pleased Our Lord, another who knew better how to govern would be in my place."

As he reached manhood, he showed that for all his monkishness he had the strength to lead a kingdom. He forced his mother Queen Blanche to step aside and let him rule. Hardly had he won full control, though, than he turned the royal power back to her. King Louis had taken the Cross and was going to the Holy Land. Queen Blanche would govern while he was away.

Saint Louis and the Seventh Crusade

It was not a promising time for a Crusade. The year was 1244, and Jerusalem was about to fall to the Turks once again. Europe had grown weary of Crusading. Emperor Frederick's Sixth Crusade had left a bad taste in many mouths, and few knights cared to go to the rescue of the quarrelsome barons of Outremer another time. The old flame of faith had come to burn low. The typical attitude of the moment was expressed by the mocking French poet Rutebeuf, who wrote an imaginary argument between a Crusader and a stay-at-home knight:

"Am I to leave my wife and children, all my goods and inheritance, to go and conquer a foreign land which will give me nothing in return? I can worship God just as well in Paris as in Jerusalem. One doesn't have to cross the sea to get to Paradise. Those rich lords and prelates who have grabbed for themselves all the treasure on earth may well need to go on a Crusade. But I live at peace with my neighbors. I am not bored with them yet, and so I have no desire to go looking for a war at the other end of the world. If you like heroic deeds, you can go along and cover yourself with glory: tell the Sultan from me that if he feels like attacking me I know very well how to defend myself. But so long as he leaves me alone, I shall not bother my head about him."

In this era of little faith King Louis IX planned to go Crusading. He fell ill early in 1244, and was thought to be dying. The power of speech left him. But then came a miraculous recovery; and Louis called for the Cross and announced his intention to go to the Holy Land. Queen Blanche, hearing it, "carried on with as great mourning as if she had seen him dead." The Queen Mother and the royal advisers tried to persuade him to change his mind, arguing that he had been temporarily insane when he uttered his vow on his sickbed. Louis wavered, but did not yield.

His preparations for the Crusade were elaborate. The Kingdom of France did not at that time possess a single satisfactory Mediterranean port, since such towns as Marseilles were in other hands. Louis built his own port of embarkation. On a barren stretch of wasteland rose the town of Aigues-Mortes in 1246, started from scratch. The rest of his planning was similarly ambitious. On Cyprus, intended as an advance base for the expedition, Louis's agents gathered wheat and barley and wine, heaping the provisions so high that "they seemed like mountains when one looked at them." The dockyards of six cities, from Barcelona to Venice, were put to work building ships for Louis' fleet. Sixteen galleys were made at Marseilles, twelve at Genoa, four at Pisa, three at Narbonne. The preliminaries for the Crusade took four years.

At last, in the summer of 1248, the day of departure arrived.

The chief chronicler of the Seventh Crusade was John of Joinville, a baron who turned to writing history in his old age, more than fifty years after the Crusade. Here is Joinville's description of the sailing:

"In the month of August we entered into our ship at Marseilles.

"On the day that we entered into our ship, they opened its gates and put inside all the horses we were taking overseas. And then they closed the gates again, and caulked them well, as a cask is sealed, since when the ship is on the high seas all the gates are below water.

"When the horses were in the ship, our master mariner called to his seamen, who stood at the prow, and said: 'Are you ready?' and they answered, 'Aye, sir, let the clerks and priests come forward!' As soon as these had come forward, he called to them, 'Sing, for God's sake!' and they all chanted with one voice the hymn, 'Veni, Creator Spiritus.' And the master shouted to the seamen, 'Unfurl the sails, for God's sake!' and they did so.

"In a short space the wind filled our sails and carried us out of sight of land. We could see nothing but water and sky, and every day the wind took us farther from the land where we were born. And I tell you that the man who puts himself into such peril when he is responsible for the welfare of others is a madman. For when he lies down to sleep at night on shipboard, he lies down not knowing whether or not he will find himself at the bottom of the sea in the morning."

The objective was the same as that of the Fifth Crusade: the Egyptian port of Damietta. After spending the winter on Cyprus, Louis and his fleet put to sea again. It should have been three days' journey from Cyprus to Damietta, but they were tossed by storms and did not arrive for three weeks. Six thousand Saracens waited on the shore. The Moslem archers let fly a dense cloud of arrows as the Crusaders approached; two thousand Turks waded out into the sea to give battle. The French crossbowmen drove them back, and the Crusading knights dragged their horses out of the holds and rode them into the sea.

"When King Louis saw the others jumping down into the sea," a chronicle recounts, "he wanted to go with them, but they did not want to let him; all the same he descended against their will and entered the water up to his waist, and all of us with him."

By midday, the Turks were retreating into the city of Damietta, leaving five hundred men dead on the shore. The next day, June 6, 1249, word came from the town that

271

Saint Louis

the entire Turkish garrison had fled, abandoning Damietta to the Crusaders. When Louis entered the heavily fortified town, he found fifty-three Christian prisoners who had been in Saracen dungeons since the Fifth Crusade, almost thirty years before.

It was an unexpectedly easy victory, and Louis gave thanks to God for his good fortune. Now the Crusaders began slowly to move up the Nile toward Cairo. By December, they had covered about a third of the distance, but were stopped at the town of Mansourah, not far from where Cardinal Pelagius and the Fifth Crusade had come to grief in 1221. Harassed by Saracen archers, bedeviled by Greek fire, terrorized by Bedouin tribesmen who slipped into their camp at night to commit murder, the Crusaders found the going slow after their first quick triumph. For nearly two months they were held motionless at Mansourah by a large Saracen army on the far side of the Nile. Then a Bedouin offered to sell them some strategic information: the location of a place where they could ford the river easily to attack the Moslem troops.

On February 8, 1250, the Crusaders started across the river. It began as an orderly march, with the Templars in the lead, and the forces of Robert of Artois, King Louis's brother, next in the battle order. Robert was a bold soldier, but he knew little about Saracen fighting methods and he was rash to the point of foolishness. Impatience seized him as he forded the Nile. Seeing the Turks on the far side, he longed to charge and cut them to pieces. He began to shoulder his way ahead of the Templars. They were annoyed and told him to keep his men in second place as the King had ordered. By way of answer Robert of Artois gave the signal for an attack.

The French horsemen spurred forward in a mad

onslaught. The Templars, unwilling to let Count Robert steal any of their glory, joined in the charge, each one "driving in his spurs and striving to outdo the others." The Saracens were caught off guard by the sudden ferocity of the attack, and they began to withdraw into Mansourah. Unaware of what lay in store for him, Robert of Artois led the Crusaders plunging into the narrow streets of the town despite an order from King Louis to halt. The King, in the rear lines of the army, was dumbstruck when he saw his careful battle plan discarded by his foolhardy, vainglorious younger brother.

Mansourah became a deathtrap for the attackers. Saracen soldiers, moving expertly through the winding lanes of the town, ambushed the bewildered Crusaders and cut them down. Three hundred of the French knights went to their deaths, including Robert of Artois. Two hundred eighty Templars perished. The middle body of the Crusaders saw what was happening in the front lines, milled in confusion, then turned and tried to flee across the Nile, "which they could not do," says Joinville, "for their horses were exhausted, and the day was so hot that we saw the stream covered with lances and shields, and horses and men drowning and dying."

At this moment King Louis rode up to restore some order. Joinville writes, "The King came up with his whole battalion, accompanied by great shouting, and with a great sounding of trumpets and clashing of cymbals; and he paused on a high road. Never have I seen so handsome a knight! For he seemed to tower head and shoulders above all his people, a gilded helmet upon his head, in his hand a sword of German steel."

His valor halted the wild retreat. The Frenchmen saw their King in the midst of the Saracens, slashing with his sword at enemy soldiers who clutched at the reins of his horse, and they rushed to his defense. By sunset the rout had turned into victory, and the Crusaders took Mansourah. Joinville tells us of the scene at King Louis's tent as night fell:

"I had his helmet taken off and gave him my iron hat so that he could get some air. Then there came up to him Brother Henry of Rosnay, the Provost of the Hospitallers, who had crossed the river, and he kissed the King's armed hand. The King asked if he had heard any news of his brother, the Count of Artois; and he told him that he had indeed some news, for he was certain that the Count of Artois was in Paradise. . . . And the King replied that God should be worshipped in all He brought to him, and great tears fell from his eyes."

The victory at Mansourah proved to be no victory at all. The Saracens had blockaded the Nile. The Crusaders, making camp between two branches of the river, were cut off from their main base at Damietta. There was no food, no water. The corpses of the slain began to putrefy. The men caught eels in the river, but the eels had fed on the rotting bodies of the dead, and disease ran through the camp. "The flesh of our legs," writes Joinville, "dried all up, and the skin of our legs became mottled with black like an old pair of boots. . . . No one could escape the disease, except by dying." It was typhoid fever. On April 5 the defeat of the Crusade had to be admitted, and Louis ordered a general retreat toward Damietta. It was a march of only thirty-five miles, but they were so enfeebled by disease that they could not make it. "The King was so ill that his teeth chattered and were loosened," one account relates, "and his skin was pale and dull and he had diarrhoea and was so thin that the bones of his back were wonderfully sharp." When the Egyptians closed in, the Crusaders could do nothing but surrender. They were taken into captivity.

Queen Marguerite had accompanied Louis on his Crusade. She was waiting for him at Damietta, in the last days of pregnancy. When news came that the King had been captured, she dreamed that night of Saracens, and cried out in her sleep. Her only guardian was an eighty-year-old knight who held her hand and said, "Lady, have no fear, for I am here."

Three days later, she felt the pangs of labor. Turning to the old knight she begged a favor: "If the Saracens take this city, cut off my head before they capture me." And the old knight replied, "Be certain that I will do it, for I had already decided I would kill you before they took us."

The child was born, a son named John. By now Damietta was in panic over the King's defeat, and the merchants of the town, men of Pisa and Genoa, announced that they were going to board their ships and evacuate while the coast was still clear. Queen Marguerite called them to her bedside and asked them not to leave the city, abandoning the women, the old, and the sick as they fled. They refused. "How can we stay here?" the hardheaded merchants asked. "We shall die of hunger in this city!" The Queen replied that she would personally purchase all the food available in Damietta and see that it was rationed so no one went hungry. She did so, at a cost of 360,000 livres—$10,000,000. The merchants stayed.

King Louis and the Crusaders, imprisoned at Mansourah, were threatened with death and torture to break down their resistance to the Saracen demands. The Saracens wanted Louis to turn over to them some of the castles of the barons of Outremer in return for his freedom. Louis insisted, quite correctly, that he had no power to give away those castles and that he doubted the Templars and Hospitallers, who controlled them, would yield them to save him. In the face of chilling descriptions of the tortures that would be inflicted on him if he did not arrange for the surrender of the castles, Louis mildly replied that the Egyptians were free to do with him what they would. At last, seeing that it was impossible to use the King to gain territorial advantage in Palestine, the Saracens began talking of a cash ransom. A price was named: a million gold bezants, or about $15,000,000 in modern money. Louis agreed to ransom his comrades. For himself, though, he did not think it was proper to pay in cash. He would surrender the city of Damietta in exchange for his own freedom.

The staggering ransom was paid, and Damietta was yielded. On May 8, 1250, Louis and the other Crusaders were freed. Five days later, they reached Acre, where the King rejoined Queen Marguerite and saw his newborn son for the first time. The Seventh Crusade, which had been planned so carefully, which had begun so gloriously with the taking of Damietta, had ended in utter calamity. A vast amount of gold had been paid over to the Saracens, many Christian lives had been lost, and nothing had been gained. The survivors of the Crusade came together to discuss what to do next. Many of them thought there was no point in remaining in the East. King Louis himself was in favor of going home, which may seem surprising, but he had obligations to France as well as to his vows as a Crusader, and his country needed him. He told the barons:

"My lords, Queen Blanche, my mother, has begged me as strongly as she can to go back to France, for my kingdom is in great peril. I have neither peace nor truce with

the King of England." But he hesitated, for, he said,
"Those people of this country [Outremer] with whom I
have spoken have told me that if I go, this land will be
lost." To go or to stay? The King was torn by the conflict.
He asked his barons to consider the matter for a week and
give him their advice.

At the end of the week, they came to him and pointed
out that of the 2,800 knights who had followed him to the
Crusade, only a hundred still remained. The part of wisdom would be to return to France and gather a new army,
"to take vengeance on the enemies of God who held you
in prison."

Each knight in turn spoke. The fourteenth was Joinville, who felt the Crusaders were bound by honor to stay
in the East. Those who wished to go home shouted angry
abuse at him. Abruptly the King brought the meeting to
an end, declaring that he would announce his decision a
week later. When that time came, Louis said, "I cannot
desert the Kingdom of Jerusalem which I came to guard
and protect. I have therefore resolved that I will stay here
for a while."

The other Crusaders were free to go home if they
cared to, and many of them did, including two of the King's
brothers. Louis and his Queen remained in the Holy
Land for four more years. There was no real fighting, but
he spent time and huge sums of money to strengthen the
coastal fortresses of Acre, Tyre, Jaffa, and Sidon. Perhaps
even more usefully, he helped to calm the quarreling barons
of Outremer, acting as a virtual King of Jerusalem. (The
real King, Conrad of Hohenstaufen, had never come to the
East, and never would.) Louis arranged for the succession
of fifteen-year-old Bohemond VI to the throne of Antioch
in 1252, avoiding another family battle there, and main-

tained order in Cyprus, where once again the early death of a king had given the crown to an infant.

Louis also sought for allies in the war against the Saracens. He turned first to the Assassins, that mysterious, fanatical Islamic sect of murderers. The members of the strange cult regarded most other Moslems as heretics, and from time to time had been willing to join forces with the Franks against them. King Louis struck up friendly relations with the sinister killers and exchanged gifts with their chieftain, whom the Crusaders called the Old Man of the Mountains.

To negotiate an even odder alliance, Louis sent monks as ambassadors deep into Central Asia. At the beginning of the thirteenth century, a tribe of warlike nomads called the Tatars, or Mongols, had united behind a brilliant leader named Genghis Khan and had spread out to raid and conquer much of the Orient. By the middle of the century, the Mongols ruled most of China and Russia. They were as impossible to defeat as the Arabs had been in the seventh century and the Turks in the eleventh. And they were not Moslems. A rumor had it that the fierce Mongols were interested in becoming Christians. If they could be converted, they would be the force that could strike the deathblow of Islam. So at Louis's request, a missionary named William of Rubruck went to visit the Mongol leader. It was an astonishing journey, one of the greatest exploits of travel ever recorded, but it yielded nothing except information about Mongol customs. The rumor was false. The Mongols did not care to become Christians. In time, most of them submitted to Islam, and the dream of using them to free the Holy Land died.

Toward the end of 1252, Louis received word that his mother, Queen Blanche, was dead. Joinville tells that "he went into such mourning that for two days no one could speak to him." But he remained at Acre, completing his work, and did not sail for home until the spring of 1254.

The Seventh Crusade of Saint Louis did not add an inch of territory to the Christian holdings in the East. Its achievements were other than military. Where Emperor Frederick had divided the barons of Outremer, King Louis united them. His saintly presence, his radiant piety, brought back for a flickering moment the early idealism of the Crusades. It did not long survive his return to France. The barons were locked in dispute over petty matters of title and inheritance, and the grand goal of overthrowing the Saracens was again forgotten.

For thirteen years King Louis occupied himself with the problems of France, never losing sight of his hope of liberating the Holy Land. In the Easter season of 1267 he sent for the faithful Joinville and announced that he was taking the Cross a second time. Joinville opposed him and refused to take part in any such expedition. France needed its King, said Joinville. "Great was the sin of those who advised the King to go," he wrote, "seeing how weak he was of his body, for he could bear neither to be drawn in a chariot, nor to ride. So great was his weakness that he allowed me to carry him in my arms from the mansion of the Count of Auxerre, where I took leave of him, to the abbey of the Franciscans. And yet, weak as he was, if he had remained in France he might have lived longer, and done much good, and many good works."

At fifty-two, Louis was an old man, worn out by disease. He insisted on his Crusade, however, and on July 1, 1270, he set forth from his port of Aigues-Mortes for Africa. Eighteen days later, what has become known as the Eighth Crusade arrived at the city of Tunis.

Saint Louis and the Seventh Crusade

No battles were fought. Plague attacked the Crusaders. Thousands died. Joinville, never wavering in his objection to the Crusade, had stayed home, so it remained for another chronicler, William of Saint Pathus, to record the grim events. In August, King Louis fell ill and took to his bed. On the twenty-fourth of the month, a priest entered the bedchamber and found the King on his knees, saying in a low voice, "O Jerusalem, O Jerusalem." The next day he was dead. His body was returned to France, and before the end of the thirteenth century it was proclaimed at Rome that Louis IX of France had been enrolled in the glorious company of the saints.

THE END OF
THE CRUSADES

THE sand was running low in the hourglass. Little time remained for the Kingdom of Jerusalem. A thinning band of Frankish settlers, in cruel conflict with one another, held the coastal strip of Palestine without making any real attempt to free Jerusalem. And soon even that ghostly kingdom would be gone.

The quarrels began again right after King Louis had left the East in 1254. Within two years, there was virtual civil war in Christian-held Syria. The Venetians were fighting it out with the Genoese for commercial supremacy in the East. The Templars backed the Venetians, the Hospitallers supported the Genoese, and most of the barons chose sides according to their own interest. For more than twenty months Acre was split by a dispute that was purely economic and had nothing to do with questions of religion.

The Saracens were divided too, which was why the Franks were able to hang on in the East as long as they did. The Mongols went on a rampage, plunging deep into the territories of the Turks and the Arabs, taking Persia in 1256, Baghdad in 1258, capturing Aleppo and Damascus and forcing Bohemond VI of Antioch to submit to them. But in September of 1260, the Mongol general Kitbuga was defeated in Palestine by an army led by Sultan Qutuz of Egypt, and the threat was ended. Qutuz emerged briefly as the leader of the Moslem world.

The man behind Qutuz's rise to power was a Turk named Baibars. Baibars, a gigantic brown-skinned man with blue eyes and a booming voice, had been born in the district of Russia known as the Crimea, and as a young man had been sold as a slave in Syria. In time his great strength attracted attention, and he was bought to serve in the bodyguard of the Sultan of Egypt. He was the leader of the forces that met the Franks at Mansourah in 1250 and slew Robert of Artois.

A few months later, Baibars was involved in a conspirarcy to assassinate his master, Sultan Turanshah. The murder was carried out before the eyes of King Louis and his men, who then were prisoners at Mansourah. Joinville told how, as the horrified Crusaders watched, Baibars and his men pursued the young Sultan toward the Nile, "and, as the Sultan was passing on his way to the river, one of them drove his spear into his ribs and the Sultan fled towards the river trailing the spear. And they all came down and even plunged into the water and slew him in the river quite near our galley where we were."

Baibars put a general named Aibek on the Egyptian throne. Later he quarreled with Aibek and left the country; but in 1257 Aibek was murdered by his wife, and in short order Baibars helped another general named Qutuz to become Sultan. Baibars and Qutuz together led the army that stopped the Mongol advance in 1260. As a reward for his services, Baibars asked the Sultan to make him governor of Aleppo. Qutuz, suspicious of his lieutenant's ambitions, refused. A few days later Baibars had his revenge. He accompanied Qutuz on a hunting trip, and when they had ridden away from the main camp, Baibars gave a signal to one of his comrades. The confederate approached the Sultan, taking his hand as though to kiss it. At the same moment Baibars approached from the rear and drove his sword into Qutuz's back. The conspirators proclaimed Baibars to be Sultan. He marched triumphantly to Cairo to take the throne.

Such was the man the Franks of Outremer now faced: shrewd, ambitious, and entirely lacking in scruples. Perhaps Baldwin I would have been a match for him, or Richard the Lion-hearted. But Baldwin had been dead 140 years, and Richard for sixty. The Crusaders had turned into Oriental princes, fond of luxury and relaxation. They were not the warriors their great-grandfathers had been. In 1263, Baibars led a small force of men into Frankish territory, swept through Nazareth, and all but captured Acre itself. It was only the beginning. In 1265 he returned and surrounded the fortress of Arsuf, held by 270 Hospitallers. Ninety of the Frankish knights were killed in the first attack; the survivors agreed to surrender upon Baibars's promise that he would let them go free. They opened the gates to Baibars, who flung them into his dungeons.

In 1266 Baibars turned against the Templar castle of Saphet. The Templars resisted for more than a month, fighting with their usual valor. At last starvation and summer heat weakened them, and they, too, negotiated for surrender. The Templars offered to give Baibars the fortress if he would permit them to go safely to Acre. Baibars agreed, and promptly beheaded them when they opened their gates.

The End of the Crusades

With the fall of these fortresses, Sultan Baibars had full control of most of Palestine. In May, 1267, he marched toward Acre, flying the banners that he had captured from the Templars and Hospitallers. Thanks to this ruse he was able to get all the way to the walls of the city before being discovered. But his attack on Acre was thrown back.

The following year he moved against the only Christian possessions south of Acre, the Templar castle of Athlit and the port of Jaffa ruled by Guy of Ibelin. Athlit resisted him, but Jaffa fell after a twelve-hour siege. Now Baibars looked toward the Frankish possessions of northern Syria, the cities of Antioch and Tripoli ruled by Bohemond VI. Bohemond was at Tripoli when Baibars invaded Antioch. After a four-day siege the Saracens broke through the walls and flooded into the city.

The sack that followed was frightful. Antioch was the wealthiest of the Frankish cities of Outremer, and it had never been entered by Moslem invaders since its conquest by the first Bohemond in 1097. Gold coins were passed around by the bowlful. Every soldier in the Sultan's army seized at least one slave. Baibars wrote a gloating letter to Bohemond VI at Tripoli, describing the sacking of Antioch in terms calculated to shock and terrify:

"Ah! if you had seen your knights crushed beneath the horses' hooves, your city of Antioch laid open to the violence of pillage and a prey for every man, your treasures shared out by the hundredweight, four ladies of the city sold for one gold coin! If you had seen the churches and the Crosses overthrown, the leaves of the Holy Gospels scattered, the tombs of the patriarchs broken underfoot! If you had seen your enemies the Moslems trampling over tabernacle and altar, sacrificing the men of religion, deacon, priest, and patriarch! If you had seen your palaces going up in flames, your castles destroyed, the Church of Saint Paul tumbled in ruins from top to bottom!"

There was no way to halt the carnage. Antioch was gone, and in Europe the only man interested in taking the Cross was King Louis of France, feeble and ailing. No one came to the aid of Outremer. The barons were in turmoil. The political structure of the Frankish East was crumbling. Already the Byzantines had overthrown the Latin Empire of Constantinople in 1261, and descendants of the exiled Greek royal family were on the throne. They certainly would not lift a finger to rescue the Franks, after the wanton sacking of Constantinople by the men of the Fourth Crusade. As for the Kingdom of Jerusalem, it was more of a spectre than ever. Conrad, the son of Emperor Frederick, had died in 1254. The crown of Jerusalem had gone to his son Conradin, who never visited his kingdom. Conradin was captured and put to death in Italy in 1268 at the age of sixteen while attempting to regain some of the territory his grandfather had lost. With his death, the barons of Outremer examined the complicated genealogy of the royal line to see who would get the throne. It went at last to King Hugh III of Cyprus, the great-great-grandson of Amalric I of Jerusalem. But Hugh, as a man of Cyprus, was never able to exert much authority over the barons of Syria and Palestine.

Bohemond VI meekly asked Baibars for a truce. The Sultan, glutted with the treasures of Antioch, agreed to let Bohemond keep Tripoli a while longer. One motive for Baibars's willingness to call off his troops was the arrival of a new Crusade in the Holy Land in May, 1271. It was led by Prince Edward of England, the grandson of Richard the Lion-hearted's faithless brother King John.

Edward was in his thirties, a capable and aggressive soldier who had the valor of his grand-uncle King Richard but a good deal more wisdom. He might prove to be a formidable Crusader, and Baibars did not want to involve himself in an attack on Tripoli until he saw what Edward would do.

Edward was met at Acre by King Hugh III and Count Bohemond VI, who told him of the desperate state of affairs. Edward hoped to unite what remained of the Frankish barons and to bring in the Mongols as allies, since they had every reason to hate Baibars. Quickly he made the disturbing discovery that the Venetians and Genoese were doing a brisk business trading with Egypt and did not want this profitable enterprise upset by a Crusade. Next he learned that the nobles of Cyprus did not choose to go to the mainland to fight. A Crusade was impossible. To preserve the safety of Acre—all that was left of the Kingdom of Jerusalem—Prince Edward signed a ten-year truce with Baibars in the spring of 1272. A few weeks later, a member of the cult of Assassins slipped into Edward's room and stabbed him with a poisoned dagger. Edward's strength was so great that he seized the knife and slew his assailant with it. But he was seriously wounded, and was forced to withdraw from the affairs of Outremer. In September, when word reached him that his father was dying, Prince Edward embarked from Acre for England and arrived to become King Edward I.

Outremer clung weakly to life. Bohemond VI died in 1275, and his son became Count Bohemond VII of Tripoli, keeping alive a name that went back to the very outset of the Crusades. King Hugh III made a pretense of ruling Acre from his capital on Cyprus. Baibars, aware that he could complete the job of destroying the Franks

287

at any time, chose to invade Asia Minor, where the Mongols had conquered the Seljuk Turks.

While on this expedition to Asia Minor Baibars disappeared abruptly from the scene. His death, in July, 1277, was a mysterious matter. Some said he died of wounds received in battle against the Mongols. Others claimed that he had perished from drinking too much koumiss, a Mongol beverage made from fermented mare's milk. A third story, more in keeping with Baibars's character, holds that he offered a cup of poisoned koumiss to one of his emirs who had offended him and then thoughtlessly drank from the same cup himself before it was cleaned.

No warrior, not even Saladin, had crippled the Franks as badly as had the cruel Baibars. In his seventeen years of power he had stripped them of their chain of inland fortresses, but for two, and had left just six coastal cities, Tortosa, Jebail, Tripoli, Sidon, Tyre, and Acre. His murderous career was no cause for pride in Islam, but he had all but crushed the descendants of the Crusaders.

The end was near. The Syrian emir Qalawun succeeded Baibars after the usual struggle of Moslem against Moslem, taking control in 1280 following the brief rule of Baibars's eldest son. Meanwhile Tripoli and Jebail, two Frankish cities, became embroiled in a short but vicious war stirred up by the Templars in 1277 and 1278, and the bitterness lasted for several years afterward. Qalawun, menaced by the Mongols, left the feuding Franks alone until 1285, when he besieged and took the Hospitallers' castle of Marqab. Doom was advancing on Outremer.

With the wolf almost at the door, the Franks made merry in Acre. King Hugh III of Jerusalem and Cyprus had died in 1284, and his son and successor John survived him only for a year. The new King was John's brother

Henry, a boy of fourteen. On August, 1286, King Henry paid his first visit to the mainland, to Tyre to be crowned and then to Acre. Tournaments in his honor were staged for two weeks. Pageants were enacted, telling tales of chivalry: the story of King Arthur and the Round Table, Lancelot and Guinevere, Tristan and Isolde. During all the pomp and gaiety, the Saracens drew closer.

In 1287, they took the small town of Lattakieh without opposition. Soon after, Bohemond VII died childless, extinguishing that long line of Crusaders. With the last Count of Tripoli dead, Sultan Qalawun gathered his army and moved against Bohemond's city. In February of 1289 Tripoli was besieged. The catapults rained stones against the old walls, and they crumbled like ramparts of mud. The Arab chronicler Abu'l Feda tells of the massacre that followed as the Saracen troops entered:

"The inhabitants fled toward the port, but very few were able to board ships. Most of the men were slain and the women and children carried off into slavery. After the slaughter was finished, the town was razed to the ground. Nearby was an islet, where there stood a church of Saint Thomas. A great crowd had taken refuge there. The Moslems rode into the sea on horseback or swam to the island. All the men who were there had their throats cut. Some time later I visited that islet and found it full of rotting corpses; it was impossible to stay there because of the stench."

Of all the Frankish holdings in Outremer, only Acre and a few small towns remained.

In Europe, no one paid attention. One of the Mongol leaders had sent ambassadors to King Edward I of England, calling for a joint Mongol-Christian Crusade against Qalawun. But Edward had wars of his own to

The Crusaders stage a tournament

fight in Scotland. King Philip IV of France received the ambassadors next and took them on a sightseeing tour of Paris, but showed no desire for a Crusade. Constantinople, Greek once more, was pleased to see the Saracens annihilate the Franks of Outremer. Only the Mongols seemed to care about defeating the Sultan of Egypt, and they no longer had the strength that had been theirs during their great outward surge under Genghis Khan.

The Franks of Acre, shivering as they considered the fate of Tripoli, hastened to renew their truce with Sultan Qalawun for another ten years. But the truce was stupidly broken by a band of Crusaders from northern Italy who arrived at Acre in the summer of 1290. They had come in response to a plea from the Pope, and like nearly all

newly-arrived Crusaders they had no understanding of the
delicate ways of life in Outremer. They were drunk and
disorderly and had come East to kill Saracens; they could
not understand why the weak-kneed Franks of Acre had
been so cowardly as to make a truce with Qalawun.

Under the terms of the truce, Moslem peasants were
free to bring their produce to the markets of Acre. One
day toward the end of August the new Crusaders, after
drinking their fill, rushed into the suburbs of Acre to
slaughter Saracens. They fell upon harmless farmers bringing their goods to market. Deciding that any man with
swarthy skin and a beard was a Saracen, they slew a number of Syrian Christians as well.

The barons of Acre were shocked. They rescued a

few of the Moslem peasants and arrested the ringleaders of the massacre. Sultan Qalawun, however, chose to make the outrage an excuse for ending the truce. He demanded that the criminals be handed over to him for punishment. The leaders of Acre, unable to bring themselves to give Crusaders over to certain execution, refused. Qalawun vowed to take Acre and slay every Christian in the city.

Death came to the Sultan before he could fulfill his vow. Setting out from Cairo with his army in November, 1290, he fell ill and died almost at once. His son and successor, al-Ashraf, pledged to carry on the campaign. By the following March, the Saracens were closing in on Acre.

Their army was immense. Frankish chroniclers told of 60,000 Saracen cavalrymen and 160,000 foot soldiers. Siege machines were collected from every part of al-Ashraf's domain. There were a hundred catapults, including one monster called the Victorious and another nicknamed the Furious. There were light stone-flinging mangonels known as Black Oxen. This array of artillery was placed around the walls of Acre. Thirty to forty thousand civilians, were within the city with about 1,000 knights, and some 14,000 foot soldiers.

On April 6, 1291, the siege began. The mangonels and catapults hurled stones and pots of Greek fire at the city. Acre answered back with nighttime raids into the Moslem camp. A Christian ship in the harbor catapulted stones at the attackers. One by one, the watchtowers of the city collapsed as the Saracen engineers mined them.

Young King Henry of Cyprus and Jerusalem arrived during the siege with all the troops he could collect: 100 knights, 2,000 infantrymen, forty ships. But even these reinforcements were useless against the vast Saracen horde.

292

The End of the Crusades

King Henry sent two messengers to the Sultan to ask him why he had broken the truce. Al-Ashraf met them and asked bluntly, "Have you brought me the keys of the city?" The envoys said they had not. "Be off with you, then," the Sultan declared. "I have nothing more to say."

The Saracens attacked a tower known as the King's Tower by piling sandbags around it until they could reach the top. On May 16 they took the tower. The civilians of Acre, seeing that defeat was near, put their wives and children on board ships in the harbor for an escape, but the sea was so rough that none could sail. They returned to their homes. On Friday, May 18, the general assault came. An eyewitness known as the Templar of Tyre tells of it:

"Before dawn broke, a great kettledrum sounded loudly, and at the sound of that drum, which made a loud and horrifying noise, the Saracens attacked the city of Acre on all sides. . . . They came on foot, in countless numbers. First came those who held great long shields, and then those who hurled Greek fire, and afterward those who shot darts and feathered arrows so thickly that it seemed rain was falling from the heavens."

The invaders forced their way into a watchtower known as the Accursed Tower and pressed onward toward the city. Those ancient rivals, the Templars and the Hospitallers, fought side by side at last, but their harmony came too late. The Moslems were in the city. The people of Acre fled toward the port, followed by sword-wielding Saracens who left few survivors. In the heart of the city were four towers belonging to the military orders. The Saracens surrounded the one belonging to the Templars, who offered to surrender. The gates were opened, and the Moslems rushed in, but this time it was the Templars who played false, shutting the gates again and killing every

Saracen who had entered. The Sultan went to the tower and told the Templars "that he well understood that his men had died through their own folly . . . and that he bore the Christians no grudge and they might come out safely in all confidence." The Templars, trusting al-Ashraf's words, came forth, all but a few who were too ill to leave. Those who emerged were seized and beheaded at once.

Then the Saracens mined the tower to kill the remaining Templars within. The defenders yielded. As the attackers surged into the building it collapsed, taking the lives not only of the Templars but of hundreds of Saracens as well.

Acre was in Moslem control. The city was deliberately destroyed, its walls pulled down, its houses put to the torch, its towers and castles demolished. Its people were slaughtered or sold into slavery.

The remaining Frankish cities soon followed: Tyre, Tortosa, and the rest. By the end of August, only a Templar fortress called Ruad, two miles off the coast opposite Tortosa, remained untaken. It held out for twelve more years, but it did not matter. There was nothing left of Outremer. The soldiers of al-Ashraf paraded through the land, destroying the buildings and fortifications and irrigation systems of the Franks. After nearly two centuries, all was over for the Franks of the Holy Land.

And so it ended. The cities of Outremer became desolate rubble heaps. Scorpions and lizards crawled over the shattered walls of Crusader castles. The barons who had survived fled to Cyprus, which remained free of Moslem rule. The island so casually conquered by Richard the Lion-hearted was the only Crusader holding that survived. For several centuries more, a shadowy Kingdom of

The End of the Crusades

Jerusalem continued to exist at least in name, for the Kings of Cyprus went on calling themselves Kings of Jerusalem as well until their time came to pass from history.

There was constant talk of the "next" Crusade, of course. It was good politics for a European prince to take the Cross and speak of recapturing Jerusalem, but few actually tried. The great victory of 1099 engineered by Godfrey of Bouillon and Raymond of Toulouse now seemed to those who looked back a miracle that could never be repeated. How had those fierce warriors done it? To march through Asia Minor, thrusting the Turks aside, to carve Christian states out of Syria and Armenia, to strike deep into Palestine and seize Jerusalem, all in less than four years—it seemed the work of demigods, not of men.

Yet the dream lived on. In 1359, King Peter I received the crown of Cyprus and Jerusalem, and within him surged the same fire that had led Saint Louis to take the Cross eleven decades earlier. He toured Europe, gathering support for a Crusade. The target was the Egyptian city of Alexandria, by then a richer prize than Damietta. Peter hoped to repeat the events of the Fifth Crusade—to take an Egyptian port and barter it for Jerusalem. In 1365 Alexandria was savagely sacked and despoiled, but once the Crusaders had seized their booty they left for home with it, and King Peter could not restrain them. The Crusade collapsed. Close to insanity, a madman who could talk only of Jerusalem, King Peter kept his people in ferment, trying to organize an attack on the Holy City. He became so troublesome, such a threat to the peace of Cyprus, that his assassination had to be arranged in 1369.

The center of Moslem power had shifted once more from Egypt to Asia Minor. A new group of Turks, the

Osmanlis or Ottomans, were starting to assemble an empire. They began to move on Constantinople late in the fourteenth century. King Sigismund of Hungary, knowing that his own country would be next to fall if Constantinople were taken, promoted a Crusade against the Ottomans in 1396. An army of a hundred thousand men assembled in Hungary, the largest force ever to do battle against the Moslems.

King Sigismund, who knew the fighting methods of the enemy, suggested a strategy of caution. Lure the Turks into Hungary, he advised, and attack them from a position of strength. But the knights of western Europe had learned nothing from the experiences of the past centuries. They insisted on a grand and glorious attack, always maintaining the offensive.

In September, 1396, the Christian army reached the city of Nicopolis in Bulgaria. A large Turkish force was camped three miles away. With blind confidence the Christian horsemen charged into the Turkish cavalry only to find that the Turks had thrust stakes into the ground to block their approach. Dismounting, they tried to advance on foot, pulling the stakes out as they went. Their robust charge scattered the Turks, and the Crusaders raced breathlessly forward to discover that the enemy had regrouped and was about to throw a regiment of fresh troops at them. The slaughter that followed cost thousands of Christian lives, and the ransom of the prisoners sent vast heaps of gold into Turkish coffers.

After the fiasco of 1396 there was nothing that could even remotely be considered a Crusade. There were only unfulfilled vows. When Henry IV became King of England at the beginning of the fifteenth century, he swore to go to Jerusalem, and Shakespeare makes him express a wish "to chase these pagans in the holy field where Christ once walked." But the closest he came was a room in his own palace at London, a room called Jerusalem, where he died in 1413.

The power of the Ottomans grew. The year 1453 saw them capture Constantinople and put an end to the Byzantine Empire. They moved onward into Europe. No one spoke of freeing the Holy Land now; the problem was to halt the Turks before they installed themselves in the capitals of Europe.

One voice cried out for a true Crusade: Pope Pius II, who was elected in 1458. He pleaded for a new alliance, but only the Hungarians, with the Ottomans clawing at their borders, supported his call. The rich cities of Italy did not care to disrupt the trade that they carried on with the Turks. The King of France was too busy. The King of England sent his regrets.

Pope Pius did what no Pope had ever done before. He took the Cross himself, in July, 1464, and announced that he would personally lead the new Crusade. He sent men to buy and equip galleys and ordered the princes of Europe to join him at the port of Ancona for the holy war.

He was an old man, wracked with fever, coming to the end of his days. No one took him seriously. No knights waited at the docks of Ancona. The Pope was carried in a litter to the port, and his attendants kept the curtains of the litter drawn, so that he could not see the men of his fleet streaming along the roads as they deserted their ships. Death came for him at Ancona, and he never learned that his call had gone unanswered. There were no more Crusades.

The Turks advanced. In 1526 they took Hungary, and three years later they were threatening Austria. In

1570 they looked toward Cyprus, which had come under the rule of Venice. A famous battle in Greece halted the Turkish progress, but it was not until 1697 that the Ottomans ceased to be a threat to Europe. They settled into a long decline, and the Ottoman Empire sleepily ruled over most of the Near East until the beginning of the twentieth century, when the Sultans at last were overthrown.

What good had it all been, the years of Crusading, the bloodshed and the valor, the cruelty and the treachery? Sir Steven Runciman, the modern historian of the Crusades, has written: "The triumphs of the Crusade were the triumphs of faith. But faith without wisdom is a dangerous thing. . . . The Crusades were a tragic and destructive episode. . . . There was so much courage and so little honor, so much devotion and so little understanding. High ideals were besmirched by cruelty and greed, enterprise and endurance by a blind and narrow self-righteousness."

He is right that the story of the Crusades is not a pretty one. The original idealism quickly was lost as the men of the First Crusade grasped for power in the conquered land. The coming of the Venetians and the Genoese turned the holy war into a quest for profit. The Templars and the Hospitallers introduced a note of ferocity. When the Crusade struck against Constantinople in 1204, a turning point was reached, transforming the whole project into something ugly and shameful. Frederick II's sly acquisition of Jerusalem was scarcely a matter for pride, and not all the sainthood of Louis IX could redeem his grand adventure and make it what it had been meant to be.

The story is marred by stupidity and viciousness. The Crusaders never were able to learn from experience, and one needless defeat followed another. Their record is a sorry one. By wrecking Constantinople, they gave the Turks an open gateway into Europe, with catastrophic results. When Pope Urban issued his call in 1095, the Seljuk Turks had an uneasy grasp on parts of Asia Minor and Syria. When Pope Pius II died at Ancona three and a half centuries later, the Ottoman Turks ruled all the East and much of Europe. There was no gain for Christianity, only a colossal loss.

But the Crusades brought changes to Europe, and history would not have followed the course it did if there had been no holy wars. The contact between East and West sent new ideas flooding into half-barbaric Europe; the Crusaders came home laden with new foods, new spices, new ways of thought, even new words. Our language is studded with words of Arabic origin, souvenirs of the collision between the Moslem world and Europe. Such words as *alcohol, alchemy, algebra, zenith, cipher, amalgam* and many more came westward. Arab science, Arab medicine, Arab geography and astronomy—these were some of the fruits of the intervals of peace between the wars.

The eastward flow of warriors altered history, too. Turbulent, unruly knights who might have upset the order of things in Europe went off instead to fight and perhaps die in Outremer. Who knows what kingdoms Bohemond or Baldwin of Lorraine might have founded if they had remained in Europe? And there were economic changes. Haughty knights, borrowing money heavily to finance their expeditions, became much less haughty when the debts fell due. Great estates were broken up. Power shifted from one family to another. When the Crusades began, men thought of themselves only as citizens of a single province or even a single city—Godfrey of Bouillon, Hugh of Vermandois, Raymond of Toulouse. By the end of the era, the old feudal domains had been transformed, and men were starting to regard themselves as citizens of France, of Germany, of England, of Italy.

There were many more subtle effects of the Crusades, but it is better, perhaps, to be content with looking at them as grand adventures, as the robust exploits of robust men, for so they began. The complexities came later. Looking at the era of the Crusades across the centuries, we can see the naked scheming, the selfish grabbing of power, the treacherous making and unmaking of alliances —and also the heroism, the nobility, the faith, all the idealistic motives that got the great project under way. That the Crusades went so far astray from their pious purpose tells us much not only about medieval man but also about all the follies of humanity.

There is an odd postscript to the story of the Crusades. For the Kingdom of Jerusalem has been born again, in a sense. Once more there is an alien state in the midst of Islam, creating some of the same tensions that existed in the medieval world.

It is not a Christian state, this time, but a Jewish one. A thousand years before Christ lived and died there, Palestine was the heartland of the Kingdom of Israel, and Jews everywhere never ceased to think of it as their home, though they had been driven into exile in the farthest parts of the globe. When the Ottoman Empire was broken apart after the First World War, Palestine fell into the control of Great Britain. The British, petitioned to create a national Jewish homeland there, agreed to turn Palestine over to the people of Israel in the course of time. The delays were many, but in 1948 Palestine was finally divided between Arabs and Jews, and the State of Israel was born.

The End of the Crusades

Today Israel occupies a precarious position in the East, surrounded by hostile Moslem neighbors just as did the Kingdom of Jerusalem eight centuries ago. Ruined Crusader castles loom on Israeli hilltops as reminders of those ancient times of strife. Modern Saracens in Egypt and Arabia lay plans for an invasion of the Holy Land; Israelis remain on guard against the day when that invasion comes. All the rest of the world eyes the explosive situation with uneasiness.

King Baldwin I would find much to discuss with the Premier of Israel. The President of Egypt and the King of Saudi Arabia would welcome the counsel of Saladin. History may never repeat itself, but certain patterns seem eternal, and the struggle for that sun-parched scrap of earth known as the Holy Land is still going on, in the atomic age as in the days of mounted knights.

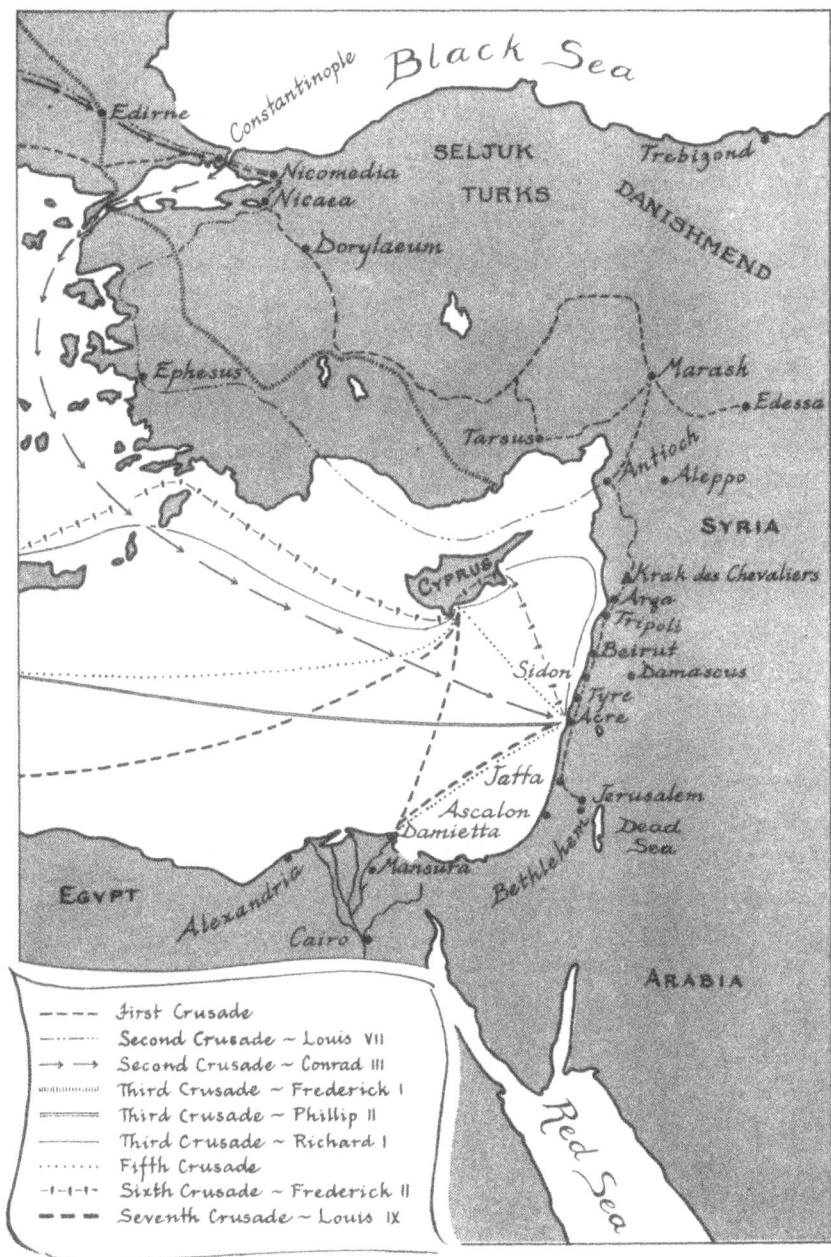

Black Sea

Edirne

Constantinople

Nicomedia

Nicaea

SELJUK
TURKS

Trebizond

DANISHMEND

Dorylaeum

Ephesus

Marash

Edessa

Tarsus

Antioch

Aleppo

SYRIA

CYPRUS

Krak des Chevaliers

Arqa

Tripoli

Beirut

Damascus

Sidon

Tyre
Acre

Jaffa

Jerusalem

Ascalon

Damietta

Bethlehem

Dead
Sea

EGYPT

Alexandria

Mansura

ARABIA

Cairo

Red
Sea

------	First Crusade
—·—·—	Second Crusade ~ Louis VII
→ →	Second Crusade ~ Conrad III
▪▪▪▪▪	Third Crusade ~ Frederick I
▬▬▬	Third Crusade ~ Phillip II
———	Third Crusade ~ Richard I
······	Fifth Crusade
-ı-ı-ı-	Sixth Crusade ~ Frederick II
▬ ▬ ▬	Seventh Crusade ~ Louis IX

303

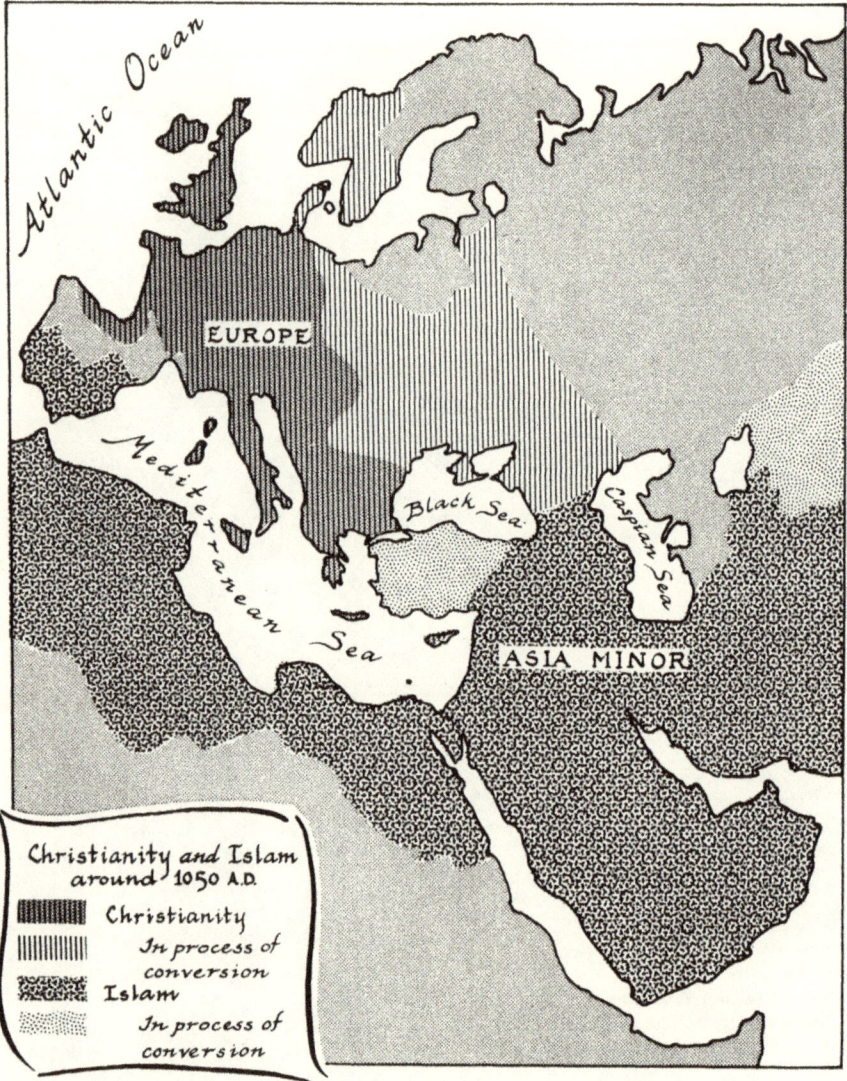

Christianity and Islam
around 1050 A.D.

Christianity

In process of
conversion

Islam

In process of
conversion

Atlantic Ocean

EUROPE

Mediterranean Sea

Black Sea

Caspian Sea

ASIA MINOR

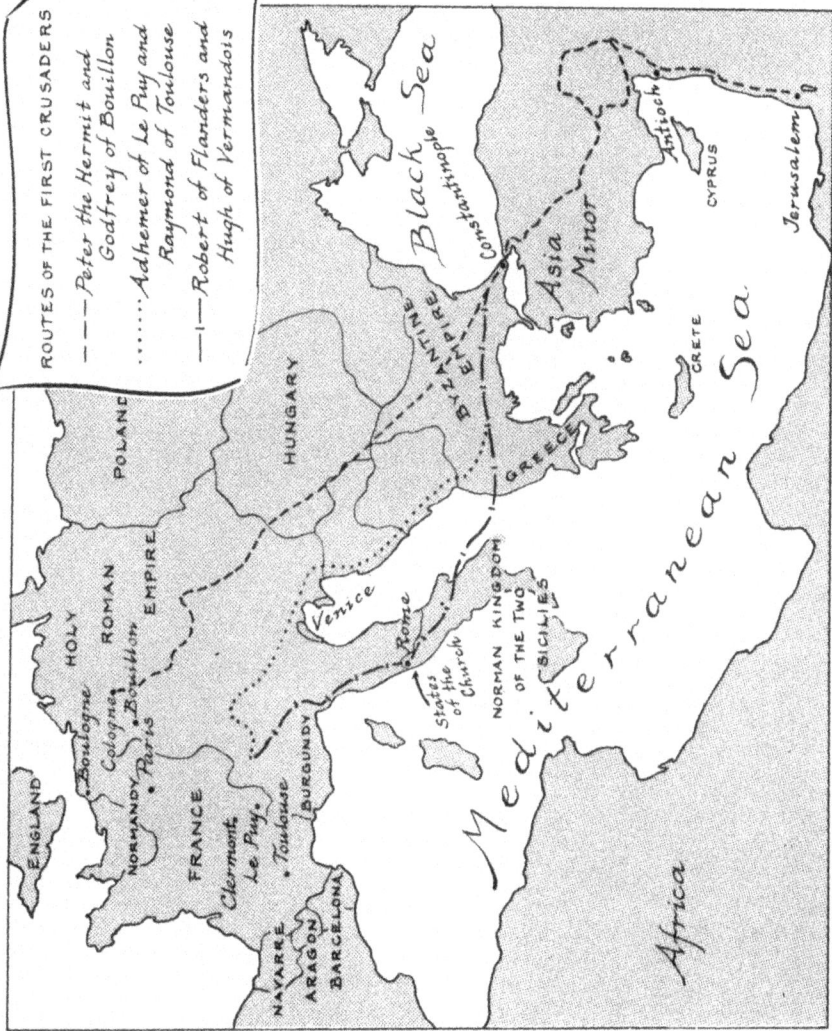

ROUTES OF THE FIRST CRUSADERS

–––– Peter the Hermit and
      Godfrey of Bouillon
·········· Adhemer of Le Puy and
      Raymond of Toulouse
–I–I– Robert of Flanders and
      Hugh of Vermandois

ENGLAND

Boulogne
Cologne
HOLY
ROMAN
NORMANDY
Bouillon
Paris
EMPIRE
POLAND

FRANCE
HUNGARY

Clermont
Le Puy
Toulouse
BURGUNDY
Venice

NAVARRE
ARAGON
BARCELONA

Rome
States of the Church
NORMAN KINGDOM
OF THE TWO
SICILIES

BYZANTINE EMPIRE

Black Sea

Constantinople

Asia Minor

GREECE

CRETE

CYPRUS

Antioch

Jerusalem

Mediterranean Sea.

Africa

bibLiogRApby

ADAMS, BROOKS, *The Law of Civilization and Decay.* New York, The Macmillan Company, 1896.

BROCKELMANN, CARL, *History of the Islamic Peoples.* New York, Capricorn Books, 1960.

Cambridge Medieval History. Cambridge, England, 1911–36.

DIEHL, CHARLES, *Byzantium: Greatness and Decline.* New Brunswick, Rutgers University Press, 1957.

HASSALL, W. O., editor, *They Saw It Happen*, Vol. I. Oxford, Basil Blackwell, 1957.

HEER, FRIEDRICH, *The Medieval World: Europe 1110–1350.* Cleveland and New York, The World Publishing Company, 1961.

IBN AL-QALANISI, *The Damascus Chronicle of the Crusades.* Extracted and translated by H. A. R. Gibb. London, Luzac & Co., 1932.

NEWTON, A. P., editor, *Travel and Travellers of the Middle Ages.* London, Routledge & Kegan Paul, 1926.

PERNOUD, REGINE, *The Crusaders.* Edinburgh and London, Oliver & Boyd, 1963.
—— editor, *The Crusades.* London, Secker & Warburg, 1963.

RICE, TAMARA TALBOT, *The Seljuks.* London, Thames & Hudson, 1961.

RUNCIMAN, STEVEN, A History of the Crusades. Volume I, The First Crusade. Cambridge University Press, 1951.
—— Volume II, The Kingdom of Jerusalem. Cambridge University Press, 1952.
—— Volume III, The Kingdom of Acre. Cambridge University Press, 1954.

TREECE, HENRY, The Crusades. New York, Random House, 1962.

VILLEHARDOUIN and DE JOINVILLE, Memoirs of the Crusades. Translated by Sir Frank T. Marzials. New York, E. P. Dutton & Co., 1958.

INDEX

Alexius IV, 231–34

Alexius V, 234–35

Alfonso-Jordon, 109

Alice of Cyprus, 128, 129, 134–36, 138

Alp Arslan, 24

Amalric, 142, 160; death, 179; marriages, 174, 180–81; rise to throne, 165; war against Egypt, 166–75, 177–79, 245

Amalric II of Cyprus, 224, 239

Andronicus, 231

Anna Comnena, 40–41, 44, 54

Antioch, 110, 125, 131; and Alexius Comnenus, 67, 69–70, 75, 89; attacked and sacked by Baibars, 285–86; attacked by Saladin, 204; besieged by Franks, 62–67; besieged by Turks, 68–74; captured by Franks, 67–68; history, 61; regained by Byzantium, 138–39; ruled by Baldwin II, 119, 123; ruled by Baldwin III as regent, 157–58; ruled by Bertrand, 110; ruled by Bohemond, 75–78, 99–100; ruled by Bohemond II, 127; ruled by Bohemond III, 165–66, 223; ruled by Bohemond IV, 240; ruled by Bohemond VI, 278, 283; ruled by Joscelin, 129; ruled by Raymond, 135–36; ruled by Reynald, 162–64; ruled by Roger, 112; ruled by Tancred, 94, 98–99, 103, 109

Armenia, 63, 98

Arnulf of Rohes, 85

Arqa, 79, 81, 110

Arsuf, 104, 284

Ascalon, 92, 117, 125, 175; besieged by Franks 158–60, 162, 266; besieged by Saladin, 183; held by Saracens, 106

Ashdod, 118

Assassins, 279, 287

Baghdad, 22, 134, 283

Baibars, 283–88

Balak, 123, 125

Baldwin of Flanders, Emperor of Byzantium, 237

Baldwin I, of Lorraine, 28–29, 37, 38, 47, 90; Count of Edessa, 62–63; death, 116–18; King of Jerusalem, 93–99, 103, 104–07, 111–14

Baldwin II, of Le Bourg, 129, 133; death, 130; King of Jerusalem, 118–19, prisoner of Turks, 99, 110; ransomed, 127; Second Count of Edessa, 94

Index

Baldwin III: attack on Reynald, 162–65; capture of Ascalon, 158–60, 162; death of, 165; King of Jerusalem, 142, 153, 157–58; siege of Damascus, 155
Baldwin IV: death, 187; reign, 180–86; victim of leprosy, 180
Baldwin V, 186–88
Baldwin II, Latin Emperor of Constantinople, 237, 267
Balian of Ibelin, 192–93, 201, 207
Bazawash, 136
Beha ed-Din, 213
Beirut, 51, 81, 200
Belgrade, 32
Berengaria, 212
Bertrand, 108–11, death, 112
Bethlehem, 81
Blanche, Queen of France, 267–69, death, 279–80
Bohemond of Taranto, 28, 40–43, 47–49; and Alexius, 48–49, 101–03; attack on Antioch, 64–65, 66–68, 73–75; attack on Marra, 77; death, 103; defeat of Turks, 58–59; marriage, 101; return to France, 100; treatment of spies, 65
Bohemond II: death, 127, 129; heir to Antioch, 119, 127
Bohemond III of Antioch, 185, 192; death, 240
Bohemond IV, 240, 258
Bohemond V, 266
Bohemond VI, 278–79, 285–87
Bohemond VII, 287, 289
Boniface of Montferrat, 226–27, 236, 237
Bordeaux, 18
Bosphorus, Strait of, 17, 48
Bulgaria, 33, 150, 296
Byzantium, 17, 22–24; and Crusades, 18, 103, 135, 150–53; capture of Antioch, 138; war with Moslems, 21

Caesarea, 104
Cairo, 170, 175, 249–50, 273
Caliph of Egypt, 170–72
Charlemagne, 22
Charles Martel, 21, 22
Chartres, 131
Christ, see Jesus
Civetot, 35, 36, 55
Clermont, Church Council at: proclamation of Crusades, 10–15

Index

Duqaq of Damascus, 26, 65, 74, 95, 108, 112

Edessa, 66; attack by Joscelin, 145; attack by Zenzi, 143–144; captured by Baldwin of Lorraine, 63
Edward I, of England, 286–87, 288–89
Egypt, 17, 23, 24, 84; invaded by Amalric, 168–69, 172, 174–79; invaded by Louis, 271–80; under Saladin, 182–84
Eleanor of Aquitaine, 147, 153–54, 156
Eschiva, 200
Etheria of Gaul, 18
Eugenuis III, 147
Eustace of Boulogne, 28, 37, 117–18

Fatimids (Arabs), 109; battles in Palestine, 104–07; enemies of Seljuks, 24–26; enemies of Turks, 78–79, 95; power weak, 158, 166
Firouz, 66–67
Francis of Assisi, 246–48
Franks, 22, 147; of Outremer, 131–32, 156, 180–88, 200–01, 284–90
Frederick II, of Hohenstaufen, Holy Roman Emperor, 245, 252–65
Frederick Barbarossa, 209–10
Frederick, Duke of Swabia, 150
Fulcher of Chartres, chronicler: at Clermont, 11; of first Crusade, 39, 41, 59, 96–97, 115, 116, 119, 124; summary of Crusade life, 131
Fulk Fiole, 202
Fulk of Anjou, 128, 130; death, 142; religious freedom, 139–41; ruler of Jerusalem, 133–42
Fulk of Neuilly, 224–25

Genghis Khan, 279
Genoa, 83, 97, 126, 244
Geoffrey of Burel, 36
Geoffrey of Villehardouin, 228, 235
Gerard, Grand Master of the Hospitallers, 120–21
Gerard of Ridfort, 181, 192–95, 199–201; death, 207
German Crusaders, 149–52, 154

Index

Index

Qalawun, Emir of Syria, 288–93
Qutuz, Sultan of Egypt, 283–84

Radulph, Patriarch of Antioch, 136
Rainald, 35
Ramleh, Battle of, 105–07
Ravendel, 63
Raymond of Aguilers, chronicler, 59, 72, 73, 74, 82, 85
Raymond of Antioch and Poitiers, 136–39, 156–57
Raymond of Le Puy, 121
Raymond of Toulouse, 28, 37, 76–78; attack of Antioch, 62–67, 75–78; in Constantinople, 49–51; death, 108; in Jerusalem, 90–93; siege of Nicaea, 52, 55; siege of Tripoli, 107–08
Raymond III, Count of Tripoli: death, 204; regent of Baldwin IV, 181–82, 187–88, 190–91; truce with Saracens, 192–95; war with Saladin, 195–96, 198
Reynald of Chatillon, 162–64, 187–88, 195, 203; breaks truce, 185, 191–92; captured by Turks, 165; death, 199; release, 181–82
Rheims, 131
Richard of Salerno, 103
Richard, the Lion-hearted, 209–11; death, 221; Third Crusade, 211–21
Ridwan of Aleppo, 26, 61, 112–13
Robert II, Count of Flanders, 38–39, 50, 52, 76, 77–78, 82, 90–91
Robert, Duke of Normandy, 38–39, 50, 78, 82, 90–91
Robert of Artois, 273–74
Robert of Clary, 237
Robert of Coudre, 202
Robert of Courson, 248
Roger, of Hospitallers, 192–93
Roger of Antioch, 112, 118, 123
Romanus Diogenes, 24
Rome, 16, 17
Runciman, Sir Steven, 41–42, 298

Sahara, 16
Saif ed-Din, 144
Saint Andrew, 70, 79

Index

www.ingramcontent.com/pod-product-compliance
Lightning Source LLC
Chambersburg PA
CBHW022114080426
42734CB00006B/128